P9-CBL-544

05/24
STAMP PRICE
$ 5.00

THE
CHINA
OPTION

THE CHINA OPTION

Nancy Dall Milton

PANTHEON BOOKS, NEW YORK

Copyright © 1982 by Nancy Dall Milton

All rights reserved under International and Pan-American Copyright Conventions. Published in the United States by Pantheon Books, a division of Random House, Inc., New York, and simultaneously in Canada by Random House of Canada Limited, Toronto.

Library of Congress Cataloging in Publication Data
Milton, Nancy Dall
    The China option.
    I. Title.
PS3563.I456C5   1982   813'.54   82-47879
ISBN 0-394-52721-6   AACR2

Manufactured in the United States of America

First Edition

To David

THE CHINA OPTION

/

CHAPTER

1

The winter chill of Shanghai is like that of London. It penetrates the bones and lodges there tenaciously, leaving the body numb at the core. The black figures of the young demonstrators moved doggedly forward through the cold. From a distance, they were rounded, armless shapes, shoulders hunched, hands in pockets, heads hooded, dark marchers in an ominous cortege.

From the ninth-floor window of the International Hotel, the view was decidedly unpleasant, partly because of the size of the crowd, but mostly because of its tone—hostile, there was no doubt of that, and in a language that seemed to take on a peculiar ferocity shouted at such volume. The demonstrators had at first appeared to be a raggle-taggle band, half a dozen front-line marchers carrying a homemade paper banner already tearing at the edges. Perhaps fifty others followed in straggling rows, their soft shoes thudding rhythmically on the pavement, their fists upraised in a gesture of protest practiced since nursery school.

As they proceeded down the street, however, the crowds on the narrow sidewalk seemed to merge invisibly with them, and the small band soon became a mass of moving figures, constantly growing tighter and expanding outward until those who did not join them were forced onto side streets. By the time they reached the front of the hotel, the demonstrators numbered hundreds—perhaps a thousand—and the entire area was theirs.

The crowd spiraled about the hotel entrance, until there came an

3

isolated shout from one of the groups somewhere in the center of the crowd: "Foreigners go home!" The cry was echoed here and there, then vanished amid muffled shouts of "No, no" and the distant sounds of argument. But when "China belongs to the Chinese people" burst out, the slogan swept the streets, hundreds of voices shouting it in deafening unity. Suddenly, the area in front of the International Hotel was a thicket of upraised blue- and black-sleeved arms. The banner, anchored firmly on padded shoulders somewhere in the middle of the street, faced the hotel's revolving doors. "China Belongs to the Chinese People" the huge black characters stated unequivocally.

The faces in the churning blue and black sea were young—faces from a thousand photographs of the Chinese masses. Perhaps many among them who made up the frightening unemployment statistics of the city simply had nothing better to do with a Saturday morning, but they didn't have the air of youth on a fling. The mood was too hostile.

One was safe of course. There was no question about that. Chinese mobs were always kept under control, and foreigners held back at a careful distance. Still, there was the feeling . . . And to have so many of them so close . . .

"Right out of Eisenstein," Paul Engleberg remarked. "The scene on the steps."

"You're too intellectual for this job, Paul," Jack Rickett replied sarcastically. "You expect this to develop just like a script, with Cossack guards firing on the defenseless crowd. That's not the way they do things here. They'll arrest the leaders, send them off for a few years of forced labor. You should leave the romantic scenarios to Warren Beatty. It's no wonder they're getting rid of you." As always, his tone was tough but unmistakably affectionate. He'd miss having Paul around.

"Remember my slogan, Jack. Never forget Teheran. Anyway, you've got to assume they're expelling me for a reason." Paul put his cup impatiently onto the coffee-stained saucer. "This business was inevitable. You can't ban the Chinese from coming into these foreign-devil hotels. It's completely crazy. The only thing I don't understand is why this hasn't happened sooner." He took his jacket off the back of the chair.

"I'm going down for a closer look. I don't know if they've heard of double jeopardy here, but I don't see how they can get rid of me twice."

Jack shrugged. "Everyone to his own taste. With increasing age and decrepitude, I prefer watching nasty crowds at a distance. Particularly when they're adolescents blowing off excessive sexual energy.

"Of course what they're asking for is perfectly reasonable. In theory, I don't like seeing them banned from foreign hotels, either, but in practice? . . . You want one billion Chinese peasants standing around in the lobby, spitting and gawking at every big-nose who gets off the elevator?" Putting another spoonful of Nescafé into his cup, he poured boiling water from the thermos and leaned back comfortably in the overstuffed chair. "This is a box seat. Perfect view of the whole drama. I'll see you at lunch and we'll find out who got the better story."

But the turbulent sea that threatened to roll through the old hotel's great front door did not do so. The demonstrators stopped precisely at the edge of the sidewalk, their massed bodies pressed tightly together to the far ends of the street. Inside the lobby, where Paul now stood, the din of a thousand voices was suddenly overpowered by the ear-splitting screech of a loudspeaker.

Standing high above the shoulders of the crowd on a barely visible makeshift platform, the speaker—thin-faced, with short-cropped black hair, probably in his middle twenties—could have been any of a hundred faces in the crowd. He shouted out his speech in the angry rhetorical style of such Chinese speeches.

"We've gone back to the colonial Shanghai our parents told us about! As children we were all taken to see the infamous sign at the old racetrack, 'No dogs or Chinese allowed.' " There was a roar of affirmation as he paused dramatically. "This time there's no sign, but the facts are the same. Are we dirtier than the foreigners who stay in the hotel?"

"No, no!" the chorus roared back.

"Are we less polite?" A wave of derisive laughter swept the streets.

"Is our money of less value?"

"Maybe, maybe it is," a distant voice responded, and there was scattered laughter amid the roar of no's.

"But are we Chinese?"

5

"Yes, yes, we're Chinese!" they thundered. "We're Chinese. China belongs to the Chinese people."

"And this hotel belongs to us," the strident voice went on, amplified to a nerve-cracking shriek. "It's not yet owned by American or Japanese capitalists. It's owned by the Chinese people, and if we want to go in, we have the right to do so!"

It had been easier to slip out of the hotel than Paul had expected. Of course, the front door was impossible. Stern figures with the unmistakable look of security men stood just inside the door. But there was that dark passageway through which food was delivered to the huge kitchen by a side entrance. Paul had gone out that way one day when he'd wanted to avoid a tiresome acquaintance he'd spotted at the front desk.

Surprisingly, there was no security there at all—just a few white-capped kitchen workers going about their usual morning tasks. Perhaps the Chinese didn't really believe any of their foreign guests would want to go out among the hostile crowd, and the security men at the front door were only meant as symbols of protection.

Paul made his way without any trouble to near the front of the building. He had no interest in going farther. In any case, the leaflet he was determined to acquire was everywhere—in every hand and pocket, on the ground, on the bare branches of bushes. An anonymous hand placed one in his grasp, just a single sheet of rough paper with "China Belongs to the Chinese People" in bold characters at the top. He scanned the text quickly, skipping the routine slogans at the beginning and end, searching for some small bit of substance. A perfectly predictable event, as it turned out: Several days earlier, a few young Chinese had come to the hotel to visit their "foreign friends" and had been denied admission—rather roughly, it would seem, for their "leader" had been arrested and the others detained for twenty-four hours.

Suddenly, Paul noticed that the roaring, swirling crowd had become stunningly quiet, and the youthful shriek had been replaced by a smooth, powerful baritone, speaking with a resonance that even the crude loudspeaker system could not distort. Paul craned his neck and squinted. He was awfully far away, but the silhouette was somehow different—taller, for one thing, and even from a distance showing a profile that must be very handsome. The speech was different too. Not just a reference to the obvious, but a series of complex historical analogies, of glorious Shanghai struggles past.

6

And then a whole chain of related contemporary events—similar incidents in Peking, in Nanking, in Canton—the peasants, the workers, the students. . . . Who was this man? Either he hadn't been introduced or Paul had missed it.

There were two young women at Paul's elbow, bundled up to their round faces in padded blue. "What's his name?" Paul asked them in his rudimentary Chinese. The women glanced quickly at each other. Then one nodded.

"Wang Weilai," the other said.

"Wang Weilai? Who's he?"

"Only a foreigner wouldn't know," the first woman snapped. "He's our leader—the people's great new leader." Then the two women moved quickly away from him.

The speech was ending. The mysterious Wang Weilai exhorted his listeners to join with their brothers and sisters throughout the country, and then disappeared into the crowd. The respectful silence was over within seconds.

"China belongs to the Chinese people," went up the cry once again, and the huge weight of the crowd began to press forward.

"No, no!" Paul heard the isolated shouts. "Stay where you are! Don't push, don't push! Discipline! We must not break discipline!" But the massive throng swayed in a single direction. Paul moved quickly back toward the passageway that led into the kitchen. Bodies moved past him toward the hotel's entrance, the forbidden front door.

Now there were other shouts, too, and yellow smoke in the air, and the acrid smell of tear gas. The crowd spun kaleidoscopically, but there was nowhere to go. Bodies collided against bodies, and then began the sickening, muffled thud of wooden sticks on padded jackets, the crack of wood on heads. Screams cut the air, curses roared and died. The dense crowd broke and fled. It was over as quickly as it had begun. On the ground lay the wounded amid the shredded and torn remains of paper banners and leaflets. The sirens of ambulances shrieked in the distance.

Paul shook his head. What a time to be leaving! He was still clutching the leaflet in his hand. Definitely something to hold on to, although he'd have to be pretty careful about trying to take it out. He folded it carefully, and as he did, something caught his eye—not the mimeographed print, but a few lines scrawled with a ballpoint pen.

7

"Foreign friend, would you like to know more about our struggle? If so, I will meet you Monday at noon on the bench that faces the old lions on the Bund. I will be eating my lunch."

No signature. Nothing. Jack was right. It was an adolescent struggle, a childish web of intrigue. And the lions on the Bund—the old British colonial symbol pointedly left in front of the former bank—high symbolism indeed for this new struggle. Still, it was closer than he'd come to making any sort of personal contact following up the leads that had gotten him thrown out of China. And damn it—Monday at noon! He was leaving tomorrow afternoon.

Then, for some reason that wasn't clear to him, Paul took out his pen and wrote a name on the back of the leaflet. Wang Weilai.

"Well, are you ready to take a crack at the Peking assignment?" Larry Metcalf ground out another cigarette in the already overflowing ashtray on his cluttered desk. He was an editor in the old style who read every story himself, while steadily chain-smoking. He was very good at his job, and took some pleasure in the image he projected. None of this contemporary nonsense about apologizing for the stale and carcinogenic air in which he worked best. Those who entered the office of the editor-in-chief of the *Washington Inquirer* did so on his terms.

"Yes, I am." Anne hoped her matter-of-fact tone gave no indication of her excitement, though she was hardly surprised. Office rumors about new assignments were mysteriously accurate, and there were those who swore that at the very moment a decision was made in some editorial mind, it was telegraphed into the cubicled hive of the worker journalists. For several days now she'd been receiving whispered hints that she'd been selected as the *Inquirer*'s next China correspondent.

She knew she was the logical choice, but logic was not necessarily the determining factor in such matters. She'd certainly put in her time—the requisite years China-watching in Hongkong, polishing up her Stanford Chinese, which by this time was quite presentable; and she'd been trained by the master of Asia journalists.

It was upsetting: She still couldn't think of Hank without a wave of depression. One of the few good marriages around. Everyone had said it, and she and Hank had smugly agreed. The third for him, the first for her. They seemed effortlessly to have solved all those obdurate intangibles like freedom, equality, your time and money versus my time and money. Even the status business had never seemed a problem. Since Vietnam, Hank had been *the* veteran Asia correspondent—the first among the best, it was generally agreed; Anne, the bright novice, straight out of graduate school. But he'd been the best kind of teacher, a role that never seemed to interfere with his being a quite wonderful husband.

That such a rational and superior relationship should have been done in by the oldest of biological forces was to her an exquisitely cruel irony. They had come back to Washington. It hadn't appeared to be a catastrophic move. Like almost everybody who'd witnessed the long agonies of Southeast Asia, Hank was burning out, ready for an editorial position and a little peace. For Anne, being assigned to a national political desk was an entertaining change.

But no sooner had they settled into a proper suburban house than Hank wanted to have children. It had to be now or never. He was forty-seven. He'd be sixty before the kids were teenagers, maybe dead before they graduated from college. For Anne it was ridiculous, heart-wrenching, and just too soon. She was at the beginning of her career; Hank seemed ready to retire from his. In a few years, she might welcome having a child, but now . . . Not now.

Unpleasant to have that rushing through her head as she sat in Larry Metcalf's office, facing him across his huge old-fashioned desk. But not illogical. This was the career she'd given Hank up for. In fact, if she didn't get the China assignment, it wouldn't make much sense at all.

"It's not quite the thrill it was when things first opened up. You know that," Larry continued. "But even if China hasn't often hit the front page in the last few years, it's still one of our most important assignments. China is China, after all."

Anne nodded. She didn't really need to be reminded of China's geopolitical significance, but it would be interesting to see just what he'd say. Especially after Paul Engleberg . . .

"What's needed is that delicate balance, you know, between paying scrupulous attention to anything that might turn out to be news —the little sociological, psychological indicators that are straws in the wind. Remember how prophetic those seemingly lightweight stories on women having their hair permanented and getting interested in fashion turned out to be." He clearly didn't expect her to reply now. "The balance between that meticulous awareness of the little ripples in the society and the obvious big events and just how" —he paused, doodling on a pad with the pencil he was never without—"just how we're going to handle them." Larry Metcalf smiled, a pleasant but definitely no-nonsense smile. "We're sending you as much for the discretion in dealing with the Chinese that you're supposed to have learned during your Hongkong years as for the fact that you're a damned good journalist and speak Chinese."

Anne maintained her serious, noncommital expression, but a closer look would have revealed something like a twinkle in her dark blue eyes.

"You know about Engleberg. I don't blame him. Nobody blames him. He's a brilliant reporter. Those were great stories he wrote, and we're not about to be second to anybody on news from China. We were proud to run them. But we can't afford to lose our foothold in China either. The Chinese have threatened not to allow us to station any of our own people there. I don't know if you knew that."

Anne shook her head. The rumor mill was reliable, but not everything slipped through. Or was Larry laying it on a bit?

"It might have been only a bluff. I know they operate that way. Obviously, though, we have no choice but to take it seriously. I don't intend the *Washington Inquirer* to get its China news from the wires, and we're hardly in a position to beg favors from the *Post* after breaking their monopoly." Larry's pleasant smile had disappeared. He was now unabashedly the man in charge.

The message was quite clear. Larry stood up and extended his hand. In the style of the day, he'd kiss her good-bye in the front newsroom with the full staff looking on, but here in the privacy of his office, where business was really business, the handshake was still the symbol of the contract. It said a woman—or a certain few women at any rate—could be taken seriously.

"The best of luck. We look forward to some great stories from you." Now that they were by the door, Larry's smile was just that of the old newspaperman seeing a buddy off to yet another capital. Anne stood outside his office for a few moments. She knew she should get back to her desk; a million odds and ends had to be taken care of, but that was such a tiresome business. And she had to admit she was excited. Larry was right. Peking was no longer the plum it had been only a few years earlier, but for someone like Anne, who had spent so many years immersed in China's history, in the aes-

10

thetic and intellectual pleasures of learning the language, it would never be just another assignment. China was still the Middle Kingdom, the repository of the treasures of the centuries, the ancient soil that was still home to one fifth of the inhabitants of the planet. No matter how calmly the giant seemed to be slumbering, it was always a mistake to assume that China was as serene as it appeared on its well-mannered surface. That was one of the lessons of its history. Anne knew that much.

Even now . . . The stories were scattered, seemingly unrelated—a demonstration of unemployed youth, a filmmaker arrested, women engaged to marry foreigners sent to labor camps—maybe there were no connections. Perhaps they were all separate manifestations of the trauma of modernization, of the sudden shock of Western contact. Perhaps, too, it was simply impossible for any outsider to put into a coherent whole the events of the enormous Chinese drama. But now Anne was going. She would have her chance.

She was a striking figure, standing alone in the empty hallway, absorbed in her thoughts: tall, slender though not thin, dressed in her customary work clothes—beige wool pants, a cream-colored silk shirt, a tweed jacket. Her long straight blond hair was pulled back severely and tied with a thin black ribbon.

Paul Engleberg had been hoping to catch her at just such a moment as this—without an army of people around. There was no reason why they shouldn't have a talk before she left. It was the customary thing to do. Certainly everyone expected it. Maybe that was just what had kept him from approaching her before—the fact that the entire staff was curious to know what he'd say. Was he going to warn her to stay out of the kind of trouble he'd gotten into, or give her some suggestions so she could pursue matters even more deeply than he'd been able to? He wasn't really sure himself.

It had all started out so simply—a straightforward news story about a Chinese actress engaged to marry a visiting American playwright. She'd been arrested and sentenced to two years at hard labor when her fiancé left on a brief trip to New York. It was a signal to all Chinese that there were clear and dangerous limits to associating with foreigners, particularly in making an individual and personal decision to live with one outside the parameters of Chinese marital restraints. The problem was that Paul Engleberg had become interested in all these implications. It had been the beginning of a series

11

of stories on human rights in China. Next, he covered a demonstration of young people protesting hunger in the countryside and lack of civil rights in the cities. Their banners simply read "For Food and Democracy." Then there was the story on the women handing out leaflets against rape and particularly against the exploitation of young women by Party officials in positions of power. That was the end of the human rights series. Paul Engleberg was asked to leave the country in the interests of harmonious U.S.-China relations.

"Don't you think we ought to have a drink together before you fly off to fill my old shoes?"

"I can't imagine flying off before we do," Anne replied wryly. "But how do you know for sure that I'm going?"

"Everyone knew. That's the way it always is. You know that. Actually, I was the first to know for sure. Larry checked out the decision with me and I gave you my stamp of approval."

Anne smiled. She'd always liked Paul Engleberg, though she'd neither known him well nor worked with him. He was thin, serious, and with his old tortoiseshell glasses reminded her somehow of a little boy on his way to the library. He was not naive, but with his old-fashioned strain of humanism, he was the logical one of the *Inquirer*'s correspondents to get himself expelled from China for writing what the Chinese didn't want written. He was also the man who was quite likely to do exactly the same thing again tomorrow.

Though they had no reason to keep their conversation from their ever observant colleagues, it seemed more comfortable to have their drink in the anonymity of a hotel bar rather than in the congenial mob scene at the *Inquirer*'s favorite neighborhood drinking hole.

"Well, you know what you're in for, I'm sure. Days, weeks of soul-crunching boredom, and then something interesting suddenly breaks through the opacity of the official line."

"And you can't write about it." Though Anne's words were negative, her face was bright with anticipation. Now, at this very moment, in this conversation with her predecessor, she felt she was on her way.

"That's just the problem. You *have* to write about it. And there's the rub. The point is *how.*"

"Ah, yes. That's what Larry was just saying."

"And it's not simply a matter of your own perspicacity. It's all tied in with the shifting sands of Chinese policy—and of course

American policy, too. You'll have to use every bit of your own diplomatic good sense." Paul smiled mischievously. "Actually, it's pretty entertaining playing the Chinese cat-and-mouse game. I enjoyed my time there."

"Are you sorry you're not still there?"

"If you mean by that, do I regret writing the stories that got me thrown out, the answer is an emphatic no. Everybody has to make a decision on those things. I knew what I was doing."

There was a lot to talk about, and Anne knew the right questions to ask. She'd stayed in Canton several times, and made the now routine tour of China's major cities, so she already had a fairly good idea of what the details of her everyday life would be like. What she wanted to know now was who to contact, what the possibilities were for real travel and investigative reporting.

The conversation was warm, even relaxed, but as they chatted, Paul Engleberg was thinking of something else. That crazy note. He'd tucked it into an inner compartment of his wallet, and it was still there. There had been no search by Chinese customs. He should have known there wouldn't be. Once the definitive slap on the wrist had been administered, the Chinese seldom went on slapping you across the border the way the Russians did. "Slap and stroke"—the old Chinese technique. Having been made aware that you'd behaved in an uncivilized fashion, you were sent on your way with meticulous Chinese propriety. He wasn't quite sure why he'd even held on to the scrap of paper—a date by a river that no one would ever keep. Maybe there was just a bit of ego involved—that this had been his lead, and only he could have used it. Still, there might be something in it. A hint of things to come? In any case, there were really only two possibilities: to give it to Anne or to throw it away. After all, it would be no good to anybody else. And he liked her. A very bright and lively woman. Hank Steiner's ex-wife. He'd known Hank from years back. Impossible to imagine his marrying anyone without brains and some guts. And why not? Let her make her own decision which way to go in China. He pulled the leaflet out of his wallet and unfolded it on the table.

"What's that?"

"A little going-away present. Maybe a link in a chain, maybe nothing at all. It was slipped to me during a demonstration outside the International Hotel in Shanghai just before I left. A protest leaflet, as you can see."

13

Anne frowned in the dim light as she looked at the worn piece of paper. "But what's this written on it?"

"An invitation from an anonymous rebel to meet for a brown-bag lunch on the Bund. Obviously, you're not going to make lunch, but who knows? Keep it or toss it away. No obligations."

"Is this one of the things they threw you out for?" Anne was looking at him intently.

"No connection at all. I didn't have the chance to act on this one, and the irony is I'd never had such a good lead before."

"Who's Wang Weilai?"

"I have no idea, except he was the main speaker at the meeting —and quite impressive. A woman in the crowd told me he was their new leader."

Paul grinned. The second round of drinks was set on the table. There was still a lot to talk about, and somehow he felt relieved to be rid of the note.

CHAPTER

2

The rebellion in Baluchistan was inevitable. Ever since Afghanistan, the probabilities had been analyzed, evaluated, and dissected. But the power alignments in the area were changing too rapidly to allow for a scenario that would hold for more than a few days or weeks at best. It had been enough for the immediate present that there was still a government in Pakistan with which it was possible to communicate, and a president who at least feigned goodwill toward the United States.

This was not the first Baluch rebellion, of course. While the Soviets stubbornly persisted in the struggle to get Afghanistan in hand, there had been series of small uprisings along the border. Tribal guerrillas moved back and forth, finding easy access to weapons, training, and political support on the Soviet side. Up till now, their sporadic outbreaks had been no match for the American weaponry pouring steadily into government armories or President Khan's commitment to saturation bombing of the insurgent areas. There were isolated voices around State (and the Pentagon as well) muttering about "the Shah syndrome," but it wasn't as if there had been a choice. It was Khan or no one—at least no one reliable.

This morning's situation was another matter. The Pakistani army base at Chaman on the Afghan border had been attacked during the night by an estimated 30,000 Baluchis said to be armed with Russian assault rifles, hand-held rockets, and artillery. Latest reports indicated that it would be only hours before the garrison there fell.

15

Even more ominously, well-coordinated smaller battles were occurring throughout the area. There were reports, as yet unconfirmed, of Soviet advisers on the battlefront, but whether or not that was the case, the signs of first-rate Soviet training and armament were apparent.

Once again, the National Security Council adviser was about to preside over his small action group consisting of several senior State and Pentagon officials and their aides, a man from the Joint Chiefs, the Secretary of Defense, and the director of the CIA. The President never appeared. Like previous commanders-in-chief, he had learned not to participate in the committee's acrimonious debates but to study their recommendations and then make his decisions. He was pleased with his choice of a title: WASAC—the Washington Strategic Action Committee. Kissingerian, but with a bit more impact; a good name for the period of his administration, tough and very American.

It was unusual for WASAC members to have to wait for the NSC adviser. The conversation was dilatory, the room quiet, and the view from the tall windows unpleasantly appropriate—the indeterminate gray of late winter.

When Stefan Zolti arrived, at fifteen minutes past the hour, he looked tired, most unusual for this NSC chief, who seemed to thrive on crises and expected his staff to perform as he did, with minimal sleep and unlimited enthusiasm for managing world disorder. He sat lightly, almost stiffly on the edge of a high-backed leather chair, his wiry body tightly coiled, apparently ready to spring.

"I have been with the President, gentlemen," he began abruptly. "He hopes you are all aware of the seriousness of the crisis and that you understand we cannot once again slap the Soviets in a way that harms only ourselves—grain embargoes, limited economic retaliation, that sort of thing. He'll take the recommendations of this committee very seriously, as he always has. However, he wishes to remind you that we are faced today with the very gravest crisis of his administration and that he personally is prepared to take serious steps."

The members of the committee leaned forward, concentrating intently as Zolti spoke. They were accustomed to his Hungarian accent, but still, it was sometimes not entirely clear what he was saying. This President, like some of his predecessors, had come to feel that "real" Americans somehow lacked the genetic instinct for

16

the subtleties of geopolitics and had brought Zolti down from Yale. There'd been a good try at bringing in men with more easily pronounceable names, but the President did not intend American foreign policy to be an international joke indefinitely. If it had to be one of these Europeans, at least it wasn't Kissinger, and he couldn't help feeling that there was a certain brilliance in following the German from Harvard and the Pole from Columbia with a Hungarian from Yale. These were the fellows, after all, whose instinct to screw the Russians came from the gut, not from the head.

Zolti sat watchfully, waiting to see who would begin. His opening statement had set a tone for the meeting. It would be difficult for the temperate gentleman from State to override the explicit wishes of the President, though Mason Graves often managed to dilute them into ineffectualness.

"Let's have the morning's intelligence briefing on the military situation and the level of Soviet involvement," the representative from the Joint Chiefs said solemnly. Zolti nodded his agreement. The general could always be depended upon to operate on the most obvious level.

There was a dreary inevitability to the recitation of the statistics: 50,000 rebel troops reported in the field, two provincial capitals captured, the main government airbase under siege, major tank battles in the desert, the number of Soviet advisers actively involved still unclear. For months, all the members of the committee had been reading memos predicting precisely this situation. Shipping massive amounts of armaments to President Khan had been a calculated risk. If he used them unwisely to suppress the Baluch rebels, or, perhaps more important, if his suppression was not successful, a Baluchistan rebellion was probably just a matter of time. Like so many of America's clients, he had used his weapons unwisely and unsuccessfully. The last remaining bulwark separating the Soviets from the Straits of Hormuz was crumbling.

The Secretary of Defense, James Schneider, was the first to speak. For him, the solution was obvious. "Fortunately, we have fifteen thousand of our own troops in Egypt," he said confidently. "We're ready to move by land and air into the Baluch areas of Iran on an hour's notice."

Mason Graves, who had appeared to be entirely absorbed in studying the design of the ceiling, started visibly. "But the Baluch areas of Iran are quite calm now. Our people have done a great job

17

there ever since we armed the rebels against the mullahs. That's one of our real successes. Why wipe that all out with some sort of ad hoc military operation?"

Zolti looked at him disapprovingly. It would be far easier to get things done if these State Department area specialists were not included in the meetings, but unfortunately there was still no way that could be managed.

"We're faced, as I'm sure you all understand, with total Soviet dominance of the area," Zolti said sharply. "The scenario that's unfolding appears to be very similar to the one in Afghanistan. Once the Russians were there, we had very few options. There was the initial shock and the fact that they've gotten bogged down, but still —they're there."

"There's no need for ground forces to go through Iranian Baluchistan," the Secretary of Defense interjected. "We're prepared for air strikes from Saudi Arabia or from one of our bases in Egypt."

"How do you propose to separate Iranian Baluchistan from Pakistani Baluchistan?" Graves asked wearily. "We may think there's a nice neat line running through the area, but the Baluchis don't see it that way. Once you have American planes dropping bombs on their fellow tribesmen, that'll settle the question for the next century. The whole region will go up in flames."

"Let's be realistic," Schneider replied. "It's not as if the government of Pakistan has collapsed. We're still talking about a tribal rebellion, even if it is Soviet supported. We should be able to crush it in a pincers movement from both sides."

"I wouldn't want to dispatch those Middle East forces anywhere without at least two Americans to keep an eye on every Arab," the general said grimly. "And from what we've seen of the Pakistani army, I don't see where we have any choice except to use our own forces."

Zolti tapped his pen impatiently on a memo pad. The committee was skirting the question that could not be raised: What if American forces came up against Soviet forces? Zolti had long ago determined that if he were to have any responsibility for presiding over the decision to begin World War III, it would not be in such an absurdly disadvantageous position as the present one.

"The discussion thus far is proceeding along extremely narrow and conventional military lines," he snapped. "Before we complete the formalities, would anyone like to recommend that this problem be brought before the U.N., and that we initiate a few economic and cultural sanctions against the Soviets? In the area of something like rock bands, perhaps?" His sarcasm, too heavy to be biting, invariably succeeded in giving a disagreeable tone to the meetings.

Graves understood that he was being baited. "You know that we must do that sort of thing, Stefan," he said flatly. "We must do it, whether or not you think it's useful, and even whether it *is* useful. It's simply part of our international responsibility."

Zolti smiled disdainfully as he asked for the ritual vote on the U.N. resolution. "We've now taken care of the diplomatic requirements and have, as I understand it, covered the following military options: one, the use of Middle Eastern and Pakistani troops in a pincers movement, which my friend the general says is out. Is that correct, sir?" The general nodded gravely. "Very good. Option two: the deployment of our own ground and air troops into the Baluch areas, which, as I understand it, Mr. Graves fears might anger the tribesmen. Right?" Graves nodded calmly. "And third, the use of air strikes, which might anger the tribesmen even more. Am I correct, Mason?" Graves didn't even bother to nod. "This leaves us with very few viable conventional military responses, as I see it."

One of the aides from the Pentagon muttered, "The Russians are doing all right with conventional military responses." There was no reaction.

Zolti leaned back. The only small man in the room, he was conspicuous among these aggressively healthy Americans who lined the two sides of the long, polished conference table. He was the product of an uneven diet, nights of study in inadequate light, and the ancient bitterness of Eastern Europe. They were the products of milk and meat, pediatricians since birth and dentists since their first teeth, tennis and running, and not particularly painful courses of study in very comfortable universities. Vietnam had been hard, as had Watergate, and the intractable problems of the opening of the eighties—the hostages in Iran, Afghanistan, Poland, the inflation that would not go away, the resources that would not come back— but they still had the conviction that there was always a way out for Americans. It pleased Zolti to have all of these well-tanned faces turned in his direction, and he waited, savoring the moment.

"We must be a little more imaginative, gentlemen. We must utilize the political and diplomatic resources that our presidents from Nixon on have so carefully cultivated for a crisis like this one."

19

He looked around the table, his eyes glistening. "The time has come to make full use of the China card."

There was an almost audible sigh as the WASAC members shifted in their stiff chairs. Zolti had at last raised the option which most had guessed would come up sooner or later. It had to. From the time of the Shanghai Communiqué, the China debate had never really been resolved. It had simply oscillated with the shifting tides of Washington politics. From the beginning, there had been a perfectly clear and simple reason for the China relationship: China's potential effectiveness as a military counter to the Soviet Union. And so the crises of the world, not the inherent importance of China, determined the ups and downs of the alliance. For the Chinese, the raison d'être had been the same: America's effectiveness as a counter to their Soviet enemy. Because the Chinese had staked everything on the American card, their demands for a U.S.-China military alliance had had an urgent consistency since Mao and Nixon first met.

Under Brzezinski's guidance, Carter had moved cautiously but steadily toward closer military ties with the Chinese. Sophisticated military-related technology was transferred to China accompanied by public statements that the United States would not provide Peking with military equipment. The real military hardware, meanwhile, was sold to China by America's European allies. However, there would be no out-front U.S. military pact with Peking. Too dangerous, too many unknowns, too many voices around Washington warning that it might provoke the Soviets into making a preemptive attack on China. Until now, the new President had seen no reason to reverse the policy.

Zolti was as determined to effect a de facto Sino-American military alliance as Brzezinski had been. The crucial moment had arrived. Even the President understood that. This time there were no other options to thwart his plan.

"The moment has come for us to begin moving, and rapidly, toward a full-scale military alliance with China—a pact on the NATO model, the old NATO model. As you're all aware, that has been the underlying rationale for our relationship with the Chinese from the very beginning. The business deals, the tourists, the scholarly exchanges—all of that was simply the frosting on the cake. I'm sure there's no one in this room who doesn't understand all this."

Zolti was now playing the role he loved best: professor of political

20

science, but with a government nodding at his feet. He understood the necessary gestures of the culture. It was part of the requisite ceremony to invite participation, but he was always impatient with it. At Yale, he had finally dispensed with it altogether.

"Each time we've moved toward the serious implementation of this military relationship, certain political forces whose main focus is fear of the Russians held us back, and every time this has occurred we've lost credibility with the Chinese. They've made it very clear they want to work with us, but they're certainly justified in doubting our capacity to come through with anything substantial. We are aware that negotiations between Peking and Moscow continue. Our weakness is responsible for that."

"I'm not so sure, Stefan," Graves interrupted. "Those talks have been going on for years, and nothing much has ever come of them. They like to keep their options open too." He looked directly at Zolti, forcing the adviser to return his gaze. "You're familiar with my views on this matter. It wouldn't be the end of the world if they managed to work out a few of those border problems. In fact, it might even delay the end of the world."

Zolti waved his hand impatiently. "You're back in some earlier stage of history. We're not talking about clashes on the Sino-Soviet border. We're talking about the crumbling of the entire area and the encirclement of China. We're also talking about the fact that whether we like it or not, China is all we've got. We go with China, or what?"

Surprisingly, it was Schneider who spoke up. "We've been going with China. We still are. There's always been only one question: How far do we go? At what point will the Soviets feel they have no choice but to attack China?"

"Mr. Schneider," Zolti said with excessive softness, "we all understand that, I think. That has been the major question under study for quite a number of years now. What we're looking at is how we'll proceed to work with the Chinese militarily and give them certain defenses against a potential preemptive Soviet strike. It is the President's wish that this meeting devote itself to agreement on that procedure. He expects to have a memorandum on his desk within forty-eight hours spelling out its major steps. Do I make myself quite clear?"

The only person of importance who hadn't yet spoken was Frederick Soames, director of the CIA. The CIA had had its troubles—

all that unpleasantness with Vietnam and Watergate, as well as the necessity for maintaining a low profile after the Helms business. For years, no respectable university graduate would consider a CIA career, but their younger brothers and sisters, apolitical and job-minded, didn't understand all that, and the Agency was once again back in operation in very much the same old way. Well, perhaps not precisely the same. There had been too many errors. The mess in Iran from '53 on had been the biggest one. And history had taken its toll. Soames had a far less sanguine view than his predecessors of the possibility of remaking the fate of countries whose histories were impelling them along some sort of incomprehensible path. One supported the anti-Soviet forces, whatever they might be—that was a given. But in a world where some of them wanted a theocratic medieval state, the options were limited.

Soames opened his leather portfolio. "You have our assessment of the Sino-Soviet talks and of the possibilities of a Soviet first strike on China, Dr. Zolti," he said, meticulously formal as always. "There's nothing new in that area. But you haven't touched on the other question that's been a problem in the China option."

"Ah yes," Zolti said impatiently. "You wish to raise the domestic political situation in China."

"I don't wish to raise it. Presumably it's my responsibility to tell you what we know about it."

"Please do then." Once again, Zolti was visibly annoyed. These were old questions, filled with intangibles and highly problematic.

"To recapitulate briefly," Soames began, "the military situation vis-à-vis the Soviets remains essentially unchanged. The border talks continue, and both sides remain in the positions they've held for some years now. However, as regards internal political developments, our reports indicate an intensification of underground activity in both Shanghai and Peking. The plan to move the unemployed youth into small businesses is collapsing. There are bicycle shops and noodle shops by the hundreds, but, in essence, there are too many people taking in each other's laundry. Demonstrations of unemployed youth are epidemic.

"The name of Wei Jingsheng, the dissident arrested in 1979, has become a rallying cry, and what appear to be hundreds of organizations are putting out mimeographed newsletters, all using his name in their titles. There seems to be coordination among these groups and between those in Peking and Shanghai. The degree of their success in other parts of the country is not yet clear, but leaflets mentioning the organization of Wei Jingsheng Guards in Canton and as far from the capital as Chungking have come our way."

Zolti interrupted. "Are you telling us, Mr. Soames, that your people are predicting something like another Cultural Revolution, or Paris in '68, or even Berkeley in '65? These reports about unemployed, alienated youth are an ongoing business in China. We can't change our geopolitical strategy every time some kid feels like issuing a treatise."

"I'm not recommending a change in strategy, Dr. Zolti. That's your problem and the President's. I'm simply informing you of what our current intelligence tells us about China. I'm sure you haven't forgotten the criticism the CIA came under for our failure to predict the unraveling of Iran. I'd like to avoid making the same error again. We collect the intelligence and try to put it into some sort of comprehensible form. What you decide to do with it is your business. May I continue, please?"

Zolti made a curt gesture of assent.

"We also have reports of peasant uprisings in South and particularly South-central China. They've been put down promptly by the Army and are referred to in provincial radio broadcasts as counter-revolutionary uprisings by Soviet spies, Gang of Four followers, and so forth, but that's simply the standard terminology. We think there may be some significance to the fact that we've now encountered three such uprisings that refer to themselves as 'The Single Spark.'"

Zolti looked at him questioningly.

"You may recall," Soames said, "that Mao's essay called 'A Single Spark Can Start a Prairie Fire' was a seminal work igniting the Chinese Revolution in the 1930s."

Zolti's displeasure was by now quite apparent. Being an academic himself, he had the greatest contempt for others who attempted the geopolitical art. "Committees like this one haven't had to take a short course in the works of Chairman Mao since Vietnam. It seems to me your bright young men working over the documents have got your analysis stuck in some earlier time frame."

"That may be. Of course, the Chinese peasants may also be stuck in an earlier time frame." Soames closed his portfolio.

23

"Is that all?" Zolti asked.

"I believe that's all that's necessary." Frederick Soames had withdrawn behind his professional mask.

"Then shall we begin, gentlemen, to nail down some particulars regarding our military relationship with China?" Zolti's small body was charged with taut energy.

"I think we should start with a few joint staff meetings." It was the general speaking.

"Ah, very good," Zolti responded. It was always refreshing to deal with the military after a bout with one of these convoluted intellectuals. "I'd like your staff to begin drawing up some specific plans for such meetings, keeping in mind, naturally, that as far as the Chinese are concerned, they're joint meetings, but from our point of view, they need not be. Do I make myself quite clear?"

The general nodded. People like Zolti always thought military men lacked subtlety. It was irritating. He was perfectly capable of understanding what a joint staff meeting with the Chinese was without having Zolti explain it to him.

"As you are well aware," Zolti continued, "we have position papers on all the areas under discussion. Our main concern this morning is to come to an agreement on which ones are primary and to recommend their immediate implementation to the President. As I see it, there are three: First, joint military planning, as the general has already so judiciously recommended. Second, the immediate go-ahead on training missions. And the third is military equipment."

They were all aware of the progression that had already taken place in the last category. The big shift had occurred after Afghanistan from what was essentially civilian equipment with obvious military applications—communications satellites, for example—to nonlethal military hardware. "Trucks, communications gear, and certain types of early warning radar," the announcement had stated. It was a signal to Moscow, of course, and the response that followed indicated that the signal had been understood—only too well. Brezhnev returned the message via the president of the French assembly, Chaban-Delmas. It was, in essence, a rather simple one: that if the U.S. armed China with nuclear missiles, the Russians would destroy the Chinese nuclear sites and the United States would have only minutes to choose between "the defense of their Chinese allies or peaceful coexistence with us." Warnings had sounded in Paris and London, but Washington's position was to take it as a bluff. This morning's decision would up the ante once again.

Stefan Zolti surveyed the gathering magisterially as the members of WASAC began to collect their papers.

"I'm sure I don't have to remind you that the press is to know nothing of our plans. We've done remarkably well in avoiding leaks from this committee. The President is extremely pleased with our record in this regard. He and I expect that it will continue."

Then he added, almost as an afterthought, "You all understand, of course, that some of the specifics will have to be worked out between the President and myself and will of necessity be secret."

They all understood. The specifics were always secret.

CHAPTER

3

An absurd nostalgia swept over Anne as she sat by the window and surveyed the room that would be her home in the Peking Hotel. It was five years since she'd been in China, and that time it was Canton, but except for southern deference to the oppressive heat— the mosquito netting over the bed, the whirring of the electric fan —it was all the same here in the North. The ugly plush sofas and overstuffed chairs modestly covered in beige slipcovers, the patterned cotton bedspread, the bright red hot-water thermos gaudily painted with flowers and phoenixes. She was pleased that she'd been housed in the old wing of the hotel. She was indeed in China.

The Peking Hotel was pre-Revolution, its worn brick exterior and curved carriage driveway perversely poignant reminders of the history of the century. A long succession of different guests had replaced one another in the high-ceilinged old dining room. The jeweled women with their powerful husbands from the old elite had given way to the gray- and blue-suited new elite of the Revolution who danced there in the fifties, when their power was fresh and filled with possibilities and even a few Western foxtrots were not to be feared. The Russians had followed; then the Africans, Latin Americans, and Asians of the Third World alliance; the Vietnamese briefly; and now the businessmen and tourists of the West, who ordered bacon and their eggs sunny-side up.

Arrangements had been made for Anne to have an interpreter-secretary who would also be her "Chinese friend"—and, of course,

watchful guardian and transmitter of her every word. It was an
official courtesy, and for Anne, a woman alone, every traditional
Chinese justification dictated it. So, upon her arrival at the Peking
Airport, she had been greatly relieved to see the woman who
stepped out of the crowd to greet her. She was short, rather round,
of the indistinguishable age that characterizes many Chinese women
between forty and sixty, but probably in her late forties. Her face
was serious, while her first remarks had an offhand briskness that
melted Anne's defenses.

"Welcome to Peking. I'm Tan Yulan," she said, offering her
small, strong hand. "I hope you had a good trip. I'm sure you'd like
to get into the city as quickly as possible, but there are a few
formalities that have to be taken care of." Her English was compe-
tent and exact, and as she spoke, she lightly but firmly directed Anne
toward the airport door that would lead to the proper reception
room. The March cold was a shock as they crossed the airfield in
the dry brightness of Peking's early spring.

What good luck, Anne thought, to have drawn a sensible middle-
aged cadre instead of one of the multitude of sweet young interpret-
ers full of half-baked platitudes about China and the world. It was
a consideration that couldn't have been accidental—nothing of this
nature ever was in China—and it boded well for her work here. It
seemed the Chinese weren't going to hold Paul Engleberg's transgressions against her. Quite the contrary. By assigning her a mature,
experienced woman, they were indicating the importance they attached to her position.

So as Anne sat before her window the next morning, smoking a
cigarette and awaiting her companion's arrival, she was filled with
pleasant anticipation. At precisely one minute before nine, there was
a light, sharp knock on the door and Anne opened it for Tan Yulan.
Over her well-tailored gray trousers and jacket, she was wearing a
dark blue overcoat of only subtly better woolen cloth than the
cotton ones worn by almost all Peking residents. Like everyone's,
it was lined with fur or sheepskin, the opulence of the skins decor-
ously hidden under a drab cotton lining. It was buttoned high to the
hooded collar, but knotted almost rakishly around her neck was a
delicate, thoroughly unfunctional scarf of pale pink chiffon. It was,
Anne knew, one of those small symbols that in a world of unisex
clothing signaled rank and femininity to those who read the code.

"Good morning," she said briskly. "Today we're going to Tian-

27

anmen Square and all the important buildings and museums there. It is the heart of Peking." Tan Yulan's tone was definitive. "I think you'll find that's enough walking for one morning—unless there's any other place in central Peking that you're especially anxious to see."

"Well, yes, there is," Anne responded cautiously. "I know that Democracy Wall has been gone for a long time, but is there any place now where people post their criticisms?"

Tan Yulan's frown was almost imperceptible. "That really is some sort of—what do you call it?—fad, I think, particularly among Americans. Criticism and self-criticism are part of our society. There's no longer any need to have a special wall. There are proper channels for that sort of thing, and responsible people understand how to use them correctly."

Anne nodded. The subject was definitely closed. However, it was better to have been up-front with Tan Yulan from the beginning. The Chinese felt more at ease when they had their foreigners properly catalogued.

As they emerged from the hotel, the sunshine was brilliant, but the cold was fierce. "I'm afraid you'll find it too cold," Mrs. Tan said. "Shall we order a car? It'll take just a minute." Anne refused politely. If she was going to have any sort of independence here, she knew it was necessary to establish her credentials from the very beginning, and that meant no pampering beyond what was obligatory. She pulled up her hood and put her gloved hands in her pockets.

The sidewalks of Wangfujing Street were packed with people, everyone—men, women, and children—heavily padded against the season. The somber blues, browns, and blacks of adult clothing were brilliantly accented by the toylike figures of children in rainbows of reds, pinks, oranges, and greens. These were the serious faces of the North, all staring—not unfriendly, but searching—at a woman so tall and wearing the fascinating clothes of the West now coveted by the younger generation.

Tiananmen Square was exactly as Anne had seen it in a hundred photographs and films—massive, sweeping, and powerfully symmetrical; the buildings Soviet Romanesque, but here, with the vermilion gates of the old pavilioned palace, quintessentially post-'49 Chinese. There were people everywhere, walking and bicycling with heads lowered against the biting cold: visitors taking pictures;

peasants staring openmouthed at their first sight of this "heart" of the nation; groups of children obediently following their padded and pigtailed teachers.

It was a happy circumstance, Anne decided, to see the Forbidden City for the first time on a day like this, for it was indeed a palace of winter, not dependent for its artistry on the exquisite gardens of the South, but of a piece with the stark North China Plain and the great overarching sky. Stone and bronze, those monumental materials, had been forged into brilliant symmetry, the genius of man shaping his world in harmony with the imperatives of nature. Just as the cathedrals of Europe directed one's eyes heavenward, so the stone steps and pavilions of the palace grounds illuminated the dialectic of Heaven and Earth.

Tan Yulan was an excellent guide. There seemed to be nothing she didn't know about this place and its history. But she also was sensitive to Anne's unspoken inclination to walk in silence. On their way out, Anne stood for a long moment before the ancient bronze crane just inside the great gate—the powerful, graceful bird worn smooth by a million hands, symbolic of immemorial China.

Anne and Tan Yulan walked with the crowd toward the red gate that would lead them again onto the square. When they reached the sidewalk, they turned left in the direction of the Peking Hotel. Anne felt strangely at home. She had seen what was on the perimeter of her new abode and liked it greatly. As they strolled slowly, a panorama of images unfolded in her mind: scarlet walls and marble bridges, bronze lions and golden roofs.

A sharp push from behind jolted her. People elbowed past. Among the stolid crowd, which only moments before had been moving patiently along the sidewalk, there was a sudden electricity. Even in the middle of the square, people suddenly broke away from their picture-taking and sightseeing and ran in the direction of the increasingly packed area. Over their heads, Anne could now see the attraction: The long sheets of a wall poster were being pasted up, a tight cluster of readers gathering around each new page.

Anne turned excitedly to Tan Yulan. "It looks as if I'm going to be able to see everything I wanted to today. That must be an interesting poster. I've never seen a crowd gather so fast." Anne started in their direction.

Mrs. Tan stopped abruptly. "You can't assume that something is important just because a lot of curiosity seekers rush to see it. People

29

always like scandal. Putting up big-character posters in Tiananmen Square is illegal, you know. Come, let's get back to the hotel. This could be dangerous." Her manner, though still mild, was nonetheless authoritative.

Anne felt her temper rising. "Are you telling me that you're going to prohibit me from reading that poster?"

Mrs. Tan spoke with exasperating patience. "I can't prevent you from doing something you insist on doing. We Chinese do not prohibit our foreign friends. We try to help them understand China. I'm merely telling you that you will learn very little from the kind of bad elements who brazenly break the law in this way."

"Thank you for your concern, but I'm going to read the poster."

"As you wish." Tan Yulan's lips were tight. "I'll wait for you here. Please try to be careful. Crowds like that one can be dangerous when they get excited. I'm responsible for your safety."

It was hardly necessary for Anne to push her way toward the wall. The momentum of the crowd propelled her forward. Intense black eyes looked at her with curiosity and occasional hostility, but the strange Western woman in their midst was of far less interest than the pages on the wall.

It was a great advantage to be tall in China. You couldn't escape the staring, no matter what size or shape you happened to be, but the extra inches were a help in viewing things over the heads of the ever present crowds. Anne realized it would be impossible for her to get close to the wall, but when she was three or four persons back, she found she could read at least the top half of the first few sheets.

The title was in the tradition of the rebellious past: "Who Are the Reactionary Monsters in Power Who Are Imprisoning the People?"

"Why have the people no rights in the People's Republic?" it read. "A dictatorship of imperial officials is oppressing the people just as they did in the dark days of the past. Everywhere people are rising to grasp the rights promised in the constitution, but whenever they do, they are arrested and imprisoned in the jails of the tyrants. In the last two weeks, 300 people have been arrested in the Peking area. Who are these people and what are their crimes?"

Although Anne's Chinese was good, she read more slowly than those around her, and she realized that, standing in one spot, tall as she was, she was annoying the people behind her who were pushing to get closer to the poster. The faces were intent and serious. There

30

was little talking around her, only angry mutterings, but there was a frightening quality to the mood of the throng. She tried to move toward the last half of the poster, but the crowd there, mostly young and male, did not budge. Many were pointing. They seemed to be picking out names from a long list and reading them aloud.

Anne was startled by the grip of a firm hand on her elbow and a woman's voice in her ear. "Come with me. I'll lead you to a spot where you can see a little more. Then you must leave quickly. This is a dangerous place for you. The people are angry and the police will arrive soon." The crisply modulated Peking dialect was that of the city's native born. Anne turned in surprise. Standing next to her, facing the poster, was a young woman. She was not quite as tall as Anne, but very tall for a Chinese woman. Her hand on Anne's elbow was long and fragile, and her face, when she turned it toward Anne, was slender, with the high, elegant bones of the North. Her short, severe haircut and worn blue jacket could not conceal that she was a beauty in the classical mold. Under thick, black, perfectly arched brows, her oval eyes were cool and assured.

Anne found herself being moved efficiently through the crowd, the young woman's hand now holding her own. When they stopped, they were close to the front, but slightly off to the side. It was as the young woman had said. Anne could get a good overall view from this spot and would then be able to leave quickly. The final sheets consisted of a listing of names, but more interesting to Anne were the titles that accompanied them: Zhu Mazhi, Chairman of the Workers' Committee of the Peking Radio Factory; Ma Wenqing, Chairman of the Southwest Peking District of the Revolutionary Youth Committee; Wang Ailin, Representative of the Young Women's Committee Against Sexual Oppression; Li Tanlu, Representative of the Underground Students' Association . . . The list ran into hundreds.

"What is this? What does it mean?" Anne asked urgently.

"Why are you here? Why are you interested in this?" the young woman asked in return. The expression on her face was neither friendly nor unfriendly, but the tone of her voice betrayed an equal urgency.

"My name is Anne Campbell. I'm an American newspaperwoman, and I'm interested in learning everything I can about China. That's not easy for foreigners to do, so I came to read the poster myself, although I was warned not to."

31

Anne caught the slightest hint of a smile. "Are you interested in learning more about the information in this poster?" she asked.

"Of course." Amazing, Anne thought. Almost a replay of Paul's experience. The rebels must be seeking out foreign reporters.

The young woman nodded. "You've learned all you can here. You must leave now. It's dangerous for you, and your being here makes dangers for others." She took Anne's elbow once again and directed her toward the sidewalk, then disappeared into the crowd. It had become enormous. Though Anne could see the direction in which she had to go, it was very slow getting there, a steady pushing and squeezing past the seemingly endless mass of bodies.

By the time she reached the sidewalk, she was totally disoriented. Which direction was the Peking Hotel—to the left or the right? Tan Yulan had stationed herself determinedly near a lamp post, but which one? Anne hadn't glanced at her watch since they'd arrived at the square. Had her look at the poster taken five minutes or forty-five? She had no idea. Yes, she'd better get herself together before she started off in entirely the wrong direction. Taking out a cigarette, she viewed the crowd from this safe distance. It had become a great blue body, swaying first one way and then the other with a roaring sound like an enraged animal. If she'd seen it like this at first, perhaps even with her usual fearlessness, she might have been influenced by Tan Yulan's warnings.

Then suddenly, as if by a violent internal convulsion, the crowd began to fragment. Black figures rushed from the periphery and, in an abrupt explosion, the throng burst out onto the square. A line of khaki-colored men swarmed out of trucks and ran, waving clubs, into the great body of the crowd, which shattered into a hundred jagged pieces. And then the crowd was gone. The police began to return to their trucks, leading blue figures, their heads down, their hands fastened behind their backs.

Anne frowned, straining to see. What had happened to the young woman? Had she been arrested? It was impossible to tell from this distance whether the dark-trousered figures were even men or women. How odd, she thought, realizing how intensely she cared whether or not the woman was among the prisoners. I don't even know who she is.

"Oh dear, I thought I'd never find you." The voice was filled with scarcely disguised irritation. It was Tan Yulan, looking weary and severe. "You're nowhere near the place you left me, but of course, you don't know where you are. I really do criticize myself for letting you be so stubborn. You foreigners always want to be where the excitement is, but we have a responsibility to see that nothing happens to you. And what a disgrace, for you to be in the middle of an illegal affair your first day in Peking! Come, we must get you back to your hotel." Her voice was not unkind. In fact, Anne thought, she must blame herself far more than she blames me, and she'll probably have hell to pay with her superiors, whoever they are, for being so negligent in supervising yet another troublesome reporter.

"I'm sorry to have worried you," Anne said placatingly. "But you see, I'm perfectly all right. I'm quite used to taking care of myself —you must understand that—and my work has often taken me into dangerous situations." Even as she spoke, Anne was aware of her hypocrisy. If it hadn't been for her unexpected guide, who knows where Tan Yulan might have found her. Probably in a police station.

"Also," Anne continued, suddenly feeling quite unsteady, "I think it's important for women not to be afraid of difficult situations. I'm sure you must agree with me."

It wasn't easy to back Tan Yulan into a corner. "There *are* situations that are more dangerous for women than for men," she responded firmly. "However, that was not the problem. This situation was dangerous for a foreigner. If you had been a man, I would have told you the same thing."

Anne smiled. There was no doubt that she would have. They walked the remaining distance to the hotel in a silence that was by no means unfriendly.

As soon as they entered Anne's room and she took off her jacket, Mrs. Tan said, "You must be very tired. You should have lunch now." She stood poised at the door, her shopping bag held tightly in her gloved hands.

"I'm really not either tired or very hungry. Just a little wound up. Why don't you sit down and have a cup of tea with me before we both go to lunch?"

Tan Yulan hesitated only briefly. Her duty lay here. She took off her coat and gloves and laid them neatly on a chair. On the glass-topped table there was a tray with a flowered teapot, two lidded mugs, and a tin cannister of tea. Mrs. Tan sprinkled tea into the pot and poured in steaming hot water from the thermos standing on the floor.

"You're a little like my daughter," she said unexpectedly. "Very stubborn."

Anne was startled. It was always difficult to imagine that the smoothly professional Chinese cadres assigned to foreigners were people with children, laundry, dishes to wash, messy domestic lives. They seemed so impersonal, so committed to their work, so free of the emotional baggage that Americans carried everywhere with them.

"But you couldn't be old enough to have a daughter my age." Anne said. "I'm thirty-two."

"She's younger than you. She's a university student now." The expression on Tan Yulan's round, serious face was pleased.

"Studying what?"

"Petroleum engineering. That field is going to be very important for our country in the future."

"Yes, it certainly is. But really, a woman in petroleum engineering. That's fantastic. Even in the United States, that's very rare."

Mrs. Tan beamed. Yes, Anne thought, she's really a very nice woman. If she acts like a mother hen, it's because she thinks I need one.

"Do you have other children?"

"No." Tan Yulan's voice was suddenly distant.

Anne immediately realized that she had made an error. She should never have asked Tan Yulan about her family. One didn't do that in China, she knew, but since the other woman had initiated the subject . . . There was silence. Anne refilled both cups with tea and took out a cigarette.

At last Mrs. Tan said gravely, "Perhaps it would be useful for you to hear about my family. You're here to learn about Chinese politics and what the Chinese people think. We tell you many things, but foreigners don't seem to believe them unless they hear them as personal stories. We don't think personal stories are necessary, but . . ." She shrugged her shoulders.

"My daughter was just a baby when the Cultural Revolution began. I was pregnant at the time with another one. My husband and I had planned to have a modern family of two.

"My husband and I were both working at the Foreign Ministry.

I was quite young and had been working for only a short time in the department of American affairs. I had been a student of English at the university. My husband was considerably older than I, in his forties, and held a more important post as a deputy minister. He'd been educated in the United States, at Columbia University, but had chosen to return in 1950 to work for the new China.

"The ultra-left line was active in the Foreign Ministry all through the Cultural Revolution, for the class struggle was particularly fierce in such a key ministry. Everyone who'd had any experience in the West was very severely attacked, and naturally that included my husband." She stopped speaking and paused as if to compose herself.

"What happened?" Anne spoke very softly.

"There were many struggle meetings held against him. He was accused of being an American spy. Of course, it was ridiculous. American spies don't give their lives to work for China the way he did. His health had been poor for years. He had an ulcer and high blood pressure. He became very sick and had an attack of bleeding ulcers, but even then they had no mercy. Time and again he was pulled out of his bed to be paraded in front of mass rallies and struggled against."

"Insane," Anne murmured. "Awful."

"The state of his health was partly responsible for what happened, but mostly it was what happened to his spirit. He couldn't bear to think that he wasn't trusted, that his work and his sacrifice hadn't been honored. He committed suicide," she concluded bluntly.

"Oh my God," Anne said in a low voice. "How terrible. I am so, so sorry. And what happened to you?"

"There were some meetings held against me just because I was his wife. I don't think anybody really believed what they said against me, but naturally my health was affected and I lost the baby. After his death, they left me alone. What did I do? . . . She paused. "I lived through the rest of the decade like everyone else, went back to my old job, and raised my daughter."

Tan Yulan stood up abruptly. It was clear that she didn't wish the conversation to continue. "I only tell you this story because you can't understand China today if you don't understand how people suffered during that terrible time."

Anne helped her with her coat. "Thank you for telling me. It's very good of you to try to help me understand things at such a painful cost to yourself."

35

"It's my duty to help you understand," Mrs. Tan said solemnly. She put on her gloves and picked up her plastic shopping bag. "You know where the dining room is, so I can leave you now. Be sure to take a nap after lunch. Everyone here does that, you know. You'll be going to a banquet tonight, and you'll want to feel your best."

Anne opened the door and watched the short, stocky figure walk sturdily to the elevator. She was overwhelmed with sadness.

After lunch Anne realized she was exhausted. Very odd, it wasn't like her to be tired in the middle of the day. Perhaps it was jet lag. There would be no problem with Tan Yulan's instructions about taking a nap. Suddenly, she couldn't think of anything except sleep.

Her sleep, though, was fitful, and she woke up feeling drugged, her head aching fiercely. There was a knock on the door, and she realized that that was what had awakened her.

"Who is it?" she shouted in Chinese.

"Hot water."

What idiocy, she thought. Why wake people up for hot water?

The room attendant was a cheerful young man with a thick, broomlike brush of black hair. He moved quietly in his cotton shoes as he replaced the thermos and put down a tray with clean cups and another flowered teapot. Seeing that she was in bed, he was careful not to look in her direction, but as he went to the door, he said almost offhandedly, "Someone sent you a note. It's on the tray."

Anne walked across the room to look. Yes, there it was: a cheap grayish-white envelope, sealed, but blank. The message inside was written in delicate, fastidious characters: "If you are interested in learning more about the subject you were studying today, you may meet me on Monday morning at ten o'clock at the Peony Gate Teahouse. It is the last building at the end of the first west lane after you pass Qianmen Gate. You can walk there easily." In the margin, there was a lightly sketched map.

Anne folded the note carefully and put it back in the envelope. What had she gotten herself into in only one day? Was she fated to be Paul's successor in more ways than one, whether she chose to or not? She couldn't let herself get expelled before she'd even had a chance to begin working. She did have a career to consider—Larry Metcalf had been very explicit. She needed more time. What did one do with a note like this? Chew it up? Burn it? Tear it into pieces and flush it down the toilet? Paul had simply kept his in his wallet. She took it out again and studied the map carefully.

CHAPTER

4

Peter Matthewson had found his first weeks in Peking very pleasant indeed. The work routine was almost immediately apparent—the documents to be analyzed, reports to be prepared, briefings on the current situation for the ambassador. So far, though, his fear that the life of an embassy political secretary might be purely bureaucratic appeared groundless. In fact, this seemed to be the job he'd been waiting for, a job with the real possibility of doing something, perhaps even influencing the twists and turns of U.S.-China policy just a bit.

Peter was far from uninitiated. He'd served the required apprenticeship for this China assignment—the Harvard graduate degree, the State Department novitiate where he'd ground out scholarly briefing papers that those with real power would probably never read. He'd been to China, too. First, a year in Nanking to do research on the Taiping Rebellion. Later, he'd been rewarded for his memo writing by being sent as an interpreter-factotum on several government junkets that did the standard tour, consumed an inordinate amount of banquet food, and returned to Washington to report that everything was under control. But this was the real thing, the tangible trophy that orthodoxy promised to those who studied hard, worked conscientiously, and were, if at all possible, bright, handsome, six foot one, and a product of the best schools.

The agreeable surprise of the new job was the fact that the ambassador was obviously prepared to give Peter more responsibility than he'd had any reason to expect—at least so soon.

"I'm glad to see you on the staff," Ambassador Carpenter had told him directly. "A straight-talking Westerner is what we need here to help us get to the heart of this Chinese double-talk. They're sensible, tough-minded people—good to work with, but they have their own way of doing and saying things, and I can't claim to understand them."

Although Carpenter wasn't much interested in the old-school-tie business, he was pleased to have another Stanford man in, as he remarked wryly, "this nest of the Eastern Establishment." Both an electronics engineer and a Stanford M.B.A., Carpenter was an industrialist of the future—his specialty was microcomputers. The clean and lively industrial parks of Silicon Valley were his home base, not the dying, smoky Allegheny. He saw no limits to the possibilities of the computer revolution for the Chinese population of a billion, and he thoroughly enjoyed the idea that his ambassadorial position might open the way for that development: bringing together the men of power from East and West; shepherding the agreements that would tie China into a network of forward-looking multinationals through the next century. But the constrictions of diplomatic procedures and the esoteric ways of the Chinese could be very irritating. It was a relief to be able to turn over to Peter any number of tiresome little diplomatic-political duties which nonetheless had to be handled well.

Like this morning . . . Peter looked at Anne Campbell's vitae while he waited for her to arrive. Thanks to the smoothness of Chinese protocol, "*l'affaire* Engleberg" (as it was jokingly known) had gone off as well as possible. There had been almost no public attention, but it had also been a mess. Before they got what they wanted—namely, Engleberg's expulsion—the Chinese had threatened all kinds of diplomatic and commercial retaliation, and there had been no way of knowing just how far they would go.

It had been hard enough to get U.S.-China relations back on track after the period of arms sales to Taiwan, and then for one reporter to threaten to upset things again. . . . It was clear Carpenter had been furious about the whole business. He had particularly disliked bending to the Chinese in their demands for restrictions on the press. Obviously, the whole thing had been allowed to go too far before anything was done. This time the problem must simply not develop

39

in the first place. However, talking with newspaper people was not something Carpenter regarded as a useful expenditure of his time. He had no doubt that Peter could handle it.

Anne Campbell. The name seemed familiar as soon as Peter heard it, and the vitae was certainly interesting: B.A., Stanford, Asian history; M.A., U.C. Berkeley, journalism. She'd graduated from Stanford two years after he had, but hadn't there been an Anne Campbell in one of his Chinese classes? One of those small, old classrooms on the quad, where the cultivated Professor Zhang wrote characters on the blackboard as her jade bracelets jingled softly. He couldn't even remember what Anne Campbell looked like, but if it was the same person, his task would be that much easier.

The embassy receptionist ushered Anne into his office at precisely eleven o'clock, and he recognized her immediately. She was taller than he remembered, and undoubtedly she'd become more polished —her sweater-dress was unobtrusively elegant on her admirable figure—but she was still prototypically California: good-looking to a fault and absolutely self-assured. Very handsome types by the time they reached their thirties, and he hadn't been around one for quite some time.

"Welcome to Peking." Peter smiled his boyish smile as he rose and extended his hand in greeting. "I think we may be old class-mates."

"I thought you looked somewhat familiar." Anne's smile was pleasant, but her tone hardly enthusiastic.

Though it would have been impossible to fault her good manners, there was, in fact, a definite coolness. The embassy's message, tele-phoned by an anonymous secretary, had been cordial but vague: Could she stop by some time soon? They just wanted to welcome her and make sure all her arrangements were satisfactory. There was no indication who "they" might be. Anne knew it wasn't reason-able, but she had been hoping for Ambassador Carpenter—an inter-esting man, if Washington gossip was to be believed—not at all the run-of-the-mill ambassador. So it had been disappointing, perhaps even a bit insulting, to be ushered into the office of this smooth-looking second-stringer.

"I'm not wrong, am I?" Peter asked. "Aren't you also one of Professor Zhang's Chinese-language products?"

"Yes I am, though I doubt she'd rush to claim me."

Peter chuckled. "I don't know how pleased she'd be with any of

40

us now that we're operating on her home turf. Remember what she used to say about not trying to use the Peking 'r' unless you'd been born to it?"

Anne smiled. "Are you following her instructions or not?"

"Of course not. I listen to the natives and copy them as well as I can. I think my pronunciation sounds pretty good, and the Chinese are too polite to tell me otherwise. Maybe I'll have to try it out on you. I imagine you'll give me a straight answer, since newspaper people aren't exactly strong on flattery."

"I'm afraid our reputation for forthrightness is greatly exaggerated." Anne spoke lightly. She felt him looking at her with just a touch of ironic intimacy, a glance that said, "We have a lot in common." Really quite an attractive man, she thought. Not at all like the Peter Matthewson of her Chinese class. Well, it was true that men improved with age.

"If that's so, it's too bad, isn't it. Courtiers of the press are the last thing we need in Washington today. In fact, I was astonished at how long it took them to take on our previous Prez—long after his policies were obviously a shambles."

"If you can call them policies." Anne smiled. "At any rate, I'm delighted to hear that you're not in favor of a lapdog press."

Somehow she'd taken the ball and run with it a bit farther than Peter had intended. "I don't think you'll find anybody here who's in favor of a lapdog press. We rely very heavily on having an independent press corps in Peking. That's the reason we asked you to stop by this morning: to offer our support and help if you should ever need it." There was still a trace of a smile on Peter's square-jawed face, but he appeared once again the polished foreign service officer. The slightly impudent man Anne had just started to like was gone.

"I'm glad to hear that," she said, hoping she didn't sound as nettled as she suddenly felt. "I've been here only a few days, but I have the impression I'm going to need all the help I can get to find out what's going on."

"You know, we're pretty constrained ourselves in some of these matters," Peter replied carefully. "There are places even the ambassador can't go, and things that none of us can see. We're obliged to show a certain deference toward Chinese feelings about that sort of thing. I'm sure you must know how difficult it's been to get the relationship back on track since the Taiwan arms-sale fiasco."

41

"Is that the machinery Paul Engleberg got ground up in?" Anne's voice was politely noncommittal.

So—they were on the subject that was the real purpose of the meeting, and it was she who had brought it up, not he.

"Actually, Engleberg wasn't ground up." In spite of himself, there was a slight edge of annoyance in his voice. "Considering that he wrote articles he knew very well the Chinese didn't want written, they handled the matter in a very civilized way."

"Civilized?"

"Yes, civilized. There was no public to-do, no Russian-style surveillance and detention. The Chinese just discussed it quietly over tea with our people and said they didn't think it would be in either side's interest to make an issue of it. They even suggested that it would probably be best if Engleberg stayed to the last minute of his two years, wrote some nice innocuous stuff in the meantime, and left with the usual farewell banquet and toasts of eternal friendship. Yes, I'd call that civilized."

Anne shook her head, tight-lipped. "So much for the independence of the press. A man writes the truth, and the measure of civilization is how effectively and quietly he's shut up. Worse yet, our embassy participates in his expulsion. That's rather important for a new correspondent to know, isn't it?"

It irritated Peter enormously that he had let the conversation take such an antagonistic turn. The message he had to communicate to Anne Campbell was nothing surprising. Surely she'd been told the same thing in Washington. She was evidently a real prima donna, yet she was somehow making him feel like a fool.

He made sure he had his voice and face completely under control before he spoke again. "I understand your position. Your job is to report the news and to find the most dramatic stories you can. That's what Engleberg was doing too. But the reality we're dealing with —we and the Chinese—is much bigger than a few demonstrations. That's not the whole truth about China, any more than every student demonstration in America is the truth for us. We all have to look at the big picture—the geopolitical picture." She was looking at him with something so close to amusement that he actually felt like hitting her—incredible!

She raised an eyebrow. "I beg your pardon. *You* have to look at the big picture. You're a representative of the United States government. I'm not. Our responsibilities are not precisely the same."

Peter forced himself not to respond directly to her challenge. "I'm sure you're a good journalist. I just don't want to see you get yourself stuck in a corner just because, like most reporters, you think the trees are more important than the forest."

"Thank you." There was a barely discernible touch of mockery in her voice. "That forest/tree dilemma is something we all have to struggle with, isn't it?"

Peter laughed in spite of himself, and realized with surprise that indignant as he was, he was beginning to enjoy tangling with her.

Suddenly Anne's severity vanished too and she was laughing with him.

"Look," he said impulsively. "Let's call a truce. I think we've both made our points. Why don't we go at the China experience from another angle. There are some great restaurants around. Let's have lunch at one of them. It's hard to stay mad when you're both dipping your chopsticks into the Peking noodles."

The diplomat's even smile had given way again to the joking grin. Really not a bad guy, Anne thought, and very winning in a rather predictable way. He probably jogged five miles a day and then read a few pages from Kissinger's *Memoirs* every night before going to sleep.

"Lunch sounds fine, unless you're afraid I'm going to leak the name of your favorite restaurant to the *Inquirer.*"

"You've got to run a few risks in this job," Peter said as he helped her into her down jacket. His hands on her shoulders were rougher than necessary for such a task, and Anne wasn't sure whether she was experiencing an embrace or an attack.

Peter's work with the ambassador was going very smoothly. Tom Carpenter was demanding, but he wasn't a tyrant. He was a doer, a problem solver, impatient with sloppiness; and Peter Matthewson wasn't sloppy. He looked forward to their work together and was getting quite used to Carpenter's abrupt, no-nonsense manner, but none of this prepared him for the ambassador's mood on this particular Monday morning. When Peter came into his office, the ambassador was standing by the tall window looking out onto the barren street. As he turned around, his eyes blazed behind his gold-rimmed glasses.

"Leave the economic reports today," he said curtly. "I have a few other problems I need you to work on—immediately." He swung his large frame into the chair behind his desk and motioned for Peter to sit across from him. "Several puzzling developments lead me to believe that something very important is happening, and I don't know what it is. I don't like that. In fact, I won't tolerate it." Carpenter's tone was ominous. "I have a hunch we may find at least a partial key in the Chinese situation. I want you to work on this and nothing else until we've unraveled all we can."

Tom Carpenter rose as suddenly as he'd sat down and walked back to the window. "I have reason to suspect that I'm being back-channeled from Washington. Ever since Zolti's man Haggard arrived, communication has been very superficial and routine. My guess is, Haggard has instructions to do a little secret policy implementation of his own."

Lowell Haggard had not been at the embassy for very long, but from the beginning, it was clear that there was something special about him. His office was physically separated from the routine flow of embassy work. He had brought his own secretary with him. He came and went as he pleased. But one didn't ask questions—or even think about them very much. Everyone understood that there were areas in an embassy's work that were strictly off limits.

Lowell Haggard was flawlessly courteous—a southerner, after all. Mississippi or Alabama? The Deep South, in any case, Peter recalled. From the top of his thinning sandy hair to the soles of his highly polished shoes, he was brushed, shined, newly pressed. A military man in civilian clothes, but definitely a military man. A somewhat mysterious figure. Hadn't someone told Peter he was a major general? Peter had heard of him in Washington but never seen him. "He's not into crisis management," Peter recalled someone saying. "He's only into war." Evidently a hawk's hawk.

"There's no need to remind you," Carpenter was continuing, "that what we discuss in this office goes no further. Embassies live on gossip. It's inevitable on these artificial little islands. There's already a lot of speculation about what Haggard's doing here. I have my own ways of finding out. I only share some of my thoughts with you so you'll have a sense of the broader context as you work on the pieces of the Chinese puzzle. I'm all in favor of a strict division of labor for people who put together computer components, but a political analyst needs a sense of the big picture."

44

"I appreciate that," Peter said. He really did. It was one of the good things about working with Carpenter.

"These goddamned southern martinets—historical hangovers! They're raised on lead soldiers and the legend of great-granddaddy's Colt pistol. They go off to VMI and on to the National War College and then we're stuck with them. They still think war's some kind of gentlemen's sport."

Peter had never seen him blow off steam like this, although Carpenter's reputation for a fierce temper had preceded him to Peking.

"A Lowell Haggard is exactly the worst sort of guy to put on a mission like the one he's obviously got. He's the sort who thinks he can figure a first-strike strategy the way he might organize a cavalry charge." Carpenter's imposing figure loomed before the window, and then he began to pace.

"I thought I'd heard that Haggard was a satellites expert," Peter interjected.

"He is," Carpenter replied impatiently. "But even a stiff dose of technology doesn't dent these guys' atavistic armor. We'll be lucky if we survive them long enough to sell the Chinese a few computers. But that's the kind of man Zolti likes to work with. They're alike —Hungarians and Mississippians—feudal knights in the nuclear age."

Carpenter sat down at his desk and was suddenly composed. "Okay, enough on that subject," he said. "Haggard is my problem, not yours. What I need from you is a solid analysis of the Chinese component so I know what he might be tying into here. There are two specific areas I want you to look into." Peter took out his notebook, but Carpenter waved his hand and shook his head. "Don't write this down," he said sternly. "Just listen.

"First, I noticed in the translation you gave me a few days ago that there seems to be a new chairman of the Chinese team negotiating with the Russians on the border question. As far as I know, the makeup of that team hasn't changed substantially in five years— certainly not the chairman, at any rate. The Chinese have always stressed to us that the negotiations are a pretty formalistic business. I want to know the significance of the change. That may be impossible, I know, but at least I want to know who this new man is, what his background is, what he represents politically."

"That probably won't be too difficult. We have a pretty good idea of who all these people are." Peter's response was consciously casual, but he was impressed. Clearly, Carpenter was as sharp as his reputation in Washington had indicated.

"Second, I want a detailed analysis of this major article from yesterday's *People's Daily*. One of the first things I was briefed on when I took this job is that when the Chinese get ready to swing into a big power struggle, they start putting metaphorical literary and historical stuff into the press, and everybody starts interpreting the symbols. I've never had the pleasure of seeing any of this during the time I've been here. Until yesterday's paper. Very interesting time for such a thing to appear. I assume you've read it."

"Yes," Peter replied. "I was going to mention it to you today, although I'm not sure I have a very solid analysis ready yet. Looks like you're right, though. Articles like that are almost always important."

The ambassador looked at Peter intently. "I know there's a lot of leeway with these interpretations. It's an exercise in Kreminology, reading between the lines. Very entertaining, if you're into that sort of thing. I don't expect you to come up with an airtight explanation. No one can be held responsible for making an error in this kind of business. But don't give me an answer you don't believe in. If you don't know, say so. We can't afford to make too many mistakes in this kind of thing."

"I know what you're saying—and thanks. Problem number one is just a matter of routine digging, and the second—well, I'll give it my best shot."

But a morning's work demonstrated that problem number one wasn't the routine matter Peter had expected. The new chairman of the Chinese border-talks team was Zhang Zhaolin—certainly not a name he could recall having heard. But he had come well prepared for work of this kind. It was, after all, the bread and butter of a China scholar's job—to have a handle on the backgrounds of the cadres periodically thrust to the top in the recurring cycles of China's byzantine politics. For what other reason, aside from publication itself, did graduate students do their statistical monographs on CCP political and military elites for the *China Quarterly*?

There were disasters in the field, of course. The case of Hua Guofeng had been the biggest one. How was it possible that a man could suddenly appear as Mao's successor—"With you in charge, I'm at ease" went the rather Victorian translation of Mao's benediction—and not a China scholar knew anything about him. The Presi-

46

dent had been in a rage, ready to sweep the whole East Asia staff out of State. The story had become a legend in Washington. Young China scholars were broken in on it. It was never to happen again.

Peter had come to Peking well prepared. His own files, accumulated over nearly ten years, were extremely thorough. He had even carried them with him on the plane, knowing that the loss of any of his other luggage would be insignificant by comparison. It had seemed appropriate to him that, should he go down in the Pacific, his files would go with him.

But of Zhang Zhaolin, there was nothing. In his file of recent clippings from the Chinese press, Peter found only one startling scrap of information about the new chairman of the Chinese border-talks team. In a minuscule Shanghai newspaper article about his appointment, it was mentioned that he was in his early forties. That was amazing. Sixty was regarded as young for a Chinese post of any significance. Zhang Zhaolin's age alone was reason to find out more about him. But Peter found nothing. He phoned the P.R.C. Research Institute in Hongkong, then his old office at State, and finally a librarian friend at the Hoover Library, but everywhere the response was the same—polite and solicitous, but absolutely no data. There was nothing to do but put the problem on hold and wait. But the lack of information was in itself indicative: A political unknown chairing the border-talks team? He had to hand it to Carpenter. The man really had an instinct for politics. Too bad Washington wasn't letting him run his own show.

Peter determined to put the nagging matter of Zhang Zhaolin out of his mind for a few hours and concentrate on problem number two. The analysis of the *People's Daily* article would be pleasant. While the tracing down of officials might be the nitty-gritty of a China scholar's work, this kind of literary and historical interpretation was far more entertaining.

The anecdote that formed the nucleus of the article was taken from the *Intrigues of the Warring States*. For two thousand years, Chinese scholars, followed by China scholars, had debated the *Intrigues'* historical accuracy, but it was by now generally accepted that a large part was history rewritten by succeeding dynasties in the long tradition of Chinese historiography. For Peter's purposes, historical accuracy was of little importance; the question was one of contemporary analogy. His desk was already littered with the tools of his trade: his favorite well-thumbed Chinese dictionaries; a modern translation of the *Intrigues* plus a copy of the original (not something he really needed to use, but he enjoyed having it in front of him for inspiration); the Chinese text from the *People's Daily*; and his own rough English translation.

The central story was an interesting one. Having been taken hostage and forced to give up five hundred *li* of his kingdom's land in order to be permitted to return to his home country and his father's funeral, the newly instated King of Chu asked his ministers what to do when the envoy of Qi arrived to claim the territory. The three ministers gave him three different pieces of advice: Give up the land and then fight for it; defend the land; or seek aid from the Qin kingdom in the west. Not knowing which advice was best, the King of Chu consulted his adviser, who recommended that the King use all three plans in order to test the wisdom of his three ministers.

And so it was done. The first minister met the Qi envoy to surrender the lands; the second followed to announce his intent to defend them. The angry leader of the Qi forces assembled his troups to attack. But the third plan triumphed. Before the enemy Qi could move, the Qin ally appeared with fifty thousand troops. The enemy forces were withdrawn and the eastern lands remained intact.

There was no mystery to the basic thrust of the article. It was entitled "The Soviet Tsars Are Up to Their Old Tricks" and was full of the familiar rhetoric about "Russia, an expansionist country by tradition," "the world's most barbarous and ferocious colonial empire," and "how the plans of the bureaucrat capitalist class in the Soviet Union for world hegemony begin with the steady expansion of their buffer territories."

Yet it seemed clear enough to Peter that under this familiar rhetoric lay some sort of reassessment of the Chinese position on the border talks, not a changed assessment of Soviet realities.

"What would have happened to the King of Chu," the article asked, "if the minister who advised surrender had had his way? And what would the outcome have been if the minister who advised military defense had faced the enemy alone? It is easy to find simple answers, but the correct ones are dialectical answers, based on the study of Marxism-Leninism. Just as, in ancient times, the mere appearance of the allied forces caused expansionist forces to withdraw, so today our correct alliance causes the aggressive forces of Soviet social-imperialism to withdraw. Those who fear such alliances place our shining socialist country in the gravest danger of

48

subjugation or destruction. The revolutionary will of the people will prevail. Those who oppose correct policies will come to no good end."

There could be no doubt that the current correct ally was the United States. But it also seemed apparent to Peter that there must be a danger, either real or perceived, to continued support of the alliance. This was the real message of the article. The assumption in Washington was that this battle had been fought out long ago— Lin Biao, the Gang of Four, all the politics of the last decade and a half had involved this issue to one degree or another. By now, China was so firmly tied into the U.S. alliance that any discussion of the matter seemed anachronistic. This strong article was something one might have expected to find in a leaflet, not as a major statement in the *People's Daily*. Still, there it was, and Peter saw no other way it could be read.

There were no return phone calls on the elusive problem of Zhang Zhaolin. Peter grew increasingly uneasy. Undoubtedly, something was happening with the border talks, and there was no way that the mysterious identity of this new chairman could be unrelated. Peter didn't want to see Carpenter until he had both problems solved, but he knew the ambassador would rather know part of the answer than operate with nothing. And certainly the difficulty of turning up any information on Zhang Zhaolin was an important part of whatever development was taking place. Peter made an appointment to see the ambassador, hoping that one of his sources might soon report back.

When the time came, however, there was nothing new.

"I'm not surprised. I sensed that we might run into some snags on this one." Carpenter was unexpectedly calm. "If anything really important is happening in the Chinese government, obviously it's going to be difficult to find out about. But you're right, of course. The fact that we're having trouble getting to the bottom of this makes it all the more critical that we do so. Keep on it until it cracks. I assume, however, that you untangled the *People's Daily* article?" It was with great relief that Peter was able to reply that he had.

Carpenter listened intently to his explanation, nodding from time to time. When Peter finished, there was a brief silence. Then Carpenter said slowly, "As you know, I'm a layman in all this. It's difficult for me to see any problem with your interpretation—particularly with this other border-talks business going on. But are you quite sure there couldn't be some other equally reasonable way to read this thing?"

"There's never any guarantee," Peter replied, weighing his words carefully. "Everything depends on what's actually happening in the internal Chinese situation. But I don't see that there could be many other interpretations of this particular article."

"All right. It certainly seems that way to me. And there's nothing we can do about it at the moment, anyway. It just goes into the hopper. But we must know more." Carpenter's voice had become urgent.

As he stepped into the curtained Red Flag limousine, Lowell Haggard was aware of Ambassador Carpenter's figure at the upstairs window of the embassy building. But it was of no importance. Haggard's prerogatives were well understood by everyone here, the ambassador most of all. There was resentment, Haggard knew, of his position as Zolti's man, but that was always the price of power.

He settled comfortably on the wide back seat, as the car started slowly through the Sanlitun diplomatic quarter. There were two diplomatic areas in Peking—the old and the new. Haggard personally enjoyed the ambiance of the old quarter, mostly because it reminded him of the South. The gracious nineteenth-century buildings stood amidst luxuriant gardens, all hidden from the street by high stone walls. The trees were huge old willows and sycamores, a rare phenomenon in treeless North China and in Peking itself, where most trees were regimented rows of poplars planted by the Communists after '49. There was a slow colonial charm in the old quarter that was not unlike Charleston or Savannah. But Haggard understood that for the Chinese, what was new was now ipso facto good. In their deference toward the United States, it would never have occurred to them to give the American embassy a building that was anything but the newest, shiniest, and most antiseptic possible. Sanlitun reminded him of those barren American housing tracts, expensive but dreadful.

PLA soldiers stood guard at the gates of each of the embassies as the car drove past. They were bright-eyed and smiling—real innocents, just like the soldiers in Chinese movies. He envied his Chinese counterparts: What a pleasure to command an army of simple, strong, young peasants. No one asking, "Why are we doing what we're doing?" No drugs, no blacks, no women getting pregnant and demanding their right to abortions. But Haggard had no illusions. There could be few naive rural soldiers in America, for even backwoods youngsters had been corrupted. It was a combination of many things—TV largely, but also the liberal welfare ideology that the damned northern Democrats had forced on the country for so long.

The United States Army of the last decades of the twentieth century had to be an army of high technology. He understood that. He was a technologist himself. But he was also a soldier's soldier. It had been his family tradition for two centuries, and he knew that in the last analysis, even in an era of nuclear weapons, there was no such thing as an army without foot soldiers. That was where the Chinese came in. He had grasped that from the beginning—had even stated it in Washington, where most people were too dishonorable to take a straightforward position. Of course, many of them hated the Russians as much as he, and understood as well as he that the combination of American technology and millions of simple Chinese soldiers was the military answer they had been praying for. Washington was a city of hypocrites—politicians weeping crocodile tears for the benefit of the gullible fools who voted them into office. It was a slimy business, but the military had no other choice than to work with them. Working with Zolti was another matter. The two men had understood each other from the moment they met. Neither was answerable to the public. Both knew that only a tiny elite was capable of planning world strategy. And for both of them, the defeat of the Soviet Union was at the heart of that strategy.

The long, black car moved smoothly out of the embassy quarter and into streets jammed with bicycles, blue-clad pedestrians, triwheelers pedaled by men with hard-muscled legs, horse-drawn carts driven by peasants wrapped in their worn, black, sheepskin-lined coats. Drivers of official cars like this one were remarkable. It would be difficult at home to hire such a chauffeur at any price. With nerves of steel he wheeled boldly through the crowds, honking the horn authoritatively as the people obediently scattered. It was odd, this custom of having drawn curtains in the cars of the powerful, but Haggard had come to like it—the secrecy, the privacy, the protection from the thousands who were everywhere, staring. It seemed very sensible to him that the rulers of a country with such enormous masses of people would find ways of hiding from them.

And singularly appropriate that men of state, their affairs conducted in secret, should be physically shrouded in secrecy too.

The Chinese understood such matters well. Arrangements for Haggard's meeting with Tang Chen had been made smoothly and quickly. One of the popular complaints among Westerners who did business with China was about the impossible perversity of Chinese red tape. But Haggard, like others in whom the Chinese recognized true power, had never experienced such problems. When they saw that it was in their interest to move with speed and efficiency, no one in the world was better at doing so.

The car turned off the busy public thoroughfare and without stopping passed through a heavily guarded iron gate. Obviously Haggard was expected. The two-lane road, which looked as if it had been swept only minutes before, wound between a double row of poplars, still bare in March. They were inside a parklike area with no one in sight. Haggard had little idea where he was, but he was only mildly curious. Tang Chen was a man who understood the requirements of power, the first of which was a proper meeting place for two men like themselves.

Haggard had initially met Tang during the historic Nixon visit to China. Haggard's role as special military envoy had even then been intended to signify America's serious interest in a future military relationship. As a symbolic recognition of Mao's position that the two countries' interests vis-à-vis the Russians were at least parallel, the Chinese had been presented with a precious gift—American satellite photos taken over the Soviet Union. They were duly impressed with the gesture. Haggard had been assigned the task of interpreting the photos to the man whom the Chinese would select as an appropriate counterpart. That man was Tang Chen.

Involved with Chinese security in a way that had never been quite clear to the outside world, he was one of those remarkable Chinese survivors, tough and resourceful. A Chinese Beria he was sometimes called, the difference being that he ended up back on top in the wake of every purge. Like Deng Xiaoping, he was known to have a network of organizational connections reaching into every province. Though he spoke no English and Haggard no Chinese, they had understood each other intuitively as they met periodically over the years, never for long, but always successfully.

The car drew to a stop before a low, beige building, a contemporary adaptation of traditional Chinese courtyard style. As if by signal, just as the car door opened, Tang Chen appeared in the doorway, hand outstretched. He was smiling in the ceremonial Chinese welcoming style, but this smile affected very little the coldness of his masklike face. His gaunt bone structure, almost total baldness, and extremely nearsighted eyes behind thick glasses were the whims of nature; but his expression was not. One could not, however, expect a man who had survived the political inquisitions that Tang had, to look upon the world with benevolence.

Tang Chen led the way to a spacious but simple room. At first glance, the furniture seemed ordinary—a sofa, two overstuffed chairs, a glass-topped coffee table. But there were subtle differences. The sofa was upholstered in a muted fabric of creamy brocade; the teapot and cups were of a fine-quality modern celadon; and several scrolls painted in the traditional style but dotted with tiny red flags hung on the wall.

A serious, square-faced young woman dressed entirely in gray wool was waiting for them. "I am Tang Meiling," she said pleasantly in careful English as she extended her hand. "I'm Tang Chen's daughter, and I will interpret for you today." Tang Chen waved Haggard to the sofa. When both men were seated, the daughter poured the tea and offered cigarettes. A Rolex watch ornamented her delicate wrist.

Tang began speaking in Chinese. His daughter's steady translation followed. "I'm very glad to welcome you back to Peking, General Haggard," he began, as always using Haggard's military title. The Chinese were quite comfortable with a military leader in a civilian role. "The interests of our two countries are well served by your visits here."

He gestured toward Tang Meiling. "My daughter has studied not only English but also the history and economics of the United States. Now that she's completed her graduate studies at Peking University, she has become an invaluable assistant to me. She has an excellent understanding of our mutual areas of interest, and though she will only interpret our discussion, I hope you will feel the same confidence in her that I do myself."

Haggard nodded. This use of female relatives was a particularly brilliant Chinese way of meshing the old with the new. The traditional family structure, with its complex network of loyalties and mutual obligations, was retained, but women were now permitted to participate. However, they seldom had real power, being depen-

53

dent on the influence of their fathers, uncles, husbands, or brothers, and were entirely expendable if the need arose. In fact, they were extremely useful scapegoats for policies for which they'd had little responsibility. Tang Chen could trust no man as he could trust his daughter. Not only was she his offspring, but even if she wished to do so, she would find it nearly impossible to build her own power base to oppose him as a son might do. Of course, American politicians did the same thing, but somehow their wives and daughters never looked as convincingly liberated as the Chinese women did. Perhaps it had something to do with the clothes.

"I'm delighted to meet your daughter. The presence of a charming and intelligent woman adds greatly to discussions such as ours," Haggard responded. Southern manners had never been anything but an asset in dealing with the Chinese.

"I think you know why I've come," Haggard then said.

Tang did not respond, waiting for him to continue.

"The close military alliance we've both been awaiting for many years is finally coming about. It took an event like the rebellion in Baluchistan to force some people in the American government to see what has been apparent to others of us for a long time. However, the process is now under way."

Tang's face indicated nothing. Haggard had no doubts about his ability to phrase things delicately, but still it would be necessary to speak with great care. The subject was explosive.

"In all governments, there are always trouble-making factions that oppose sensible policies. You understand, I'm sure, that that's the reason we haven't been able to work more closely with you on military matters until now. We sympathize with the fact that you must also have such problems, although your Premier Deng did a remarkable job of creating stability after the chaos created by the Gang of Four."

"Throughout world history, there have invariably been reactionary forces mounting struggles against the forces of progress," Tang responded ponderously. "We must always be alert to such people. That is true in all countries."

"That's right," Haggard agreed. "Your government has done a great deal to alert the West to the dangers of conciliation, to the possibility of a Munich in our time."

"We've done our best to warn the world about the danger of capitulation to Soviet aggression. You understand this problem.

Many of your fellow countrymen do not. They foolishly continue trying to have détente with the Soviets. Détente is nothing but a trick."

How refreshing it was to talk to an intelligent man. The winds of Washington politics were always changing. There were a few men who understood the tricks of détente, but he'd found no one who had been quite as undeviating as Tang Chen.

"As you know, we never involve ourselves in your internal affairs," Haggard continued. "We have absolute confidence in your ability to handle your own conciliators. However, we've recently observed something that causes us some concern, and so my government thought it best that I come and discuss it with you directly."

"We respect directness and frank speaking." The answer was routine.

"We notice that there seems to be quite a bit of activity recently in the border talks with the Russians. There also appears to be a new chairman on the Chinese side—a man we don't yet know."

"The border talks have been going on for fifteen years or so," Tang replied noncommittally.

"We understand that, and we appreciate your reasons for wishing to keep them going—forever, if necessary." Tang smiled slightly. "However, it seems strange that there should be an increase in activity just now—if indeed that is the case—and of course, we're concerned about any change in personnel."

Once again Tang nodded, but didn't respond. Haggard knew he would get no direct answer to his questions—certainly not at this meeting, at any rate. But he also knew that all the questions must be made quite explicit, and that Tang Chen must have no doubts about the U.S. position.

"We hope that we're as sensitive to your problems as we know you are to ours. I'm sure you understand that even the slightest indication that China and the Soviet Union were resolving the border problem would completely change the atmosphere in Washington. You're aware that there are certain politicians who fear arming a China that might return once again to the Soviet camp. They must be assured that there is no change in China's relationship with the Soviet Union. I regret having to raise these unpleasant matters, but I do so out of responsibility to my own government and friendship for yours."

Tang spoke. "We're well aware of the quality of your friendship.

55

It has been consistent over the years. We want to continue it."

The meeting was going well. Now was the moment to lay a few more cards on the table. "As you know, it's sometimes difficult for the people of one country to understand the politics of another. For example, although I personally approved of your action, there were Americans who objected to your inviting Nixon to China in the middle of the Watergate business. Watergate was very difficult for foreigners to understand, I'm afraid."

"Nixon was your greatest president," Tang stated categorically. "He understood the importance of recognizing China."

"Yes, I know. Many Americans don't understand that, though. In the same way, some of your political struggles have been difficult for us to interpret. The Lin Biao affair, for example."

"That's quite simple. Lin Biao worked with the Gang of Four in a plot to overthrow Chairman Mao. He was a pro-Soviet counter-revolutionary who was killed in a plane crash fleeing to his masters. That in itself proves the case."

"I'm aware that that's your official explanation. However, you know some of our CIA people had a somewhat different interpretation. I don't expect you to comment on it. I mention it only because it seems to me it might offer a solution to our current difficulties."

Tang didn't respond, but Haggard hadn't expected him to.

"First of all, let me say that our analysts initially had some difficulty in understanding why, in the spring of '69, that Chinese border patrol opened fire on a Russian patrol in an area where both had been stationed for many years; also in an area where Soviet troop strength was heavy; and finally, in a situation involving Zhenbao, a useless little island."

Tang was frowning. Haggard had known that his approach was a daring one. If his frankness backfired, there could be problems. But he felt sure he understood the man he was dealing with.

"Our study of your internal political situation, though, led us to some interesting conclusions. It seems to us that Mao and Zhou, convinced that the Soviet Union was China's main enemy, had already decided upon the opening to the United States. However, their decision was apparently reversed in February 1969 by the military and the radicals. Lin Biao and his allies wanted to keep the door open to improved relations with the Soviets. It would appear that Mao and Zhou were blocked on this very important policy decision."

"You know I cannot agree with all of your CIA's ideas, General Haggard. However, it is certainly true that Chairman Mao and Premier Zhou had to go through many difficult struggles to carry out the correct line of uniting with the United States."

Though Tang's voice was expressionless, Haggard had become sufficiently sensitized to Chinese innuendo to pick up on the significance of his words. "Exactly!" He felt confident now. "Our analysts further observed some interesting results of the Sino-Soviet border clash. First, it gave a great boost to Mao's authority. And although we don't have as much information on this as we'd like, logically it must have seriously damaged the arguments of Lin and his friends who were pushing for improved relations with the Soviet Union. Finally, of course, the increase in tensions with the Soviets created a favorable climate for the opening to the United States."

Tang smiled. Was it one of those Asian smiles intended to create a proper social atmosphere? Was it contemptuous? Amused? Appreciative? It was impossible for Haggard to say.

"If our interpretation is correct—if the border clash served our mutual interests as we think it did—I can only say that Mao and Zhou were incredibly brilliant political and diplomatic strategists."

"That is not a matter of opinion, General Haggard. Their brilliance as strategists is renowned, not only in China but in the entire world. You may rest assured that we will take the necessary measures to insure the continuity of their policy. The alliance with the United States is central to that policy. You do not need to fear the influence of any contemporary Lin Biaos."

Haggard's mission was successfully completed. He leaned back and for the first time truly enjoyed the flavor of the excellent tea. The two men spoke of Baluchistan, of the situation in the Middle East, the most recent petroleum discoveries in China, and most important of all, about the details of the new military alliance. Tang wanted to hear about the Americans who were to be represented on the joint planning staff. No doubt he already had his own detailed sources of information on all of them but was curious about Haggard's personal assessment. However, of the most intense personal interest to him was the nuclear weapons delivery system.

It was a thoroughly pleasant visit of confidants, drinking many cups of the fragrant Dragon Well tea, the finest in China; smoking Panda cigarettes, the finest in China; and discussing the subject dearest to their hearts, the destruction of the Russians.

CHAPTER
5

Anne felt good. Now that most of the ceremonial preliminaries were over, her work could legitimately begin. She had smiled constantly and been duly praised for her excellent Chinese during the obligatory welcoming banquet. She had even enjoyed the assembly-line ritual that the officials who dealt with foreigners had run through a thousand times, but miraculously managed to give an appearance of freshness and sincerity. The trips to the Great Wall and the Ming Tombs, to the Summer Palace and the Western Hills had been interesting, though they were sights too often read about, described, seen in slides to have real meaning. At any rate, it was over, and she could at last get on with what she'd come for.

Though Tan Yulan undoubtedly understood the necessity of keeping a close eye on a charge who eagerly sought out riots, Anne's admirable decorum during the following days had not escaped her either and had been duly noted in the psychological profile that she was carefully compiling. Foreigners got points for control and public conformity regardless of what they might be concealing. The atmosphere between the two women was courteous and amicable, though there had never been a return to the personal conversation of that first day.

By nine o'clock this Monday morning, Mrs. Tan was settled at her new desk working on the statistics for Anne's first story. The subject, consumer goods and prices, was eminently suitable. There was now some serious inflation. Tan Yulan hadn't been hesitant about admitting it. In fact, she seemed rather proud that China now shared this problem with the rest of the world—the "advanced world," as she said. Of course, such a story would also show the increasing excitement in the cities over the consumer market and the changes that a wage-incentive system were making in the society.

There'd been no difficulty in coming to an agreement about their work for the day. Mrs. Tan would stay in Anne's hotel room, which was now also their office. Anne would go out and take a look at shoppers, go to some of the smaller shops—perhaps on Qianmen Street—talk to a few people, "fill out the story," as she explained. No doubt she'd be back in plenty of time for lunch. She was specific about the details, but Tan Yulan, already hard at work, did not seem interested.

Anne had studied the map carefully before tearing the letter into tiny pieces and flushing it down the toilet. She had also seen to it that they passed by Qianmen Street on their various drives through the city. So she set off in that direction without hesitation. As she approached Qianmen Street she realized with pleasure that she was truly in old Peking. The bleak socialist-modern architecture of the newer sections had made hardly any inroads here. The shabby wooden buildings seemed piled upon one another. In the dusty shop windows, cloth shoes, fur hats, and the mysterious claws and bones of Chinese medicine shared space with enamel washbasins, neat rows of fountain pens, and striped socks. The fragrant smell of the fried bread and millet that was Peking breakfast mixed with the thousand aromas of a Chinese market street.

Finding the first west lane was no problem. On her earliest walks with Tan Yulan she had familiarized herself with the north-south, east-west axis on which the ancient city had been laid out to harmonize with the traditional dictates of the Chinese cosmos. Some of the *hutongs*—the little alleyways that zigzagged off the streets of every old neighborhood in the city—were impossible to locate, appearing suddenly from behind crumbling stucco houses and disappearing into narrower dirt paths where toddlers in split-bottomed pants played. Fortunately, the map had been very precise. The shops of Qianmen straggled around the corner, and the first west *hutong* seemed simply a continuation of the main street.

The Peony Gate Teahouse, located at the end of the alleyway, was already buzzing with the day's business. A mostly male clientele in faded blue were crowded in, some standing, some squatting or sitting around tables on small wooden stools, large bowls tilted under their chins as they shoveled down noodles. Clouds of steam and cigarette smoke filled the cramped space. Talking, laughter, the clatter of pans and plates, cheerful slurping and spitting made up the convivial pandemonium of a Chinese neighborhood restaurant.

Anne had been expected. No sooner had she pushed into the room than a round-faced man in a soiled apron appeared to greet her. His manner was very casual, as if the appearance of a tall, blond American woman was an event of no great import.

"Your friend is waiting for you," he said, motioning for Anne to follow him up the narrow, uneven stairs. At the top of the staircase, he held a faded swath of blue and white cloth up for Anne. This was the "back room" that existed in almost every Chinese restaurant for the use of the occasional foreigner or other anomalous visitor who couldn't be comfortably assimilated into the common dining room. A small, opaque window in the back let in only a dim yellowish light, and it took Anne a few moments to adjust.

The single round table was covered with the inevitable white tablecloth. Behind it sat the woman from the demonstration. Dressed entirely in dull black, her exquisite, pale face sharply outlined by gleaming black hair, she was a monochromatic cameo framed by the dramatic emptiness of the shaded white room. The aproned cook disappeared, only to reappear seconds later with a plate of steaming white-dough dumplings. After he left them alone, there was silence. It seemed to Anne that she was expected to take the initiative.

"Thank you for inviting me. This must be very complicated for you. I was worried about what might have happened to you after you left me the other day."

As before, the young woman didn't respond directly. "It's very important for us to get information out to the world, particularly to the United States." She spoke calmly, but her voice was intensely serious. "We know there are a few American reporters who are interested in learning the truth about China. Since you took a certain risk in reading the big-character poster the other day, I felt perhaps you were one of them. We must take chances."

It was disconcerting to be informed so flatly that her trustworthiness wasn't taken for granted when, in fact, Anne hadn't determined to what extent she was prepared to participate in the drama she'd stumbled upon.

"I'm interested in learning the truth about China," she replied carefully. "But there seem to be many truths. I do want to know about the poster I saw, and even more importantly, what it represents—what people, what politics, and so forth. What I really want to learn about is how these people and politics fit into the Chinese picture as a whole."

A trace of a smile appeared on the young woman's face. "We used to explain that people's ideas depended on their class position. That's not the fashionable way to explain things now, but it's still true. Your interpreter and the officials you meet will give you the position of the new bourgeoisie—government and party officials, certain intellectuals, members of the technological and bureaucratic elite—the small class that benefits from the westernization of China. We will tell you the thinking of the millions of unemployed young people, the peasants who are being driven into beggary, the workers who are being exploited in capitalist factories without even the right of workers in capitalist countries to strike, the middle and lower cadres who are made to take the blame for the policy mistakes of the leadership. . . ." She stopped and looked intently at Anne as if to judge her reaction.

"I'm very interested in what all these groups think," Anne said. "But when you say 'we' will tell you about them, who do you mean by 'we'?"

"The people who put up the posters, the people who struggle," the woman replied matter-of-factly. There would be no hints. Anne would either have to commit herself or withdraw from the encounter.

"All right," she said decisively. "Where shall we begin?"

"With the background to the poster you saw."

Anne nodded. She'd have to do her own sorting out, but this informant certainly had something to say.

"The poster stated that three hundred people had been arrested in the Peking area alone within the last few weeks. What were these people arrested for?" The young woman paused dramatically. "All over China, because of the new capitalist policy of this regime, people are suffering like they did in the old society. At first, many people were convinced when all of China's problems were blamed on the Cultural Revolution and the Gang of Four. It's true that many problems arose from that period, but the new policies didn't solve these problems. In fact, they've made them worse. People have

61

memories. There are problems now that are far more severe and even quite new when compared to the problems of twenty years ago."

"Can you give me some examples?"

"That's what I'm going to do. For several years now, people on the local level have been struggling and protesting. The economy is in serious trouble. Some very big mistakes have been made. Favoritism and corruption are rife. Most career opportunities are reserved for the children of people already in power. The dictatorship from the center is becoming stronger every day, and what it wants is the biggest possible profit from the people. So young people fight for jobs and a fair chance to enter universities. The peasants fight for food. In some cases, for higher prices for their crops; in others, just for the right of survival, since the commune system is being broken up and many once again have no land. The workers are losing their 'iron rice bowl'—a guaranteed job—and they're being squeezed every day to produce more for less money." She stopped and then added, "And for everyone there must be democracy, for without the right to speak and write freely, we cannot even begin to fight. The democratic rights that were promised in the constitution have been taken away again. As soon as Deng Xiaoping showed them off to the West, he didn't need them any longer. But we've kept them and use them anyway."

Anne waited.

"What's been happening in the last few months has so frightened the authorities that they're rushing to put thousands of people in jail. All these people are joining together. It's the new revolution. That's the meaning of the poster you saw." She stopped and sat quietly, her face as self-possessed as that of a cultivated Tang lady in an ancient painting.

It was all incredibly naive. The young woman might perhaps be as old as Anne herself, but in her innocence and indignation, she seemed like an idealistic eighteen-year-old. If she hadn't been so beautiful, would it all have had such a pure and touching quality? It was quite unreal—and yet, it had happened. The huge crowd had gathered; Anne had seen the police arrest dozens of people. And it wasn't as if the scattered protests the woman referred to were not known, especially to journalists. But a revolution, *the* revolution? . . .

"Is this basically the same movement that started with the Democracy Wall and people like Wei Jingsheng a few years ago?" Anne asked.

"Yes, it's related. That was the beginning. It's in honor of his vanguard role that groups all over the country use Wei's name in their titles. But at that time there was very little connection between the starving peasants and the young people struggling for democracy. Only a few people understood that they belonged together.

"I brought along the manifesto that was issued by our coalition two weeks ago. It was this manifesto more than anything else that led to the arrests described in the wall poster." The young woman placed on the table in front of Anne several coarse pieces of paper covered with closely written, mimeographed characters.

"How public is this?" Anne asked.

"It's all over the country. Millions of people have read it. In Peking, everyone knows about it. But the authorities haven't acknowledged its existence. As far as I know, foreigners know nothing about it yet."

It was remarkable, but Anne knew it was also perfectly possible for millions of people in China to be aware of secrets unknown to literally any foreigners at all. When one faction or another decided that the time had come when it was useful to leak something, then and only then did the secrets emerge. So for whatever reasons of accident or logic, she had been selected. Was it the best or the worst luck that could possibly have happened to her? She couldn't help but think of Paul Engleberg's fate.

"I'm afraid you'll have to read the document here. I'd like to give it to you, but if anyone discovered it in your possession—and that's very likely—you'd be watched more closely, and then it would be very hard for you to learn anything."

Anne nodded. Strange. You didn't feel that the luggage was searched, that the phone or the room was tapped, and yet—how to overlook the significance of the constant companionship?

"Perhaps it would be more convenient if I read the manifesto aloud," the young woman said diplomatically. "Then if you have any questions, you could ask them as we go along." She cleared her throat and began to read in the dramatic style copied from Peking Radio and no doubt before that from Peking opera. Her natural voice was light and melodious, but when she read, it became shrill and didactic. She had chosen a good place for their meeting, however. The roar of voices and the clatter of dishes continued unabated

63

downstairs. The two women could have shouted at each other and still not have been overheard.

Anne had experience, both as a student and during her years in Hongkong, with the style of such manifestos, whether they were the product of the student movement of May 4, 1919, the Red Guards, or the dissidents of Democracy Wall. Because its rhetorical introduction invariably had a ritualistic tone to the Western ear, it was tempting to tune it out, waiting for the real content to begin. But Anne knew better. She listened and followed the characters closely as the historical analysis began.

China had been a feudal society for thousands of years and would probably have continued in the same way if it hadn't been for the military intrusion of the West. Foreign pressure had torn apart the traditional structure of Chinese society, creating a semifeudal, semicolonial country with a people more cruelly oppressed than they had ever been. They had struggled for national liberation and independence for a hundred years. Finally, in 1949, under the banner of the Chinese Communist Party, "the Chinese people stood up." They had achieved their national independence at last. But China had gone too quickly from feudalism to semifeudalism to socialism. It was now clear that Chinese socialism was feudal socialism, retaining its basic structures from the past.

"We do not want capitalism," the young woman read in a ringing voice. "But having skipped the historical stage of capitalism, China's revolution lacked the great concepts of the French Revolution— liberty, equality, and fraternity—and the English and American Revolutions' concepts of the rule of law. The emperor of socialist China"—so this was now Mao's title, Anne thought—"never understood democracy. He believed it was a method of mobilizing the people for a limited time in order to consolidate the power of the ruler and his faction. Both his allies and his enemies learned from him, and now all ruling groups in China attempt to use the democratic movements of the people for their own political interests. But the painful lessons of these movements have now been learned. Although the democracy that we have been permitted so briefly has always been taken from us, in the process, we have learned what democracy is."

The young woman stopped dramatically. Her look was triumphant but questioning, as if asking for confirmation.

"It's incredibly interesting," Anne said. "Very exciting." Could

64

this possibly be more than the self-important games of student revolutionaries?

The woman began to read again.

"Everyone in China now understands the Gang of Four. They represented the simple feudal idea of absolute rule by the emperor's family over an obedient people producing happily for the state. But in criticizing this backward idea, the people were hoodwinked once again by the new mandarins appointed by Deng Xiaoping. They are in favor of capitalism. There is no secret about that. And many of the Chinese people, believing that with capitalism would come not only higher productivity but the democracy and freedom they had sought for so long, supported Deng's plan enthusiastically. But this leadership also used democracy as a tactic, not a principle. We now see that China has the worst of both systems. We have the dog-eat-dog profit motive of the so-called free-market system of capitalism and the centralized government control of the socialist one-party dictatorship."

No, Anne thought, this did not have the feel of a schoolchildren's document.

The youth, the Cultural Revolution generation, had been used for their political value and then dumped in the countryside. Many were now living underground in the cities, denied work permits and ration tickets. Of millions of high school graduates, only a handful were being admitted to college. Everyone was looking for jobs, waiting for jobs. Anne nodded. It was the story told by the hundreds of young refugees who poured into Hongkong every month. Rising expectations in a crowded world.

The communes were being broken up, and once again peasant families were fending for themselves. They had believed that private plots and a free market would make up the difference, but their bits of land were too small, the products too minimal. Once again, the rich got richer, the poor got poorer, and landless laborers ended up as beggars.

The workers were now subject to the survival of the fittest. A few did well, but many were losing out. Without even the relief benefits that had been won in the West, many became like the peasant laborers and the displaced students—"homeless wanderers in our own land."

"And what of the army?" the young woman read dramatically.

Strange question, Anne thought. The Chinese army was something the West simply took for granted—the millions of young peasant volunteers, their infinitesimal wages and unquestioning obedience. Anne was tense with concentration.

"Our army is becoming the tool of a foreign power. We entered the alliance with the United States to protect ourselves from the Soviet Union. But Deng Xiaoping was outfoxed. The Americans wish to use our fine Chinese soldiers as their surrogate army. American officers and military experts rush arrogantly around our country like colonial overloads, ordering about the sons and daughters of the great Chinese people as if they were mere coolies."

Anne felt suddenly cold. From the shadows of the past came the specter of the Boxers, the old Chinese xenophobia rising once again.

"We were promised that the Americans would help us achieve modernization quickly, but what they're really interested in is the militarization of China. We cannot afford both. We're being forced into a military role which is not determined by our national security interests, but by the strategic interests of the United States. They make no secret of their game. They call us their China card. What a disgraceful role—to be a card that can be discarded when it is no longer useful in the war games of the Russians and the Americans."

The tone was becoming decidedly ominous. Anne interrupted. "But what about the Soviet threat? They have a million troops on your border. The United States didn't create that situation. We aren't responsible for the fact that China has to maintain a large combat-ready army."

"I'm almost finished," the young woman said, pointing to the paragraph that remained on the paper before her. "This states our position on the question."

"We people—the Russian, American, and Chinese people of the so-called triangle—are being frightened to death by our leaders. If they have their way, we will all blow each other up. We must resist them. We now have a relationship with the United States. Let us put this relationship on a proper footing of equality and respect. We are not willing to be their cannon fodder or their card, but we will be their friend. In the same way, we must begin to repair our relationship with the Soviet Union. It is to the benefit of neither their people nor ours to spend our national treasure on weapons to destroy each other and our energies in nationalistic hatred which serves to consolidate the power of those who understand only war."

The closing slogans followed one another in a rhetorical flourish,

66

but Anne had tuned them out. She heard, as if on a radio from another room, only the sound of the clear, clipped Mandarin, the precise articulation of standard phrases. She was startled to realize that the young woman was looking at her expectantly.

"It's quite overwhelming," Anne said slowly. "It's extremely interesting, but . . ." She stopped speaking. The young woman said nothing. "I guess what I'm asking you is whether this is just your idea—you and the others who think this way—or whether there's any sign that this kind of change might really happen."

The young woman folded the manifesto neatly and tucked it in her plastic bag. She took a sip of cold tea from the mug and cleared her throat. When she spoke, her voice had returned to its normal tone.

"The most difficult problem for us is the Russians. We've lived with that hatred for so long and been so thoroughly propagandized that it's hard to make changes in people's thinking. But nothing is impossible. After all, look how quickly the change in attitude toward America occurred after so many years of enmity."

It was true. The turnabout that both Americans and Chinese seemed to accept so easily had happened virtually overnight. Enemies had turned into friends with only a shift in official statements and a switch in media coverage.

"Actually, a rather positive development is taking place right now. There's a new chairman of our Chinese border-talks team, and he represents—what is it you call them?—you know, the gentle birds."

"Gentle birds?" What *was* she talking about?

"Oh yes, pigeons—eagles and pigeons," the young woman said, pleased to have found the right phrase.

Anne couldn't help laughing. "Oh dear, well almost. Doves—hawks and doves."

The young woman laughed with her, but no doubt not for the same reason. "We like the phrase," she said. "To compare people with birds. We often do that in Chinese." The laughter had helped. The solemn atmosphere was somewhat lightened.

But the news itself was significant. "You mean there's a faction in the Chinese government that wants to negotiate seriously with the Russians over the border?" Anne asked. It shouldn't have been surprising. It was logical that such a faction should exist, though it certainly hadn't been visible up to now.

67

"Yes. There has been one for a long time."

"Who is this new chairman? Has he been on the team all along or is he someone completely new?"

"Someone new," the woman replied. "I doubt that you've heard of him. He's much younger than most of the present leadership and represents a different kind of thinking. He's not one of the old men with the thinking of the past that our manifesto refers to."

"What's his name, his background?"

"His name is Zhang Zhaolin. Anyone who was active in the Cultural Revolution knows his name, but few outsiders do. He was a Red Guard leader from Sichuan. He was sent to the countryside like all of us, but he was too much of a leader to stay buried. He did such remarkable work in the village in bringing together the urban youth and the peasants to raise production that the Party had to recruit him. He continued to move up until he was on the provincial Party Committee in Heilongjiang Province. But he has never fallen into the corrupt ways that are so common in the Party now. The people trust him—we do, the youth who have been through the same experience as he. His is one of the few voices that speaks for us. And the peasants trust him too. They know he understands the real problems."

"So how does such a good man manage to rise so high so fast?" Anne asked dubiously. "That's not the way it usually works, is it?"

"The Party needs him. They know the danger to themselves from millions of alienated people. Of course, the Party thinks it will incorporate him into the structure and make him like the rest of them, but so far that hasn't happened. His position is very difficult, very delicate. But we're encouraged by his appointment. It means there are people in power who want a shift in policy. No doubt their reasons aren't the same as ours, but for the moment we can work together."

The masters of the shifting alliance, Anne thought. She hadn't understood how deeply imbedded in the culture the concept was until she read the great Chinese novel the *Romance of the Three Kingdoms*. Alliances existed for the needs of the moment and were easily dissolved when those needs changed.

The young woman looked at her watch. "It's time for us both to leave," she said as she stood up. But it was impossible to leave matters like this—to have heard this much and then simply return to the Peking Hotel for lunch!

"I really appreciate your taking the time to read and tell me all you have," Anne said hurriedly. "But I can't just send a story back to my newspaper recounting what I've heard from a document. Is there any way I could talk to people who are involved in these movements?"

The young woman showed no surprise. "That would probably be possible. Who do you want to talk to?"

Anne had interviewed many Red Guard refugees in Hongkong. That seemed like the part of the story that was already known. "I'd like to talk to workers or peasants," she said, trying to make a decision quickly. "But any actively involved people who you think might be interesting . . ."

The woman stood thoughtfully in the shadowy half light.

"I don't suppose you've heard anything about the Tianbei strike in the China-Cal Electronics Plant," she said tentatively.

The Tianbei zone—the first free-trade zone in north China. Anne was astonished. "You mean a strike in an American-owned plant?"

"That's right. This is the first strike in a Western plant. It's just started. You might like to interview some of the strike leaders," the young woman said noncommittally.

"Of course." Anne's voice cracked with excitement. "When? Where?"

The woman had started toward the stairs. "I'll let you know as I did before," she said. "But you should think of a way to cover your absences with some kind of consistent explanation. If you go out too many times as you did this morning, it will start to look suspicious."

Anne started to follow, but her companion gestured for her to stay.

"Please wait here for a few minutes. The man who brought you in will see you out. It's better if we leave separately." And she disappeared through the blue and white curtain.

Anne poured herself a cup of cold tea and looked about the dingy room as if seeing her surroundings for the first time. On the wall, a faded picture of Zhou Enlai—forever young, forever handsome— curling at the edges. What would he have thought of all this? Probably, if he were still around, things wouldn't have come to this. The background noise had not subsided, but the little room seemed uncannily quiet to Anne. Suddenly she realized that she didn't even know the young woman's name.

69

CHAPTER

6

The International Club was another of Peking's little foreign ghettos. It had been for years, even when its habitués were a handful of international waifs and strays, drinking against the isolation and boredom of Peking life. Now Peking had become part of the global circuit, and every evening the staid old bar was jammed wall to wall with businessmen, travelers, and correspondents—all hoping to learn from each other what was going on in China, where they were still bored and isolated.

Anne had spent a lot of Friday evenings at similar gatherings in Hongkong. It was part of a correspondent's job to be where people talked, and she was well aware that in Peking, where the Chinese guarded against personal contacts with such care, it was essential to talk to everyone who had anything to say and endure those who didn't.

On the other hand, the Friday night flesh hunt was a bore. Being married had been nice in more ways than one. A woman was simply relieved of a lot of tiresome mating ceremonies initiated by unimaginative men. Not that she had anything against the games men and women played; she just wasn't interested in the Bogey-Bacall script still current in the Far East. Nonetheless, she felt relaxed as soon as she heard the roar of voices speaking English, French, German, and Japanese. After only two weeks, she was already feeling the strain of performing the full-time role of foreign friend, and had wished Tan Yulan a pleasant weekend with a feeling of some relief.

Anne was not unaware of the turning of heads as she entered the room. Women were always at a premium at gatherings like this one, particularly if they were attractive, but she had come to terms with that reality a long time ago. She was what she was, looked the way she looked, and lived her life the way she wanted to live it. As she worked her way toward the bar, she was pleased to see a few familiar faces and note several hands raised in greeting. The international fraternity of Asia correspondents was, after all, not that large. She ordered her usual Scotch and water.

"Well, well, so you made it to the Forbidden City at last," whispered a bored-sounding voice in her ear. It was Michael Crimmins, someone Hank had known well in Southeast Asia. Red-haired and elephantine, lethargic in manner but with the intimidating wit of the British, he had written for them all—the *Manchester Guardian*, *Le Monde*, and both *The Times* of London and the *New York Times*. A first-rate journalist, he was capable of being intensely concerned one moment and totally cynical the next.

"Yep, I made it," she replied noncommittally.

"So you see, there is an end of the rainbow for good journalists who mind their manners and say the right things to the right Chinese in Hongkong—and I imagine a few things were said to the right people in Washington as well." His tone was sardonic, but it was hard to dislike him. Crimmins understood how power worked, but he didn't hold his colleagues responsible for its uses.

"It's not the big accomplishment it used to seem, Michael. Now the Chinese let in anybody with money to spend."

He laughed. "True. But their enthusiasm for journalists still has its limits. They weren't too pleased with your predecessor, I believe."

Anne shrugged. "That's just the name of the game, isn't it?"

"Naturally. Have you completed the initiation rites—the Great Wall, the Ming Tombs, Tiananmen, et cetera?"

"I have, and even if I'm already tired of hearing the same thing over and over, I do like the Chinese, here, in their own country. They're very impressive."

"Of course they are—and charming, too, no doubt about it. That's the reason some of us keep hanging around, I guess. And

71

pretty soon, according to the ancient arrangement, you end up bringing tribute to the Middle Kingdom. They don't even twist your arm, because they know that sensible barbarians will see the superiority of Chinese civilization. That's why they so dislike Engleberg affairs. You're supposed to know what not to write without being told. It's all a little awkward if that kind of action has to be taken."

"I guess you just have to decide whether you want to pay the price of blowing things open."

"Exactly, my dear. And knowing your intrepid American audacity, I can't imagine that you've been here for two weeks without encountering a few of those things."

"You must know about the posters that were put up in Tiananmen on Monday and the arrests. I got a glimpse of all that when we were taking our ritual walk around the city."

"You'll find that happens every now and then. There are a lot of grievances in a country as poor as this one," he responded nonchalantly. "Everybody wants to get into a university; here more than anywhere it's the route to power. The ones who don't make it—and there are millions—take to the streets.

"When I first came here, I did the same thing you're no doubt now doing. I rushed into the fray and wired off what I thought was a red-hot story. I don't bother with that sort of thing anymore. It's more useful to keep your ears open at embassy cocktail parties."

Anne tried to sound casual. "I'm sure that's true, but it seems there've been a lot of demonstrations in the last few weeks—and not just students."

"It's spring, my dear, spring. Everybody's still in their long underwear, but you'll notice, the first bits of green are on the trees. There's that surge in the blood that accompanies the season, particularly in North China, where winter lasts forever. People like to get into the streets."

It was difficult for Anne to judge Crimmins. Was he putting her on, being honest, or simply steering her off the track to protect his own hunches?

"So you don't think it's worthwhile to report a story like that?"

He smiled in his disdainful way. "Look, news is hard to come by here, but if you irritate the Chinese by reporting something that's not very significant anyway, all you've done is make things harder when something important does come up. Probably the most interesting thing about your mob scene is the proof once again of how well the government has everything in hand."

The noise level in the room was rising. There was a constant ebb and flow of bodies. Anne and Michael's conversation now had the addition of a trim, graying man in a navy blazer who was nodding at Michael's remarks.

"Trouble in the streets and they just march people off to jail never to be heard of again," Michael continued. "No public defender, no Amnesty International. No one interferes, or if he does, he gets marched off too. Only one thing matters, the Four Modernizations, and anybody who gets in the way of that steamroller goes." Michael took out and lit another cigarette. "Actually, it's quite impressive. In a few decades, they're going to have it all over the rest of us with our messy pluralistic democracies."

"You're absolutely right," the man in the blue blazer chimed in. "I don't know if I'd go quite as far as you just did. America is still the most dynamic country in the world, but there's a lot we could learn from these people, and this business of cracking down on troublemakers is certainly one of them. You sign a contract with the Chinese guaranteeing labor discipline and they mean it, by God. Look at the way they handled things when a few Chinese workers began to get the idea of organizing unions. They were smashed immediately. But at the same time, the Chinese press began running articles on how to reform the problems that led to the trouble in the first place. I call that good social engineering.

"I'm finding it a lot easier to get things done here than I ever did in Detroit, even though their technical level is lower. It's the combination that's going to do it—American technology and Chinese discipline."

"Detroit?" Anne said questioningly. "I didn't realize Detroit was still on the map. I thought it had simply been plowed under. Are you here to sell the Chinese cars?"

"No, trucks. That's what they need. Perhaps in time, cars, but personally I hope not, until we get the gas problem solved. No need for them to use up valuable oil that way. They're perfectly happy with their bicycles. We're putting up a big plant in Wuhan. We set the conditions. The workers, even with the government taking sixty percent of their pay, make more than the going wage. The Chinese get some foreign exchange. Everybody's happy."

"But do you think that's going to work? Foreign enclaves on

73

Chinese soil? That's a pretty tricky business, you know. The Chinese have a way of changing their minds."

The man from Detroit looked at her with mild surprise. "The Chinese want the arrangement as much as we do. Maybe more. Of course, there was a big loss in business confidence after the Chinese started cancelling contracts. That's no small matter. But I think we have to look at the long-term potential. You just don't ignore a market of this size."

A booming voice interrupted their quiet conversation. "And my God, if you've done any business in Africa or the Middle East, these people have their feet on the ground!" The voice fit the speaker's huge size. He was wearing a shirt of some kind of slippery, shiny fabric, cinched at the neck with a heavy silver and turquoise bolo tie. He wasn't wearing a cowboy hat, but the hand-tooled western boots made up for that omission. It was remarkable, Anne thought, that Texans always looked like caricatures of Texans.

"Forget about the cancelled contracts. The important thing is the oil. They're finding new deposits every day. The Middle East is a snake pit. Those crazy sand niggers are going to blow each other up, and what's left of the oil at the same time. And the Mexicans, Christ . . ." He shook his head derisively. "Nobody who's worked with them as long as I have looks forward to that business—mañana the delivery, take a little siesta, play the music, eat the tacos . . . Besides, they hate the United States, always have. These people here, it's all work, work, smile, smile, no fucking around. A few bowls of rice every day and a little walk in the park on Sunday. They're the best thing that ever happened to us. Of course, it may take a few years. We let a lot of valuable time slip by."

"They had a revolution," Michael remarked laconically.

The big man shrugged. "I'm a businessman. I'm interested in selling drilling equipment. I don't give a good goddamn who buys it. Everybody has revolutions."

He'd been sizing Anne up as he talked. "Haven't I seen you in the dining room of the Peking Hotel?"

"Perhaps. There's quite a mob of Americans there and I'm among them." She stared back at him with unmistakable coolness.

"We'll have to have dinner together one of these evenings." He narrowed his eyes and smiled in what he must have thought was an intimate manner.

74

"Not too likely. Newspaper correspondents have heavy schedules."

"So that's what you are!" His enormous laugh roared across the room. "One of those pretty, feisty females making trouble all over the globe. That's all right. We like spirited ladies where I come from. You've got to remember, a man like me sees a lot, hears a lot that might be interesting to you. Just take a rain check for dinner. You might decide to use it. I'm going to be in and out of that moldy old hotel for quite a while."

"I like staying in a moldy old hotel," she said. "But I know it's not to everyone's taste."

"Look, I've worked everywhere. You think China's bad, you should try Qatar, Oman, that whole wasteland out there. The Chinese are back in some other century, but they're learning. The women are going to fashion shows. The teenagers are scrounging around for Levi's. When I first came here a few years ago they served warm beer. Good beer, but warm. Now they've learned to ice it."

"That's right," the auto man agreed emphatically. "You can do anything with people who have some brains and are willing to learn. Of course, the Chinese have gone a little crazy in their new enthusiasm for making a profit."

The Texan roared with laughter. He had belted down a steady succession of straight bourbons in the few minutes since he'd joined them. "Crazy is right! Did they stick you in the Diaoyutai state guest house for $3,000 a night and a surcharge every time you flushed the john? That was quite a surprise, even for a Texan."

The auto man frowned. "Yes, that's been a bad business. Some of our executives got stuck with that arrangement. We had a $36,000 bill for three men for a week. We just had to make it clear to the Chinese that if that continued, we'd pull out completely. They got the point."

Scotches for Anne had been arriving with regularity. She felt annoyed that she'd neglected her usual principle of buying her own drinks. The conversation was tiresome, but somehow hypnotic. She decided to give the businessmen about five more minutes.

The auto man was now totally absorbed in the subject. "But one good thing about their hotels. No riffraff in the lobby, no ragged people hanging around the doorways trying to play on American

75

guilt and get a handout like in Latin America, where you've got to watch your wallet every minute and every second person is a guerrilla or some other kind of fanatic. Here, the only Chinese who can get through the front door have been checked and double-checked. It's not even automatic that the people you work with can come see you. That's a little annoying sometimes, but I'd rather have it that way."

The Texan chuckled. "Yep, they've got that sort of thing together all right, even the local cathouse—another service added since I first came here. No Chinese need apply, not unless they arrive by car, and those Chinese are our Chinese."

"What do you mean, arrive by car?" Anne didn't like to appear surprised, but she was. Official brothels in China?

"Just what I said. That's the rule of the establishment. The poor slob who arrives by bike, or, God help him, on foot, is out of luck. It's a self-selecting clientele. None of this 'we were all created equal' bullshit for these people."

"Aside from the elegance of the carriage trade, how would you rate the facilities?" Michael asked. His bland expression never changed, but Anne knew he was enjoying the conversation. He found American businessmen one of the great entertainments of any international gathering. "Can you use your American Express gold card?"

"Not yet, but it probably won't be long. The Chinese are trying hard. Pretty girls, very pretty girls, and with the natural talents all Chinese women have. They used to try to train it out of the ones here, but it's an instinct, you know. They learn fast, just like oil drillers." He laughed again.

Michael began to ease his way toward another circle. Anne was about to follow him when she saw Peter Matthewson.

"I followed the voices and seem to have found the American contingent."

Peter had met the two businessmen in their dealings with the embassy, but it was obvious he'd come looking for Anne. The circle widened and separated. Suddenly they were alone in the middle of the packed room.

"You must be slumming," Anne remarked. "I thought the embassy had its own more exclusive Friday cocktail hour."

"It does." Peter looked tired, but his boyish grin was quite intact. "I just had to get away for a few hours. I wasn't sure I'd find you

76

here, but I'm delighted I did. Our lunch was the highlight of my week. Aside from that, it was downhill all the way."

Anne gestured in the direction of the two businessmen. "If this is how you spend much of your time, it's not surprising. What a bore."

"I do meet them, but it's not really my department. They're not so bad, though. You probably still suffer from the sixties stereotype of the multinationals. They make the world go round. It's as simple as that." He'd put his hand on Anne's arm in a firm but casual way. She wasn't sure whether she found it pleasant or irritating. Probably pleasant. He wasn't a man to push you, but still, he did make his interest felt. And he was right. Their lunch together had been fun. A little sparring, a little flirting . . . If she'd met him in Washington, she'd have dismissed him in a minute, but here, strangely enough, he interested her.

"Aren't you about ready to get out of this international cesspool and eat a decent dinner at one of the restaurants on my private list?" He was looking at her with an expression that was at the same time self-assured and appealing. And he did look quite worn out, that oldest of the old stand-bys of male sex appeal, Anne thought, but it always worked if you were willing to let it. There seemed no particular reason not to let it work.

"Sold," she replied, aware that they were already on their way to the door.

After a brief phone call to make a reservation, Peter led her to the embassy car which was waiting outside, the driver smoking and talking with his colleagues.

"How do you like this arrangement? The driver waits patiently for as long as you're occupied, all night if necessary, and then he's right outside when you're ready to move on to the next spot."

"Wonderful," Anne replied wryly. "Much better than Washington. How much are they paid for that kind of devotion?"

"Ah, there's the rub. We pay plenty. That tightfisted bureaucracy called the Diplomatic Services Bureau is squeezing us for everything the market will bear. But the workers get only about ten percent of the so-called salary."

"Why do they put up with it?"

"Who knows? Because they have no choice, presumably. And they've been convinced that serving foreigners and helping the government accumulate capital is their role in the modernization program."

They got into the back seat of the car and Peter gave the driver directions in confident Chinese.

"It must be a very easy place to get an inflated sense of your own importance," Anne remarked. "You begin to understand the mentality that finally causes all colonial powers to go into a state of myopic idiocy."

Peter smiled and put his hand on hers. "Why don't you just enjoy the perks of a Peking assignment? They have their own way of doing things, and there's nothing you can do about it anyway. Our first ambassador and his wife rode their bikes everywhere when they were here, and what difference did it make? The Chinese just thought they were a little freaky. You can't remake a culture, you know."

"I'm not trying to remake the culture. I just have the impression that Chinese reality may not be so monolithic as all that. I'm really surprised to hear so much 'they think this' and 'they think that.' Simpleminded businessmen I expect, but not simpleminded diplomats, God help us."

Peter smiled. A woman with a sharp tongue could be very refreshing. The car turned suddenly into a narrow *hutong* and stopped before a small, nondescript building. The color of Peking, Anne had decided, was dust—the yellowish dun of the fine loess dust that periodically blew over the city from the Gobi Desert and made the earth from which the stucco buildings of the old quarters of the city were built. This was such a street and such a building, but its front door was painted the brilliant cobalt blue of Chinese porcelain.

The stout beaming host greeted them genially and ushered them into a small room where the lone round table was set for two. Bare except for a few plants on the windowsill and a single scroll painting of the traditionally austere and graceful bamboo and orchids, the room was warm and immensely cozy. Their tiny porcelain cups had already been filled with that soothing and exhilarating libation of winter dinners, hot yellow Shaoxing wine.

"You do know how to entertain new arrivals," Anne said delightedly.

78

It had been a bad week, but Peter felt himself already beginning to unwind. Anne's pleasure in the restaurant pleased him, and he always enjoyed the ritual of ordering the dinner. He took pride in his knowledge of Chinese food, his expertise in assembling a felicitous assortment of dishes. He and the smiling waiter talked seriously about the fish. It would be a whole beautiful carp, mouth open, eyes staring, floating majestically in a pond of delectable sauce.

The vegetable proved more of a problem. It was, after all, only March. One must wait a little longer for the fresh, perfectly ripened vegetables that would pour into Peking from the surrounding countryside. Still, Peter was familiar, was he not, with that wonderful Chinese cabbage dish? Indeed the same drooping variety stacked for winter storage on every windowsill in North China, but cooked lightly in a sauce so creamy, so buttery, so richly delicate that it was transmuted into something beyond a mere vegetable.

The little cups were filled and refilled with the hot, luxurious wine, and the dishes began to arrive, a succession of glorious creations, borne triumphantly by their beaming friend, placed like fragrant steaming offerings on the table to be admired and lovingly consumed. The food was superb, and Peter and Anne, warm and a little drunk, were suffused with well-being, nurtured by Chinese solicitude.

"Do I feel better!" Peter announced in the middle of the shrimps and garlic. "It's really nice being here with you. I don't know why I didn't have sense enough to break out of that crazy place over there and get in touch with you sooner."

"It's lovely—and the timing's just right. Does everybody who comes here feel as if they're on the moon? Is it true, as the Chinese have always said, that they're at the center of the world and that's why everything else seems so remote?"

Peter deftly picked the last shrimp off the plate with his chopsticks and put it in Anne's rice bowl. "You're right, that's the way it is, and I kind of like it. So what is it you need to be connected with out there—the number of towns that have fallen to the Baluchi rebels? I can tell you exactly—the number is six in the last week, and what difference does it make? It'll just go on and on the way Afghanistan has. Zolti will recommend that the President try some sort of smart-ass military foray, which will exert the usual inexorable pressure to push the area into the Soviet orbit. It's all pretty predictable."

"You amaze me. For a member of the American diplomatic

corps. . . . You mean it really doesn't matter to you what happens in Pakistan?

"Of course it matters, but there are parts of the world where we have very little leverage. Southwest Asia is one of them. That's the Russians' backyard, just as Central America is ours. There's a kind of Monroe Doctrine operating, whether anyone states it publicly or not. My feeling is we should try not to play our cards too badly in traditionally Russian-dominated areas, but we usually do, just because the options are always too limited and we have no understanding of the area. We should hire British advisers, but of course, we couldn't humiliate ourselves by admitting they know things we don't."

"But China is different." Anne's voice held just a hint of mockery.

"China *is* different. You know that. America was the only Western power that didn't try to screw them after the Boxer Rebellion. They have long memories. They don't forget anything that ever happened. And now they really want us. They tell every American who appears on their doorstep, 'We love you. Help us develop our industry. Teach us English. Take our engineering students. If you want us to drink your lousy Coca-Cola, we don't give a damn. Let's talk about the big things.' "

"I know that's all true. I read the same things you do. I even write some of them. But it's hard for me to believe that there's as much agreement here as our policymakers want to believe. Simply from a straightforward American interest point of view, don't you think we're looking at it a little one-sidedly?"

"For example?"

The cabbage had arrived, swimming lucently in its pool of golden sauce. They tasted it with rapt seriousness and in only a few moments had polished off the plate. Anne placed her chopsticks across her rice bowl.

"I learned from the New China News Agency bulletin that they put under my door yesterday morning that the Chinese have launched another six-thousand-mile intercontinental ballistic missile into the South Pacific."

"Right. Pretty impressive. Don't tell me you disapprove of the Chinese having a deterrent against the Russians?"

"That's one of those 'when have you stopped beating your wife' kinds of questions, isn't it? And no, that wasn't my point. The most obvious question is who's providing the telemetry technology for

80

those missile shoots? It must be us, but very few Americans have any sense of the significance of a decision like that. As usual, huge military commitments are being made secretly."

"Sorry, no comment, Ms. *Washington Inquirer*. That's not my area, you know."

"Don't be so paranoid. I'm not going to get you drunk and try to steal military secrets. We're just talking about what we read in the paper. No inside dope whatever. Anyway, my second point has nothing to do with the news per se, only with its interpretation."

"Like what?"

"Like the quote from an American commentator who noted that Chinese missiles could now reach Moscow."

"That, my dear lady, is a fact, not an interpretation."

"Indeed it is, as is the fact that the very same missile going the very same distance in the opposite direction could reach Los Angeles. But in spite of a long history of flip-flops in Sino-American relations, that pretty obvious observation wasn't included."

"Since when does any country make public statements that include all the reasonable interpretations of any event? That's not the way policy positions work."

"I know that. What worries me is whether the people making those policy decisions are thinking about all the implications, not necessarily stating them. I'm not so sure they are. Americans are big on honeymoons, and I have the impression the Chinese know how to play that game."

Peter laughed. "Under every wild-eyed idealist there exists a total cynic. I'm not half so sure as you seem to be that the whole business is so manipulative."

The table was by now covered with the wrecks of their glorious dishes. The two diners picked idly at a stalk here, a crumb there. Peter added a little more wine to each cup.

"But byzantine, yes," he burst out sharply. "In fact, Chinese court politics is a real pain in the ass."

The euphoria of wonderful food and wine, the warmth of Anne's company seemed to evaporate. It was really getting to his ego, this unsolved problem. Peter was surprised to see Anne looking at him questioningly, even sympathetically. And she did have the sense to know when not to say anything at all. Suddenly, there seemed to be no reason not to tell her about the situation. He was well aware of what was considered a security matter and what was not. News

81

that appeared in the *People's Daily* was not. She was, after all, in the newspaper business herself, and there was some strange pull that he just didn't feel like resisting.

"Have you been reading about the reopening of the border talks with the Russians?" he asked.

"Of course. I always keep up with things like that."

"There's a new Chinese chairman."

"Right. His name is Zhang Zhaolin."

Peter's eyes revealed his surprise. "Pretty good. You do keep up. Okay, we know his name. Everyone who reads the *People's Daily* knows his name. But do the rest of the readers know what we don't know? Who the hell is the guy?"

There was nothing more fragile than the wounded male ego. Anne was conscious of proceeding with the gentle and calculated assurance of one approaching a skittish horse. It was clear that the information she'd so dubiously accepted from the beautiful rebel was indeed something special if the American embassy's political officer didn't know anything about it. And there was something else. Peter Matthewson, minus his diplomat's façade, was singularly winning—the man whose boyish grin had somehow pulled her toward him that first morning in his office.

She replied with nonchalant matter-of-factness. "He's a provincial party official—middle level, I think—from Heilongjiang, not known outside China, but apparently quite famous among his generation. You know—Sichuan Red Guard leader, banished to the countryside, but so outstanding that he somehow made it on his own talents up there. That's where a lot of the sixties students got dumped, in the northeastern border lands, a really wild frontier. He must be quite remarkable to have built a political career out of a Siberian exile."

There was no indication that Anne's information was anything but the most mundane chitchat, but Peter was acutely aware of her tact. Somehow, in the course of the dinner, they had moved closer together; the absurdity, perhaps, of two people reaching across a large round table to share the same dishes, and then the other, less prosaic magnetism of the sexual sparks that seemed to be flying around the small, warm room. Suddenly, Peter put his hands on Anne's shoulders and deliberately, firmly kissed her hard on the mouth. It was so extravagant, so presumptuous, that it could have been interpreted as a parody if one chose to. But on the other hand, it was a very real kiss. Anne, disconcerted, though not unpleasantly, understood that the interpretation was up to her.

She drew her head back, but only slightly, and smiled. "My God, look where a little of the right information can get you! No wonder people get hooked on being spies. Before you get absolutely carried away, wouldn't you like to know what Zhang Zhaolin's position on the talks is likely to be?"

Peter dropped his hands from her shoulders. His expression was amused, intimate, but also intent. This was, after all, not entirely a matter of fun and games.

"You mean you know that, too? They should make you Secretary of State."

"Reporters always know more than the Secretary of State. The problem is that the facts we pick up don't necessarily fit into the strategic game plan, and so they end up in the shredder. Anyway, it looks as if the Chinese border team has a dove as its new chairman."

This time there was no hiding Peter's shock. "You mean pro-Soviet?"

"No, I don't think so. It sounds as if he represents a faction that just wants to get the Russian border threat off the Chinese back so they can get on with other things."

Peter shook his head impatiently. Now he was all business. This was too serious for joking around.

"I'm not questioning what you say, but that move just isn't in the geopolitical card game. There can be shifts in the triangle, but if the Chinese move away from us—and there have always been people who predicted they would—they'll go back into the old Soviet camp. That means a global shift that's ominous for us."

"I'm not so sure." Anne spoke confidently. After only a few days in Peking, she had been able to get information that had eluded the American embassy. It had to mean something. "I'm getting the feeling that there are forces operating here that our policymakers either don't know about, don't choose to know about, or aren't analyzing correctly. I could be wrong, but I don't think we have much to fear from a man like Zhang Zhaolin."

Peter smiled amiably. Enough of this. No point in letting things get too intense. "I hope you're right. Nobody wants to see the world get blown up. Anyway, you've been great. I don't know what your sources of information are, and I don't care. If you think they're reliable, that's enough for me. You might even have saved my reputation. I hope you don't mind."

"It's no big thing," Anne responded lightly. "I've probably just given you a few days' lead on some facts that U.S. intelligence would have turned up very shortly anyway. Obviously, this man's identity is no big secret."

Peter chuckled. "Obviously not. We've just had every China research office in the world working on it all week."

"All that means is that it's a Chinese secret. Even Chinese secrets get leaked in time."

"Yeah, but sometimes a little too late to do us much good."

The table had finally been cleared, and Peter poured the last two cups of the now lukewarm wine. There were some disconcerting elements to Anne's news, but Peter did not intend to worry about them right now. They were someone else's problem. The main thing, the wonderful thing, was that the border chairman's identity was solved at last. It had all been done so lightly, so casually, creating no indebtedness or nasty sense of obligation, and yet it had forged a funny kind of bond between them. How many people in the world would even care about the identity of the chairman of the Chinese border-talks team! Crazy!

But it wasn't that. It was how it had happened. She was quite a woman. He'd liked the way she looked the minute she walked into his office, and now . . . Her amused dark blue eyes met his, and neither of them made any attempt to draw back. Only their hands touched, intertwined fingers pressing more insistently. The small room was overheated and smoky from the coal-ball fire in the iron stove. The vapors of the yellow wine drifted mellowly through warm bodies.

This time there was no ambiguity about the kiss. It was fierce and lingering, and Anne did not withdraw.

"I hope I'm not wrong," Peter murmured, "but I have the feeling we're in agreement about all this. Shall we continue?"

"I've never been to bed with a diplomat before," Anne answered contentedly, her eyes half closed, "but you're quite persuasive. Yes, by all means, let's continue."

CHAPTER

7

Breakfast at the Peking Hotel was symbolic of all the strains and contradictions of China's headlong rush into the triumphant embrace of the West. The slow-paced colonial style that had prevailed for so long was not easily displaced by the schedule-oriented requirements of businessmen and women accustomed to computerized kitchens producing standardized eggs and toast. Here, the eggs and toast didn't always arrive together, and the coffee was invariably too weak. The white-jacketed young men and women who waited on the tables were polite and smiling but not overly concerned with the pressures of time as they chatted together near the kitchen door. And no one who breakfasted in the cavernous old dining room was in Peking without a purpose. The tourists had tight schedules that began early each morning; one didn't spend what a China trip cost without squeezing out every dollar's worth of temple and commune. And the business of the world's buyers and sellers of oil, guns, baskets, bristles, feathers, and electronics often began over the breakfast table.

It was always a lively scene, but as Anne entered the room this morning she sensed a greater than ordinary intensity. From the table of American and British correspondents that she joined strange place names rose. Turbat, Gwadar, Pasni—the dusty towns on the Pakistani coast of the Arabian Sea.

"The most serious crisis since the Cuban missile crisis, your President said," a British correspondent remarked to Anne.

85

"Does anybody know what that means?" she replied. "Carter was the one who started defining everything that way."

The Englishman laughed. "I'm not responsible for the poverty of your language. I'm just reporting the news: That's what your President said. What's actually happened is that the Baluch rebels have accomplished what all the experts said couldn't be done—sewn up the coastal area of Pakistan adjoining Iran."

"And Iran?" Anne asked.

"The rebellion is evidently spreading there."

"Anybody could have predicted how that gamble would come out, that crazy risky business of arming the Baluchis to the teeth in the attempt to overthrow Khomeini." The speaker was Jack Rickett of the *Chicago Times*.

"I even did a few pieces on that myself—relegated to page seventeen of the late edition, naturally. It was another of those short-term deals. Use any forces available to get rid of this week's enemy and don't worry about what they might do with the hardware next week."

"There was no choice, Jack," was the measured comment of the *New York Chronicle*'s man.

"Oh Jesus, no choice," Jack snapped impatiently. "It's just that it wasn't an easy choice. Everybody knows that area's the Soviets' turf, and that the Baluchis don't give a fuck about anything except Baluchistan."

"Big Soviet troop movements in southern Afghanistan," her neighbor murmured in Anne's ear. "Hard to see how we're going to avoid the big one this time."

The Balkanization of the area, the crumbling of the borders, the hot line activated . . . The voices rose in volume. More coffee was called for.

"Look," Pete Rosso interjected, "it's looked like World War III almost every week since the end of World War II. That's just the reality of the second half of the twentieth century." Pete was the perfect reporter for *Progress*, the newsweekly with a circulation of 30 million, the new Bible of Middle America. For decades, its editors had harangued against Communist Chinese terror and backed Chiang Kai-shek, but they had made their policy turn with ease and enthusiasm. Pete himself was astonishingly, ingenuously sincere.

"There's no saving that Southwest Asian situation, but China is the big one. This country represents the limits to Soviet expansion, and they know that. Let all those little tribal people have their day. In the long run, everything falls back into spheres of influence anyway. And China is one of those spheres of influence. It's lucky they're with us now. After all, they've been around this part of the world quite a bit longer than we have."

"And quite a bit longer than the Russians."

The voices rose and fell. It was impossible for reporters to talk without a tone of contentiousness, but through it all there ran a thread of affirmation until Michael Crimmins waved his water glass and shouted, "Hip, hip, hooray for the Sino-U.S. alliance." As the laughter and applause was subsiding, he added softly, "And don't forget to keep your bags packed."

A few people began to get up and leave. Every scrap of news or rumor that could be exchanged had been. Anne, finishing her toast and coffee, found herself subject to the inevitable summation delivered by Marvin Burger, by respectful consensus the dean of Far Eastern correspondents. For an American newspaperman he was a scholar, knew Chinese and Japanese well, and was an encyclopedic source of information. When he spoke, you listened.

"We all joke about this alliance, because we're journalists and we're used to looking at politics objectively, without much commitment—and that's the way it should be," he was saying in his ponderous voice. "But as it happens, we're also Americans, and what Pete said is important. The greatest stroke of historical luck we could have had was that the Chinese Revolution turned itself inside out and came over to us. We know what our job is as journalists. But as Americans, we're also responsible for supporting this alliance and seeing that nothing happens to it. A lot depends on that."

Burger stroked his perfectly cleft chin. Perhaps it was that chin —together with his thatch of thick, flawlessly shaped, totally white hair—that was responsible for his striking air of authority.

"I'm not one to make apocalyptic statements. You all know that. But in my opinion, the very survival of the world may depend on the careful preservation of this relationship with the Chinese."

"So, Marvin, you think the alliance is solid and everything here is solid—that we can depend on that?" It was the first time Anne had spoken.

"The situation here is as solid as we can hope for anywhere these days, and we have a responsibility to do whatever we can to strengthen it. I'm not talking about propaganda. A good reporter knows what to do. We're all good reporters." He rose from the table, and the remaining breakfasters rose with him. It was time to get to work.

Anne was thoughtful as she rode the elevator back up to her room. She had few doubts about her ability to analyze events. It was a feeling that hadn't come just from her experience as a journalist but from everything in her life that had produced her easy intellectual confidence. She wasn't arrogant. It had simply never occurred to her that she wasn't as bright as anybody she might be likely to encounter.

Still, she felt puzzled. It was as if she were seeing implications that other reporters, quite as skilled and perceptive as she and considerably more experienced, didn't see. Or perhaps more troubling, didn't find worthy of serious attention. Still, a change in the chairmanship of the Sino-Soviet border-talks team, a strike in an American-owned factory—these were important; there could be no question of that. The problem was the source. No matter what Marvin Burger said, supporting American policy had nothing to do with it.

It was shocking to her that young dissidents were being arrested every day, but it was true—that wasn't news. Burger would tell her that the Chinese had been doing the same thing for thousands of years. They simply didn't recognize the right of citizens to express ideas in opposition to the state. He'd also say—had said many times, in fact—that Americans who rushed naively about the world imposing their own political traditions on cultures that didn't even understand them had no business in the newspaper field. He would, she knew, look with amused disdain at the manifesto she'd seen and suggest that a Chinese visitor to Berkeley might learn as much about American political realities from leaflets picked up at Sather Gate.

Still, there'd been no mistaking the importance of the information she'd given Peter. What was most pressing at the moment, however, was not to sit in judgment but to get on with the investigation. She must write up what she knew about the border talks tonight; it would be her first major story from Peking. And then she must get to her interview with the strike leaders. The next step was up to her. Surely it wouldn't be too difficult to find some way to cover her absences, but for the moment she had no ideas.

When Anne arrived at her room, Tan Yulan was already hard at work, checking price indices for Anne's articles on the consumer economy. They exchanged good-mornings and a few words about the progress of Mrs. Tan's research for the day. It seemed that everything was going well. Anne put on her jacket. She had a nine-thirty appointment.

Tan Yulan looked up from her desk, smiling. "Perhaps I wasn't thorough enough in explaining the hotel regulations to you," she said pleasantly.

"What do you mean? There don't seem to be any problems."

"There's a regulation that all guests staying here must be registered."

"Of course. I registered when I arrived. Don't tell me I have to reregister every week!" What nonsense, Anne thought. The Chinese, who could be so efficient, were also capable of creating more bureaucratic red tape than anyone on earth.

"Your registration is taken care of for as long as you're in Peking. However, if you have an overnight guest, that guest must also be registered." Tan Yulan's gaze was conventionally polite but unwavering.

Anne could feel her face becoming hot. She was angry, furiously angry. She sensed that if she unclenched her fists, she would pick up the nearest object and throw it. But she quickly realized that she must appear to Tan Yulan as a discomfited and guilty child, embarrassed at being caught. That wouldn't do. Anne sat down.

"I believe what you're telling me is that I'm under twenty-four-hour-a-day surveillance and the Chinese government has appointed itself guardian of my morals. Let us please understand each other on this matter. We have a working relationship—one characterized, I hope, by mutual respect. Your personal life is your private affair, and the same is true of me. I'm a visitor to your country—a friendly one, I'm sure you know that—and don't consider myself subject to the same supervision as a Chinese citizen. I'll do my best not to break your laws or offend your customs in public, but what I choose to do with my private life is simply not your concern."

Anne had spoken quietly, but she realized her voice was trembling. Seldom overwhelmed with anger this way, she was annoyed to find herself unable to handle it with her usual self-control.

Tan Yulan maintained her imperturble expression. The Chinese who took care of foreigners all had the impersonal, solicitous calm of hospital nurses or psychiatrists, Anne thought with sudden, childish venom.

"We don't have any interest in your personal life," Mrs. Tan said distantly. "I haven't mentioned the matter. It was you who brought it up. I was referring simply to a matter of regulations which exist for the protection of the guests."

Anne sighed. It was, as Hank had always said, a no-win game with the Chinese. One's perceptions were not inaccurate. Foreigners were watched, maneuvered, excluded—but always in the name of their safety, health, and comfort. Those outraged guests who finally went into screaming tantrums found themselves the instruments of a self-fulfilling prophecy—barbarians indeed, surrounded by a superior people who were kind, concerned, and civilized.

"And what protection might that be?" Anne asked wearily.

"Suppose there should be a fire, an earthquake. There was one, you know, that shook this very hotel. It's very important to have a record of where all foreigners are. Suppose you were missing and your government should ask us where you were. It would be very embarrassing, wouldn't it, if we didn't know."

Anne laughed coldly. "Embarrassing—yes indeed, it certainly would. I can't think of anything more embarrassing than losing a foreign friend—absolutely humiliating." She took a cigarette out of her bag and lit it. "So I take it that what you want is a record of where we are at all times. Is that correct? But whatever degenerate activities we engage in is our own business."

Tan Yulan flushed. Anne knew that she was pushing harder than she should, but was perversely pleased to affect this perfectly controlled woman just a little.

"I'm only responsible for informing you about the regulations," Mrs. Tan replied primly.

Anne got up and zipped her jacket. "That's fine. I assure you there will be no problem with the regulations in the future."

The two women bid each other good-bye with careful politeness. But as soon as Anne was outside the door, she could hardly hold back her laughter. It was all so ridiculous, so absolutely absurd. But best of all, she had gained from this comic episode an idea of how to solve the problem of her cover. The details would have to be worked out, but at least she now knew what she was looking for. Having categorized Anne as a promiscuous foreigner, Tan Yulan would expect more of the same behavior. So what she had to find was a cooperative man who would provide such a façade—and on a fairly regular basis. All the Chinese stereotypes about the sexual excesses of foreigners would lend themselves to this simple deception.

But who, and where? Peter was out of the question. He was, after all, working at the embassy. And besides, she suspected he might take the matter too literally. The night with him had been lovely, but at this point an occasional lovely night was just about right. A newspaperman like Michael might play the game with her, but he would guess why too. Probably impossible. A businessman? They were everywhere, but hardly interested in a sham proposition. Even more impossible.

There had to be a solution. If only Hank were here, she thought with wry sadness. He had always understood what she wanted to do, her ideas, her intentions. He would know how to help her. But what a ridiculous thought. With a wrench of the heart, she forced him away. Something, someone would turn up. He had to, and quickly, before the strike ended.

Anne had been looking forward to her appointment that morning. Charlie Rudd was a longtime acquaintance of Hank's, a man considerably older than he—Hank had said he must be in his sixties —but one with whom he had shared experiences that had been important to both of them. Like Hank, Charlie had spent most of his youth knocking around Asia, drinking a lot, sleeping rather frenetically, it seemed, with every variety of Asian beauty, and writing hard-hitting news stories. Somehow, he'd found himself in Shanghai when the Communists took the city, and for reasons which no one who knew him could explain, he'd decided to stay. Over the years, though, he'd taken trips out—to Hongkong, sometimes to Singapore or Tokyo. It was in Hongkong that he and Hank had met, exchanged stories, and decided they liked each other. It was a strange friendship. After that they ran into one another only occasionally, with years intervening, but there was always a bond.

"He's the one person you have to meet when you go to Peking," Hank had told her. "There's nobody who knows more, who's seen more than Charlie Rudd. He won't tell you everything he knows. He's got to live with the Chinese, after all. But what he does tell you will be true. Besides, you'll like him—and, of course, he'll like you."

"What's he doing in China?" Anne had asked.

Hank shrugged. Who knows? He loves the Chinese. You see it all the time in Hongkong—those Westerners who are never comfortable in any other culture even though they can never really be part of Chinese society. I've got a little of it myself." He had looked at her with amusement. "And so do you. What was a nice Stanford girl like you doing learning all those difficult Chinese characters?"

"I know. But that doesn't mean I want to live there."

Hank's laugh was a little bitter. "Well, that's where you're going now instead of settling down happily with me. Anyway, that's what Charlie Rudd decided to do many years ago—settle down with the Chinese, for better or worse. Frankly, I think he also had a streak of idealism that he never wanted to admit to when he was playing the old Hemingway role that foreign correspondents were into in those days. He thinks the Chinese Revolution is great. He knew all the dead heroes. You could probably even get a book out of him if you set your mind to it."

When Anne had phoned and identified herself—"Hank Steiner's ex-wife" (My God, was that really who she was!)—Charlie Rudd immediately said, "Come right away." A morning appointment had been arranged. "My health isn't what it used to be, and I've fallen into that decadent Chinese habit of taking naps in the afternoon. They seem to get longer and longer. The chances that my head will be in some kind of shape are better in the morning."

Anne recalled Hank's comment that Rudd's protected Chinese life both hid his alcoholism and kept him from ever having to come to terms with it. "When you meet Rudd," Hank had said, "you'll see the positive and negative aspects of being kept by the Chinese for thirty years."

The air was crisp, but not so cold as it had been. The antiquated but still functioning taxi wound through the narrow streets of old Peking. Anne was enjoying the ride, simply for its own sake. Their route twisted and turned through back alleys, past the domestic life of the real Peking. It was a world, it seemed, of the very old and the very young. In the doorways of the shabby but neat adobe houses were wrinkled, white-bearded men who appeared to be as ancient and worn as their surroundings. Sometimes one held the hand of a solemn, round-faced toddler or pushed one in a low bamboo cart— a combination stroller and shopping cart—in which babies were ferried about. Women of indeterminate age—women retired at fifty in China, Anne recalled, so perhaps they weren't really as old as they looked—threw basins of water on the hard dirt paths and swept the thresholds with the short grass brooms used everywhere in Peking. Everyone stared impassively at the unusual sight of a taxi driving down their uneventful street.

Charlie Rudd's house, like all old Peking houses, was virtually indistinguishable from the others on its narrow street. There was simply a gray wall, and in its center a great, faded red door. But when the door was opened, Anne saw that she had stepped into a China she had not yet seen, the sequestered world of the traditional Chinese family. Once inside the red portal, she encountered yet another, this one with the high threshold once believed to keep evil spirits from entering the household. The interior courtyard was enclosed by high, whitewashed walls.

She followed a white-jacketed old Chinese man over gray stepping stones to the main door of the one-story house. This was a garden of stones, so beautifully shaped they appeared to have grown out of the rockline Peking earth, and of ancient, elegant jars and pots in shades of black, brown, and mustard. From some of the containers, the green-touched branches of emerging spring appeared, but all in all, this was a garden of stark abstract beauty, like the finest of Chinese paintings, untouched by color.

Charlie Rudd was waiting at the door, just as Hank had described him—tall, thin, his horsey face wrinkled and wrecked, but with smiling eyes. He kissed Anne on the cheek with familiar warmth.

"Well, well! So my old drinking buddy has sent me a charming visitor. Come in, come in."

He waved Anne to the overstuffed, beige-slipcovered chairs that seemed to be the only chairs in which foreigners ever sat in Peking. But the ugly chairs, vestiges of the Soviet fifties, were not the leitmotif of the room. Lustrous rosewood furniture—probably Ming, Anne decided—handsome chests with magnificent brass hardware, high-backed chairs, delicate tables crafted with perfect refinement, and everywhere, the treasures of the millenial Chinese past—a great Tang horse, its saddle streaked not only with the prevailing yellows and greens of the period but with the earliest of Chinese blues; celadon bowls, glowing oyster to gray to palest green and turquoise; on the walls, upon the dull gold silk of antique scrolls rose the majestic peaks, crags, and waterfalls of the masters of Chinese painting; on the floor were the muted reds and blues of well-worn tribal rugs.

"How wonderful," Anne exclaimed, gesturing about the room. She sat perched on the edge of the chair in her excitement. "I've never seen so many treasures in one place outside a museum."

"I've been collecting them for a long time." Rudd smiled. "Yes, there are some treasures, to be sure. I'll give you a guided tour later on if you're interested in that sort of thing. You'd be surprised how few people are. Most of my visitors from the outside world can't tell the difference between these things and the decorations in a Hongkong Chinese restaurant."

The old man who had led Anne through the courtyard was pouring steaming tea from a *mille fleurs* teapot into tiny, handless cups.

"The Chinese don't approve of individuals keeping treasures like these to themselves, and they're right. They've had enough of their past carted away to the mansions and museums of the West," Charlie Rudd continued in his twanging voice. "I just regard all these things as loans—company for an old big-nose hermit. I've willed them all back to China when I go."

His tone was self-deprecating, perhaps even a little self-pitying, but it was clear that Charlie Rudd wasn't just an eccentric bachelor picking up attractive chinoiserie. She was sufficiently well versed in Chinese art herself to understand that she was in the company of a connoisseur, no doubt a real authority in the field. What an unexpected bit of luck! This was an aspect of China that she'd never expected to be able to pursue here beyond routine visits to museums and the now astronomically expensive antique shops. Peter knew a great deal about Chinese literature and calligraphy, but had little interest in Chinese art. None of the journalists she knew cared much about it either. Strange that Hank either hadn't known or hadn't mentioned anything about this side of Charlie Rudd.

"I love Peking," Anne stated simply.

"Yes, I do too. That's one of the reasons I've stuck around all this time. I hear that a lot of your newspaper colleagues aren't so crazy about it, though."

It was Anne's turn to smile. "I imagine you'd understand that better than most people. Peking can be a pretty boring place to be if you're used to Hongkong or Singapore—or just about any major city in the world."

"The capitalist world," he added. "Of course, I understand it. I've always had to get out periodically myself. But these guys—and ladies, beg your pardon—are only here for a short assignment, and this is a rather important place."

Although she'd met Charlie Rudd only minutes before, Anne felt no hesitation in speaking frankly.

"Everybody understands that it's an important place. There's not a reporter in the world who doesn't want to come here. But then people get so frustrated. The official line comes down. Everybody repeats it. There seem to be brief periods when the Chinese are allowed, even encouraged to associate with foreigners. Suddenly, there's some kind of switch and it's cut off again."

Charlie Rudd's brown eyes were bright behind the opaque thickness of his heavy horn-rimmed glasses.

"Look around you." He gestured toward the treasures of his room. "This is the China of four thousand years—a civilization that produced marvels of human achievement while our ancestors were running around the forests of Europe in bearskins. Except for vassal states and nomadic enemies, the Chinese were alone in the world— or thought they were—for thousands of years. To them, we're still the red-haired, big-nosed barbarians who, for reasons they've never been able to grasp, were able to conquer them with technologically superior weapons. They don't know whether to hate us, fear us, love us, or respect us. They constantly switch from one to the other."

"And how is one supposed to deal with that problem?"

Rudd shrugged. "I regard myself merely as a passenger on this boat. I watch from the sidelines. Take them on their own terms. When they wish to tell me something—and they often do—I listen with interest. When they don't wish to have anything to do with me—and that happens periodically—I entertain myself with my borrowed toys." He waved his hand in the direction of the Tang horse, and then added, "And drink a little."

"And that's the price of getting along with the Chinese? Doing just what they want you to do?" Anne asked dubiously.

"That's the price."

"But I heard that a number of long-term foreign residents like yourself have been very involved in Chinese politics, especially during the Cultural Revolution."

Rudd laughed wryly. "And you must also have heard that a number of them paid with their necks—went to jail and came out behaving like lambs, even spouting a diametrically opposite new line. Not much point in that. No, I sat on the sidelines and watched the fireworks." He paused to refill the teacups. "Perhaps I'm more influenced by Chinese history than some of the others have been. The Chinese have always used foreigners in the same way—drawn them into their politics for their own factional purposes and thrown them away when they were no longer useful. I've never been terribly attracted by martyrdom." He ran his gnarled fingers over the carved jade water buffalo on the tea table. "I'm a little too sybaritic for that entertainment, I'm afraid."

"But you've watched this country develop under the Communists from the very beginning, and you knew all the giants—Mao, Zhou Enlai, Zhu De. . . ."

"Yes, they were the giants. It's a strange phenomenon in history, isn't it, that at certain critical periods a country is given giants: not just one, but many, as we were given Washington, Jefferson, Franklin, Madison, and the rest. And once that historical allotment has been used up, there are no more. Very strange indeed." A shadow came over Rudd's face, and for a moment there was silence in the room.

Then he went on, his voice almost solemn.

"And the Peking, the China, that all of you take for granted today —this clean, safe, and boring city is the miracle those giants built. Soon those of us who saw 'the bitter past,' as the Chinese call it, will be dead, and no one will remember that in the same cities of China less than half a century ago the garbage trucks used to pick up the corpses of the poor from the streets every morning."

"So you don't see any giants about to appear on the scene," Anne inquired, interrupting his reverie.

"Probably not. But I see China, eternal China, surviving as it's always survived. It's not fashionable these days to speak of superior civilizations, but that's just liberal nonsense. China is a superior civilization. They'll still be around when the rest of the world has figured out some ingenious way of doing itself in."

"And our relationship with them?" Anne persisted.

"Our?"

"America's."

"Ah yes, America's. That's what we are after all, isn't it—Americans. From the Chinese point of view, we've been around for a very short time, and I think they doubt that we have much capacity for

96

sustained existence. For them, I would imagine, a relationship with America is an infinitesimal event in eons of Chinese time."

Anne was amused, but slightly irritated as well. "I can't deal with eons. I don't imagine you could either until you underwent thirty years of Chinese conditioning. How about looking at the question in terms of decades."

Rudd smiled. "In whatever time span you select, the question is essentially the same. Alliances come and go—with the Kuomintang, the Russians, the Vietnamese, America. The Chinese are, and always have been, interested in other countries for only one reason —the benefit of themselves. Of course, that's true of all countries, isn't it? Perhaps they're only a little more sophisticated in the application of the principle."

Rudd stood up as if to unwind from the weight of the subject. He was very tall, Anne realized, and stoop-shouldered from years of bad posture. In the Chinese fashion, he wore a dark brown silk jacket indoors. The room was cold.

"It's very hard for someone who's just arrived here, like me, to make intelligent judgments about the mood, the importance of what I see and feel."

"Such as? . . . "

There seemed no reason not to tell Charlie Rudd her doubts and anxieties. "Young people are demonstrating, demanding democratic rights. You hear about strikes, peasant protests. And yet I'm told that this kind of thing is atypical, that it doesn't represent what most Chinese feel. It's hard to know how to evaluate it all."

Rudd sat down and peered at her in a kindly way.

"Look, my dear, I can't tell you how to evaluate everything you see and hear, but you must keep one thing in mind: The 'giants,' as you called them, are dead or dying. You're in China at the end of the reign of a great emperor. Such times are always difficult. China's centuries of feudalism aren't easily shaken off. I myself doubt that they ever will be. These succession struggles go on for decades. I don't expect to see the resolution of this one in my lifetime." He paused, but Anne didn't interrupt. "Power. It's everything in China. In the West it's money, but here it's power. There is no Chinese of talent who doesn't, at some time in his life, play for power."

"So that's what it's all about—the protests, the strikes, the uprisings—somebody's play for power."

97

"Yes and no. The people struggle—for food, for political rights —just as people everywhere struggle. Sometimes they win and sometimes they lose. During an unsettled period they have greater possibilities, and perhaps greater need as well, to struggle." He shook his head. "But the unity of the old leaders was a source of great strength to the people while they struggled together against their poverty. It's a bitter thing to see torn apart. We've all suffered from that."

Anne contemplated Charlie Rudd's worn face. It was indeed the face of a man who had suffered; who, although surrounded by objects beyond the reach of most men, had somehow shared in the trials of the Chinese people. Suddenly, she realized she had found the man who would help her.

She explained her problem. Not precisely where she wished to go or who she would see—she didn't know that herself—but simply that, by an accident of fate, she had access to some interesting developments, to some of the struggles she thought he'd been referring to, and how she needed him to help her.

Rudd chuckled. "You flatter me greatly, my dear. My Chinese guardian angels will be astonished, for among the various problems they've had with me, illicit relationships with ladies haven't been included. I've always taken care to conduct that phase of my life outside the borders of the People's Republic."

Suddenly, Rudd was serious. "As you may have gathered, though the closest I've gotten to newspapering in years is polishing editorials in the *Peking Journal,* I still feel like a journalist at heart, but I don't like the kind of insensitive snooping a lot of our colleagues do here. I want you to understand that I'm willing to help you not just because you're a beautiful lady highly recommended by my good friend Hank Steiner, but because when I look at you I don't see a lust for power in your eyes. And I'm very familiar with the way that looks." He went over to the Tang horse and put his hand on its smooth back.

Anne felt strangely embarrassed. Rudd was charming and cosmopolitan, and it was apparent that he'd enjoyed their conversation as much as she had. Under it all, though, this great seriousness. . . . And was she deceiving herself? Was she really being dishonest with him?

But when Rudd turned around, his face once again wore a look of friendly amusement.

"So . . . excellent. From this moment on, please regard this house as your pied-à-terre, and me as your chevalier, both at your service at your convenience."

He bowed his bony frame in mock deference and extended his hand to Anne, still seated in the big armchair.

"I suggest that we begin with lunch. You'll find, I think, along with all my other hedonistic tastes, that I've managed to acquire the best cook in Peking. He'll be delighted to have you here, for he finds it rather depressing to waste his talents cooking for one person, appreciative though I am."

Anne smiled as she took his hand. "And after lunch, the guided tour?"

"After lunch, the guided tour."

CHAPTER

8

Once her arrangements with Charlie Rudd had been made, Anne was restless and impatient—unreasonably so, she knew—but the routine stories she was doing on the economy and new developments in the film industry seemed boring and prosaic. She and Tan Yulan had worked out a steady, formally pleasant relationship. The work went smoothly, the days evolved a rhythmic regularity, and Anne began to feel that she would live in her Peking cocoon forever.

However, once again, the note arrived with the hot water at nap time. It said simply, "Arrangements have been made for your appointment on Thursday evening at eight o'clock. Please inform me where you wish to be picked up." She handed her painstakingly lettered reply to the bushy-haired attendant, his direct glance as he said, "*Hao ba*," the ubiquitous Chinese affirmative, leaving no doubt that her note would be delivered.

Rudd was delighted when she called to suggest dinner on Thursday. With more initiative than she'd expected, he said, "I hope I can prevail on you to spend the night."

Anne's newspaper colleagues often speculated as to whether or not their phones were tapped. It was the conventional wisdom that the Chinese preferred human to electronic surveillance, but clearly Rudd thought it best to cover all bases.

She laughed. "I can see that spontaneity isn't much in style here, even among Americans. I'm not used to scheduling things to quite that extent, but I'll keep it in mind." Her answer was also designed to cover all bases.

They had a delightful dinner—simple northern food perfectly cooked with lots of garlic and ginger, served casually in heavy grayish blue and white Ming dishes. "Family style," Rudd commented. "You'll be getting enough banquets from other sources." They talked nonstop—about the Northern Sung painting that hung over the sideboard; the use of garlic throughout the world; Chinese concepts of music; the architecture of Peking. Strange, Anne thought, if it hadn't been for her providential meeting with the young woman, she would probably never have come to know Charlie Rudd except for a few formal afternoons of tea.

They didn't refer to her arrangements for the evening until Lao Li, the ever attentive old man, had set the dish of mandarin oranges on the table, signifying the end of the meal.

"I'm being picked up at eight."

"Where?"

"At the end of your street. Where it turns into that back entrance to the park. I thought I'd just slip out the back door. I hope that's all right with you." Anne spoke in an offhand way, but she had surveyed the neighborhood carefully on her last visit.

"Fine, no problem. The people around here are used to seeing me and my crazy foreign friends wander in and out." They were silent for a moment as they peeled their oranges. "You know that I'm going to give you a bit of fatherly advice, don't you?"

"Let's just say it doesn't surprise me."

"I think it's fine for a young reporter like yourself to do some snooping around. I haven't forgotten the joys and rewards of that sort of thing myself. I also have confidence in your integrity. Otherwise, I wouldn't lend my cooperation to these little games. That goes without saying."

Anne nodded seriously.

"I don't want to know what you're doing or what you're finding out. I'll wait until I read it in the *Washington Inquirer*. I just ask you to remember our conversation of the other day. Everything here is politics; everyone is and must be political. There's no such thing as news for its own sake. Everyone wants to utilize the influence and the access of Western journalists. Mao himself started that a long time ago when he got the news of the Communists' very existence out to the world by way of Edgar Snow. You have to try to under-

101

stand who is attempting to use you and why, and whether, like Snow, you think your discoveries are worth anything to the Chinese people and the rest of the world." Charlie Rudd's deeply lined face looked weary and quite old.

"I guess I made that decision before I asked you to help me."

"I'm sure you did," he said, pushing aside the bowl filled with peels. "I'm sure you must also understand that there are always potential dangers involved in snooping around in China."

"Fools rush in . . ."

"But at the same time, there are gods that protect the innocent." Rudd's severe tone suddenly became kind.

"If I qualify."

"If you qualify." Rudd paused. "I think you'll find everything you need in your room. Lao Li is pleased to have a female guest so he can get out the best phoenix towels and sandalwood soap. He's very proud of China's modern domestic goods and thinks I'm inappropriately interested in musty old things. If you're here and up in the morning, I always have breakfast at seven. If that's not convenient—until we meet again."

He got up and patted Anne affectionately on the shoulder. "I'm off to my cave. I always do a little mystery book reading—that's the foreigners' opiate in Peking—and have a few drinks before bed. I've gotten interested in P. D. James lately—really pretty good. She writes in the grand old English tradition. It's nice to read trash with a little style."

He left the room, his tall frame hunched over.

Anne stared after him, this strange and erudite man quietly rotting away among his treasures. She shook herself out of her thoughts and looked at her watch. It was ten minutes to eight. Like all the products of Chinese civilization, adopted or otherwise, Charlie Rudd had been precisely attuned to the needs of his guest.

There was a sharp edge to the icy night air, and though it was only a few minutes' walk to the park entrance, Anne's face was stiff with cold. While the Peking Hotel was kept at a temperature considered appropriate for foreigners, Anne had learned how to dress for the coolness of Rudd's Chinese home—double sweaters, tights under her wool trousers, thick socks inside her boots.

102

The narrow street was quite deserted, and the dark, bare branches of poplars projected menacingly in the shadowy night light. However, Anne had only a few seconds to shiver uneasily, for at precisely eight o'clock a car slowed down and stopped beside her. It was the kind of car often seen in Peking—a Polish copy of a cheap 1950 Chevrolet imported before the Sino-Soviet split, a vehicle meticulously overhauled and prodded into use decades beyond its intended life span.

The driver reached across and opened the door. Without a question, Anne got into the front seat. As it started up, the old car rattled and shook. It seemed to Anne that it must be arousing the entire neighborhood, that doors would fly open and frightened, angry Chinese faces would soon appear. But nothing of the kind happened. Instead they wound in and out of a labyrinth of shabby neighborhoods, attracting little interest. The driver handled the car smoothly, wheeling through the bumpy, poorly paved streets and around unanticipated corners at a speed that Anne thought at least reckless, if not impossible.

In the dark, Anne could just make out the shadowy outlines of the driver's bulky, hooded figure. "It's very cold this evening," she said, hoping her conventional conversational opening would break the silence.

"Yes, it is. This sometimes happens in March," a musical female voice responded. "I hope you're dressed warmly. There's a hooded overcoat like mine in the back seat. Please put it on. It will keep you warm and cover up your blond hair." It was her rebel contact.

"You drive very well. I didn't know Chinese women drove cars."

"Most don't," the young woman replied. She seemed disinclined to talk about herself, but Anne persisted.

"This is now the third time we've met, and I don't even know your name."

"My comrades call me Xiao Hong. You may call me that if you like."

The affectionate Chinese diminutives *xiao* and *lao*—"little" and "old"—were used not so much literally as with a sense of personality or relationship, while *hong* meant "red." It was a name thousands of young girls had been called during the first heady days of the Cultural Revolution. Anne wondered if the young woman had adopted it herself, perhaps in reference to her past or present political activities. But there was no point in asking. It was obvious that

103

Xiao Hong was not going to volunteer any further personal information.

They rode in silence. The streets of old, one-story, walled houses had given way to dimly lit blocks of stark apartment buildings in the style of the new regime.

Xiao Hong spoke unexpectedly. "Do you know anything about the Tianbei free-trade zone?"

In fact, Anne did. The first free-trade zones had been set up in the south, on an island off Fujian Province and in an area just over the border from Hongkong—natural locations for utilizing the most accessible source of foreign investment, the entrepreneurs of Hongkong and the so-called overseas Chinese businessmen who moved in and out of that city. Both zones had proved to be great successes. The attractions for international business were irresistible: inexpensive land with leases of up to a hundred years; a cheap and disciplined labor force guaranteed by the Chinese government; untaxed production imports; untaxed corporate earnings for the first five years; and guaranteed tax holidays into the far future.

There had been a good deal of healthy skepticism at first about the ability of the Chinese to deliver on their promises, and the Americans, Japanese, and Europeans were, by and large, content to sit back and watch the initial Hongkong ventures. There was also the nervousness that followed the Chinese contract cancellations of 1981. But when it became apparent that the free-trade zones were paying off handsomely, at least in the short run, the rush began.

It was then that Tianbei, the first northern free-trade zone, was opened. The site was the logical one: the Shandong Peninsula near Tianjin, once a foreign enclave dominated by the Germans, and long one of the major industrial centers of North China. There was no shortage of skilled workers in the area, and though few were familiar with the newer Western industries and technologies, they proved trainable. Hotels, restaurants, and movie theaters sprang up to provide for the thousands of technicians and executives who poured in from around the globe. Most of the plants produced components for precision instruments, electronics, and optics. There were a few of the predictable textile factories of developing countries, and even some heavy industry, primarily shipbuilding, which coordinated nicely with the traditional shipbuilding industry of the port of Tianjin.

The economic and trade articles Anne was working on would

104

inevitably lead to a discussion of Tianbei. As a matter of fact, she'd planned to go there within the coming few weeks.

"It's hard to believe there's a strike in Tianbei."

Anne's remark involved a bitter laugh. "You mean there couldn't be a strike in a free-trade zone where Chinese leaders promised the foreigners an obedient labor force?" Anne said nothing. That was exactly what she'd been thinking.

"The strike in the China-Cal plant started a week ago," Xiao Hong continued. "It had just begun when I told you about it."

"What's the problem?"

"Speedup. Worker representation. And"—Xiao Hong paused—"the rape of a woman worker by the American manager."

Anne was stunned. Surely no one could have been so stupid, so unaware of what the response to such a colonial crime would be. How could anyone fail to understand its implications in a society where the old xenophobic wounds throbbed insistently beneath a fragile skin of politeness and accommodation?

"It began as a sit-down strike and a demand by the workers that the management recognize their right to representation. But since yesterday, everything is different."

The silence between them was filled with tension.

"The workers were locked out. The police came. Four workers —including two of the ones you were going to meet—were killed. We don't know how many were injured."

Anne felt strangely dazed. How was it possible that she could be the only foreigner aware of such a critical event? Everyone knew how much depended upon the success of these new foreign enterprises—the enormous capital investments of the multinationals and the current regime's entire modernization plan for China to at least the end of the century, not to speak of the alliance with America.

"I see dozens of Western and Japanese reporters every day. Every one of them watches developments in China very closely, just as I do. The Tianbei zone is swarming with foreigners. How can something this important be going on without anyone here knowing about it?"

"Perhaps you're a little naive for a reporter," Xiao Hong replied quietly. "It's extremely important for both governments to keep this quiet. When such powerful forces want events hidden, they're quite able to do that, at least for a time."

"And why have you selected me?"

"We had to take a chance. Perhaps we were wrong about you and you'll be afraid. But for us, it's just as important to get the story out as it is for the government to keep it quiet. We know there are Americans who will support us. Some of us have studied the American labor movement. We know you have a history of glorious strikes."

Anne sighed. It was impossible to doubt the young woman's sincerity. But her assumptions . . .

"I don't work for a labor paper, you know, or a left-wing paper. I write for the *Washington Inquirer,* which might be considered one of the major establishment newspapers in the United States. And I'm not even an ideological journalist."

"Everything is ideological."

Xiao Hong put her foot on the brake decisively. They bounced over the curb and jerked to a stop by the side of an austere workers' apartment house like the dozens they'd been passing.

"We're here?"

"Yes."

"I have no idea where we are."

"The southern suburbs of Peking. You don't need to know more than that. It's better for you not to know too many details."

They walked noiselessly across the uneven dirt yard to the front door. Xiao Hong pushed it open, and Anne followed her up a narrow cement stairway. There was no light except for what came through the tiny window at the top of each flight of stairs. Anne stepped carefully, her hand on the rough wall. Each small landing was a dark clutter of bicycles, baskets, and brooms. Anne counted the floors. They must be on the fourth floor. Probably the top. The hall was entirely dark, but Xiao Hong seemed to know her way. She knocked lightly on the second door.

They were inside and Anne was gently pushed onto a hard wooden stool before she had any sense of people or place. It didn't take long, though, for her eyes to adjust to the dim light—the usual low-wattage bulb hanging by a cord in the middle of the room. She hadn't been in one of these apartments before, but she knew there were millions just like this in the cities of China—cement floors, unpainted plaster walls, a wooden table, a few stools, and a hard bed or two covered with thin mattresses, the customary colorful quilt rolled up at the foot; on the table beside her, the predictable thermos and a few painted metal mugs. Someone poured hot water, for most

106

Chinese the "white tea" of everyday life, into one of the mugs and handed it to her.

There were four Chinese in the room: Xiao Hong, half-hidden now in the shadows. Another young woman, very small, round-faced, her hair ever so slightly curled, her glasses round and wire-rimmed. And two young men, one tall with the classically handsome, heavy-browed good looks of a young Zhou Enlai; the other stocky, square-jawed, dark-skinned. They sat in a solemn circle facing Anne, their faces tired, their expressions grim. Anne realized they were all about her age.

The stocky young man spoke. "We had expected to have a different kind of meeting with you. More comrades had planned to come, but . . ." He paused. "Xiao Hong has told you about yesterday."

"She has," Anne answered.

"A number of our comrades have been arrested. Others are in hiding. Several are dead. The two of us, Shilan"—he gestured toward the small young woman—"and I, came here to Peking to talk to you. Your story to the world is very important to us."

He reached into a bag on the floor beside him. It was filled with papers. "Xiao Hong says you're worried about whether you're hearing the truth. That's reasonable. Foreigners are told a lot of lies about China. Chairman Mao used to say, 'No investigation; no right to speak.' We have nothing to fear from the truth."

Anne was startled. She didn't know anyone quoted Mao anymore.

The man pulled a number of black-and-white photographs from the bag and laid them on the table.

"These are pictures that one of our comrades took yesterday. In two of them, the name of the plant is visible in the front of the building. We know this sort of evidence is important for you."

He pushed the photographs under the weak beam of the overhead light bulb, and Anne drew her stool up to the table. There was no doubt about the sign, in English and Chinese: "The China-Cal Electronics Company." The photos were very clear, probably taken with one of the good Japanese cameras that seemed to be fairly common in Peking. It was a classic strike picture: police with long clubs, guns drawn; workers fighting back, running. It could have been photographed anywhere in the world, except for the sign.

"May I take these?" Anne asked. "I'm sure my paper would like to have them."

"We brought them for you. Do whatever you think is useful with them."

It was hard not to like the young man. His expression, tough and wary when Anne first came into the room, had relaxed, and he looked at her directly as he spoke.

"I'd like to have as many details as you can give me," Anne said to him, taking out a notebook, "about the plant, the working conditions, and what led up to the strike."

He looked at the tiny young woman, and with a businesslike assumption of responsibility she began her report. She was a master of details, reeling them off crisply: 1,200 employees, half men and half women; many experienced middle-aged workers, the rest recent high school graduates with excellent academic and political records. But that wasn't the important part of what she wanted Anne to understand. The main attraction of the jobs, and the reason there had been great competition for them, was that the workers were to be trained in the most modern techniques and would work with the most up-to-date machinery. They'd seen themselves as a future industrial elite.

"And isn't that true? Aren't you the new industrial elite?"

The square-faced man laughed caustically. "Right. We know how to do more work in less time than anyone else in China. Maybe the world. We're being turned into human robots."

In a sudden angry chorus, he and the woman spoke, each interrupting and adding to what the other was saying. Since the workers weren't familiar with the new technologies of the factory, they'd had no basis at first for analyzing the operations. They'd been told that they would learn new skills and assumed that that was taking place. The shock came when they began to realize that most of their work involved mind-numbing manual operations. Not only were the workers not learning new skills, but it was becoming apparent that in time they might lose those they already possessed.

Anne was quite familiar with the situation. No one who had written as much as she had about the economy of the Far East was unaware of how free-trade-zone factories operated. No doubt the China-Cal Electronics Company produced only partial components to be shipped back to California for final assembly. Such companies carefully guarded their production secrets in a world where workers in Singapore, Hongkong, Djakarta, and Tianjin knew only one small part of the total operation.

108

"What kind of contract were you working under?"

"The only contract was between the Chinese government and the American company," Shilan stated bitterly. "All we ever knew about it was what the cadres of our government chose to tell us, which was almost nothing. The Americans said something about 'reasonable working conditions,' but that can mean whatever they want it to mean."

"And what about the working conditions?"

"That's what finally became the big problem. Our morale was low once we understood that we were to be just unskilled assembly-line workers. Most of us had no choice but to accept that, though. There's a lot of unemployment in China. It's hard to get any kind of factory job. But then, as we mastered the operations, the pace speeded up."

"The speed, the intensity, the concentration are unbearable," the man said angrily. "A nightmare of work, fall into bed, and then the same thing the next day. On Sundays we can't do anything but sleep."

"And the rape?"

"The rape was part of it. If it hadn't been for the speedup, the rape might never have happened." Shilan's clear voice had become almost inaudible. "She was my roommate in the dorm, a very intelligent, hardworking person. Like many of us, she'd studied electronics in high school and wanted to get a job in the factory. Whenever she had an extra minute, she studied electronics. She was one of the first to realize that we'd never learn about electronics there, and she felt betrayed. She was very outspoken and led the workers in protesting the speedup. Then she was called in by the manager. He's a middle-aged American, always looking at the women workers. We didn't think she should go alone, but he insisted. She was never afraid of anything." Shilan stopped speaking, and there was a long silence.

"Unfortunately for her, she's also very pretty. The manager made advances. He even told her that if she'd go to bed with him he'd see that she got moved to a better, more interesting job. When she refused, he raped her."

Anne wrote rapidly in her notebook to cover up her discomfiture.

"A committee was set up. The American management refused to talk to us. They would never deal with the workers directly. They always expected their Chinese lackeys to do that. Naturally, the rape

109

was denied. My friend was fired after the manager wrote a long report on her insubordinate behavior and unstable mind. It will be impossible for her to get another job."

"There'd been talk for a long time about the need for worker representation," the young man interjected.

"A union?" Anne asked.

"A union, a workers' committee, a revolutionary committee—call it what you like. We just called it a workers' committee. The rape and firing of our comrade was the last straw. Everyone understood then that we had no rights at all, that we could just be thrown away by the management whenever they felt like it. That was last week."

"Our grievances are just ones. We're all willing to work hard, to do a good job. But the Chinese people didn't fight a revolution to be treated once again like serfs by foreigners."

"What's the situation at the plant right now?"

"It's closed. The workers are locked out. We know there are plans to bring in other workers, but that won't be easy. If we have the chance to talk to them, we know we can make them understand."

"Organization and propaganda work are going on at this moment among the workers at all the other Tianbei factories. If strikebreakers are brought in, we hope for a general strike in the entire zone." The voice was self-possessed and authoritative. It was the other man. Anne had hardly noticed him until now. He had been silent, his handsome face somber. Who was he? Not one of the strikers, it seemed.

"A general strike?" Anne's voice reflected her skepticism. "Do you have that much power? Do you realize what that would mean? Perhaps the end of foreign investment in China!"

"Foreign investment in China must exist with just and equitable conditions for the Chinese people or it will not exist at all." The voice was cold.

Anne waited, knowing that this man had more to say.

"In their leaflets the workers are beginning to refer to their historical predecessors—the workers in Hongkong in 1922, in Canton and Hankou in 1924. This may be the spark that starts the second Chinese Revolution. That will not be decided by us. It will be decided, as it always is in history, by the response of the ruling class to the just demands of the people. We all know the stories of Louis XIV, of George III, and Czar Nicholas II."

110

Anne had stopped writing. She stared, fascinated. Wasn't this precisely the power syndrome Charlie Rudd had spoken of? She was aware that Chinese boys acted out fantasies from *The Water Margin*, dreaming of being the bandit hero who would become emperor. It was said that Mao Zedong himself had been such a peasant boy, spinning his dreams and ambitions from traditional legends and Chinese literature long before he had ever heard of Marx and Lenin. Who was this eloquent, self-assured young man? A village primary-school teacher who would forever plot revenge against the state that had denied him admission to graduate school, or indeed a new Zhou Enlai?

"You must understand that the workers of Tianbei are not alone," he continued. "When you met Xiao Hong in Tiananmen Square, you saw a big-character poster that listed the names of hundreds of people who have been arrested in the last few weeks—people from all walks of life. She read you the manifesto that represents the views of millions throughout the country. You have not yet talked to the peasants who represent the main body of the Chinese people."

"Will I be able to?" Anne asked.

"If you can find a way to take a trip to Henan Province, we'll arrange it. For now, the most important thing is for you to write the story about the Tianbei strike."

It had all been said so quickly, so casually, but the Chinese imparted important information in just such seemingly offhand ways. They would arrange for her to meet peasants in Henan Province.

The room was suddenly still, and Anne was aware for the first time of the sound of a large alarm clock ticking loudly. In the dim light, it appeared that it was almost eleven o'clock. As if by common agreement, everyone in the room rose. Each in turn shook her hand formally, thanking her for her help with grave courtesy. Just as Charlie Rudd had warned, she had been cast into a role she had neither chosen nor accepted.

The car trip back went quickly and in near silence. She asked Xiao Hong only one question, "The tall young man . . .?"

"Wang Weilai. He's one of the national leaders of our movement. Everyone in China has heard of him."

Wang Weilai—the name written on Paul Engleberg's leaflet! How incredible!

When the car stopped, she realized they were at the back gate of Charlie Rudd's house.

"No one will notice the car. It's too late and dark for you to walk alone from the park."

Anne started to open the car door, then stopped. "I want to go to Henan. I'll let you know as soon as I can figure out how to do it."

"Don't wait too long," came the terse response. "The situation is developing very rapidly."

There was little light in the narrow lane that ran behind the back wall of Rudd's house. Anne ran her gloved hand along the high gate from top to bottom. She knew there was a latch. She'd used it to get out. She felt an instant of panic, forced herself to concentrate. Her fingers touched the latch. The gate swung open and she stumbled inside, slamming the heavy creaking gate behind her. She leaned against it, and then froze.

There was a shrill screech of tires as a car accelerated rapidly in the direction of the now distant sound of Xiao Hong's car. Anne was overcome with a wave of nausea. She let herself slide slowly to the ground and sat with her head against the rough wooden gate, breathing hard in the frigid midnight air.

Neither she nor Xiao Hong had been aware of anyone behind them, nor of a car parked in the back alley. But certainly they had been followed. So soon.

It was impossible for Anne to sleep before the story was written, and even after she'd typed the last word on the old Royal portable Rudd had thoughtfully placed on the rosewood writing table, she lay awake. The story had to be written. There was no question about that, but she couldn't cable it. It would have to be hand-delivered to the *Inquirer* office in Hongkong or Tokyo. She had done that kind of favor for fellow correspondents. Surely it wouldn't be too difficult to find someone who would do it for her. But it had to be done immediately, early tomorrow morning. And after it arrived in Washington, what then? Let the Washington office make the next move. They'd know they had a hot story. And the car in the alley-way? Anne did not permit herself to think about it.

She slept badly and departed at six, leaving Charlie Rudd a note of thanks. She didn't want to have breakfast with him. It would be too much of a strain, keeping silent about the events of last night.

He would be diplomatic, she knew, but she wasn't up to his cultivated tact this morning. And as for the car, she didn't like the idea of hiding that from him.

She found the dining room of the Peking Hotel empty except for a few scattered breakfasters. She started toward an unoccupied table near one of the long windows, but was intercepted by an assertive voice.

"I didn't know you newspaper folks got up so early. You might as well have breakfast with me if you feel like company." It was the Texan.

Anne's natural response would have been to avoid him, but something caused her to sit down. She started spreading jam on the toast he passed her.

"I'm always glad when I manage to get up at six, but it doesn't happen very often," Anne said. "Are you usually up at this hour?"

The Texan was steadily eating his way through a substantial serving of bacon and eggs. "I'm an early riser. Comes from being raised on a ranch. But this morning I'm a little earlier than usual. Got a plane to catch."

"Where're you going?"

"To the Tianbei zone."

Anne's impulse had been a good one. "I haven't been there yet, but I'm anxious to go soon. There's a tremendous amount going on, I hear."

The Texan nodded between mouthfuls of toast. "I like what I see there. In fact, that's why I'm going—to investigate the possibility of setting up a plant."

"As I recall our conversation of the other evening, you're quite pleased with the labor situation here." Coffee for her had arrived. She realized she was very tired.

"It looks good to me, and I've spent a lot of years in a lot of places."

Anne spoke carefully as she stirred her coffee. "I heard a bit of street gossip. You know, we really have to scrape the bottom of the barrel to get any news here. There's talk about some sort of a strike up there in the last week."

The Texan was clearly startled. His broad red face took on a guarded expression.

"You reporters are really a menace. You'll pick up anything for a story. Street gossip isn't news, you know that."

"Sometimes it is and sometimes it isn't. You just have to keep your ears open and take your chances."

"There was a little problem in one of the plants—electronics, I think it was," he said casually, "but nothing of much importance. Everything's under control. It doesn't do anybody any good to blow these things out of proportion."

"Is the plant operating again?"

The Texan shrugged. "Don't know why it shouldn't be. The Chinese know how to handle these things." He began to put on his jacket. "Sorry to run off, but planes don't wait, even here. Keep dinner in mind. Maybe when I get back from Tianbei I'll have some real news for you. There are some big banking developments going on out there, you know."

Anne watched him walk out of the room. Although he didn't know it, he had confirmed her story. She would have sent it anyway, but now she was quite free of doubts.

It seemed part of her fate that she should meet Michael Crimmins in the lobby, on his way to Tokyo to cover an economic summit meeting. Of course he would deliver her story to the *Inquirer* office there. He was amused, but she had been prepared for that.

"You seem determined, with that marvelously characteristic American arrogance and naiveté, to get yourself tossed out of China just like your precursor. But at least you have a good sense of people. You've chosen as your courier one of the most trustworthy men around, a man who wouldn't think of trying to steal your story— and not just out of an archaic sense of British honor."

Anne laughed. "I know I can trust you, Michael, or I wouldn't have asked you in the first place. But why do you say that?"

"You're giving me a story you can't send over the wires, presumably because it's something the Chinese wouldn't like. If that's the case, my London paper wouldn't like it either because of its ties with Washington. What's the point of my stealing something that hasn't a chance of getting into print?"

"You're very sure of that. I'm not."

"Of course you're not. Otherwise you wouldn't go to all this trouble. But I'll make you a little bet. The *Inquirer* won't print it, whatever it is. How about fifty dollars?"

"Fine, I accept." Anne chuckled. "The thing you're overlooking, Michael—though far be it from me to help you win your bet—is that the story you're carrying may be too hot not to print."

114

Michael opened his well-worn briefcase and put Anne's manila envelope inside. The enclosed photos made the package a stiff little bundle.

"My dear, you've mistaken the slogan of another of your great papers. It's not 'All the News That's Hot to Print' but 'All the News That's Fit to Print.' A great deal of news, it seems, is not considered fit to print. That's one of the first lessons journalists are supposed to learn. Your education seems to have been somewhat neglected. On the other hand, that little piece on the new border-talks chairman in Wednesday's 'International Roundup' must have been yours. Clearly, somebody thought it was fit to print."

Michael kissed Anne on the cheek. "I'll see you in two weeks. Try not to get yourself arrested or expelled before then."

The "International Roundup"! It wasn't possible that the *Inquirer* could have stuck her story in that grab bag of one-paragraph odds and ends. She'd written it up as a major, front-page, speculative piece, analyzing the appointment of Zhang Zhaolin as a signal of potentially changing big-power relations. It was a first-rate article, one of the best she'd ever written, and perhaps, she had hoped, the first step in building a reputation as a political analyst rather than merely a good journalist.

The elevator rose to the sixth floor with excruciating slowness. Anne dashed down the hall to her room, unlocked the door impatiently, and flew to her desk. Yes, there it was with the other mail, Wednesday's *Inquirer*. She flipped impatiently through the first section. The "Roundup" was usually somewhere around page 9 or 10.

But even Michael's advance notice hadn't prepared her. It was nothing, absolutely nothing. Only one sentence! She couldn't believe her eyes. "A new chairman, Zhang Zhaolin, has been appointed to head the Chinese team which has been holding talks with the Soviet Union regarding the disputed Sino-Soviet border since 1969." As if it were all quite routine and insignificant. It was even subtly misleading, the "since 1969" somehow implying that this was simply the continuation of an old, hardly newsworthy proceeding.

She knew there were a dozen legitimate reasons for articles to be cut. She'd been a journalist long enough to have come to terms with the ego problems involved. Maybe they didn't think Anne Campbell had earned enough stripes yet to speculate on geopolitical questions. More likely they just didn't want any speculation on this, period.

115

Maybe. But there were too many possible maybe's. You couldn't permit yourself much second-guessing when your stories were cut or rejected.

After all, she couldn't complain that her work hadn't been taken seriously. Last week they'd handled her article on the consumer economy as a front-page feature. So forget it. It was the only thing to do, just forget it. She had other things to worry about anyway. How to get to Henan, for example.

CHAPTER

9

The men from the engineering giants, the oil and mining conglomerates, the electronics and machine-tool companies entered the embassy tight-lipped that Thursday morning. The bankers arrived, appropriately, last. Their well-tailored suits were their international uniforms, their attaché cases their symbols of office.

It was for moments like this that the President had favored a multinationalist over a career diplomat for the China post, and he had been right. Thomas Carpenter was not unfamiliar with labor problems. In fact, as the smooth labor record of his own company indicated, his particular executive genius lay in his capacity to head off potential difficulties before they could become crises. Here he hadn't been in a position to do that, and it outraged him. The very circumstances that had triggered the Tianbei explosion—a rape! Such barbarism had no place in the modern corporation, no matter where in the world it was operating. But the fault lay higher than that. Long ago, flawed judgment of such a magnitude should have been spotted by someone higher up.

Still, it wasn't as if he hadn't pulled several lagging corporations out of slides in the States, and strikes were something he was very definitely not afraid of. The situation was undoubtedly salvageable if everyone involved had enough cool to stick it out. After all, these so-called socialist countries were firmer about handling strikes than their capitalist counterparts. The problem was simply one of containment. In the Santa Clara Valley a strike had been a strike, subject to the politics and social currents of the region and possibly even the nation, but not the world. In Tianbei there was no such luxury.

Communiqués on the Baluchistan fighting were piling up on his desk with depressing frequency. Worse yet, something was happening in the Chinese power structure, no doubt about it. By eight o'clock that morning, Peter had already placed on his desk the latest in what had now become a series of historical allegories in the *People's Daily*. The ambassador had only had time to read Peter's attached comment: "Important switch in position. Today's article praises a minister of the Tang dynasty who had the wisdom to negotiate an agreement with an old enemy." It was a decidedly unfavorable turn of events.

"We'll start with the good news," Carpenter said. "The strike at the China-Cal plant is over. The Chinese authorities have come through as effectively as we expected. Their actions entirely confirm their agreements with us—both the contractual ones and the verbal assurances that I assume you've all received. The strike leaders have been arrested, and the remaining work force has been shipped out to the countryside. At present, the plant is occupied by PLA soldiers who will remain until a new work force is brought in and trained. Needless to say, it'll probably take some time to accomplish that and get production back on line again. However, the military will remain in control for as long as necessary."

The faces around the table indicated little emotion. These were men accustomed to taking the bad with the good. The world was their territory; one developing country much the same as the next. When wages rose, they moved on. When revolutions took place, there were inconveniences, even disruptions, but they adjusted, and, in time, there was usually a way to resume business. After all, look what had happened in China. The shocking cancellations of foreign contracts had led many of them to pull out their large staffs, leaving only token representatives. But, as most of them had expected, they were back again.

"Now the bad news," Carpenter continued. "Although the China-Cal strike was handled about as well as we could have wished, it looks as if strike fever is spreading through the Tianbei zone." There were now a few frowns. "Leaflets calling for a general strike have been found in several plants, and there are reports from police spies of secret workers' meetings. The situation in the shipyards looks particularly unstable."

The shipyard was an enterprise of America's largest engineering construction firm. None of this was a surprise to its foreign-operations officer. He'd been in hourly communication with both the yard and the Chinese authorities for days now.

"There's no doubt that something's brewing," he said. "There definitely are meetings going on, and the workers seem to be preparing for some sort of shutdown. The Chinese have offered to bring military control into the entire zone, but we're afraid that will just set the whole thing off. They seem to think they can handle the workers by what they call 'ideological means,' so Chinese management is running mandatory meetings day and night. God knows what they're telling the workers—probably something about the Four Modernizations, with a few threats about meeting the same fate as the electronics workers thrown in. That's their business. We told them, use whatever methods you want with your own people, just as long as they work." He shook his head, his expression grim. "So far, we see no signs of success. It just hasn't blown yet."

"Is the issue money?" someone at the end of the table asked. "Or are they making political demands?"

Carpenter responded. "Of course it's money, but in their leaflets, worker representation seems to be the other big item."

"Our workers seem to see themselves as the Chinese counterparts of the Polish shipyard workers," the construction man added. "It's that more than anything else that has us worried. We could manage a wage increase, at least in the short term, though it would certainly force us to rethink our long-term projections. But we don't intend to live with a Chinese Gdansk."

A succession of speakers followed. Some had a far greater stake in the China venture than others. In the last analysis, though, they all faced the same options: to give their China investment more time, knowing that an unrealistically optimistic calculation could mean heavy financial losses, or once again to begin thinking about pulling out. There were limits, after all, to the patience of the giants.

"We can't come to any definitive conclusions yet," one of the bankers said decisively. "The Chinese government has done everything it could in the China-Cal strike. They've certainly fulfilled their contractual obligations. What we don't have is an accurate assessment of the strength of the workers. We have no indication whether they'd be able to push matters as far as the Polish workers did, or even if they'd want to. What we do know is that there's high

119

unemployment, a hundred people waiting in line for every job that's vacated. And the government won't hesitate to use clubs if the carrots fail. However, you never can tell about these things. Anything's possible."

He directed his final remarks to Carpenter. "I suggest we give the Chinese a month to get the entire Tianbei situation under control. Desirable as this whole business is for us, it's not a matter of life and death. We've had a base in Taiwan for a long time. The Chinese won't need much reminding to understand that we can always go back to the old arrangements."

There were a few chuckles, but the seriousness of the atmosphere remained unchanged. It was for moments like this that the U.S. embassy existed, and that a Tom Carpenter had been appointed their ambassador. As the meeting broke up, they made their assumptions about his role very plain.

"Let's give this everything we've got for the next few weeks."

"Tianbei has to be top priority for a while."

"Let's see where the President's commitment is when the heat's on."

Carpenter chatted briefly with each man leaving the room. As a corporate man himself, he identified with their concerns, but his mind was already on the next business of the morning, his eleven o'clock meeting with Lowell Haggard.

Haggard had observed every diplomatic propriety in requesting a meeting with Carpenter. He was aware of the delicacy and inherent awkwardness of his position and had no intention of exacerbating the situation with an unseemly display of arrogance. However, this was the first time he had requested a meeting with the ambassador—an immediate meeting—and both of them understood that it was a command performance. Carpenter was not accustomed to being commanded, particularly by someone whose authority came from unspecified, if perfectly understood, sources. He had agreed to Haggard's suggested time, but coldly, and as he left this serious but congenial meeting of colleagues—old friends, many of them—he felt his anger returning. First, though, there was the matter of Peter Matthewson—and that irritating memo from Washington.

The departing courtesies had taken somewhat longer than expected, and Carpenter was running a few minutes behind his usually precise schedule. Peter was waiting for the ambassador in his office.

Carpenter didn't waste any time. "You know about the Tianbei strike."

"Yes."

"I've just come from a meeting with the representatives of the companies based there. So far, the situation is under control, but it's going to be tense for the foreseeable future. By some miracle, we've managed to keep it out of the press. The Japanese have had a few stories about unrest in the area, but their stuff is still way too speculative to be dangerous."

Carpenter paused. "We have only one problem. That young woman from the *Washington Inquirer* managed to interview some of the strike leaders—they've since been arrested—and got a pretty hot story. The *Inquirer* did the right thing. They put the story on hold, but we want her to stay away from the whole business." Carpenter seldom used the imperial "we," Peter noted unhappily.

"I understand you've become friendly. I'd like you to use whatever influence you might have. I'd prefer to handle this in a personal manner if that's at all possible."

Peter hadn't had to learn the art of the poker face for his diplomatic career. It was simply the way he had always contained his feelings. But this time he knew he had revealed more than he would have liked. It was acutely embarrassing. There was the loss of dignity in his relationship with the ambassador. Carpenter certainly couldn't take as seriously an aide who was asked to perform a "personal" assignment of this kind. Even the expression "whatever influence you might have" was degrading. He had simply been given an order, and it was assumed that he'd carry it out; but it was different from other orders. He felt personally assaulted.

Damn Anne! She was unbelievably arrogant. All those careful diplomatic warnings, protecting her feelings and her professional integrity. Such bullshit. She did exactly as she damn well pleased anyway. It was really childish. He didn't agree, he didn't approve, and here he was, somehow responsible for her actions. It wasn't a role he wanted, and not only because of his relationship with Carpenter. He could just see the expression on Anne's face—that amused, superior, even slightly contemptuous look he'd observed the first time they'd met in his office. Which was more unpleasant —to be an errand boy for Carpenter or a spineless bureaucrat in the eyes of Anne Campbell?

121

There was something else, too. He had to admit it. He'd never had any misconceptions about the kind of woman Anne was—not at all the kind he usually got involved with. That undoubtedly had something to do with the excitement of their little affair. Like most men, he liked women who agreed with him, and he'd never had any trouble finding them. Sooner or later, though, there was always a letdown, a cumulative boredom, and a now routine drifting apart. Surely his and Anne's different personalities had something to do with the nice change of electrical excitement that had thrown them into bed together in a kind of heightened tension that was entirely new for him. He hadn't tried to analyze it, but he most definitely did not want to give it up. He couldn't imagine not seeing her again, couldn't imagine the absence of her extraordinary smile, her cool but intimate look, her long, perfect body in his arms.

Peter picked up the phone and dialed her number. He understood that he was playing games with himself—making a date immediately, according to the letter of Carpenter's request. The spirit of the request was another matter. Let them find someone else to tell Anne Campbell to lay off the hottest stories.

Although Lowell Haggard had suggested his office for the meeting, he gracefully acceded to Carpenter's preference for the office of the ambassador. Such small questions of status and protocol were matters of indifference to Haggard. His only concern was real power. Having it, he could afford a certain amount of formal deference to Tom Carpenter. He was entirely aware of the ambassador's displeasure over his special position. It was unfortunate. Carpenter was obviously a capable fellow. But the powerlessness of ambassadors these days was hardly a secret, and those who were attracted by the superficial charms of the job had to expect to pay the price. The important thing was that Carpenter go along with Zolti's directives, or at least not use his own political channels to block them.

Haggard arrived precisely on the dot of eleven o'clock, but it wasn't until ten after that Carpenter appeared, ushering out one of the young men Haggard had seen around the embassy—one of State's China-scholar types. Thank God for a classical military education! The longer Haggard was forced to be in the company of these fuzzy-minded academics who advised the diplomats, the more pleased he was to return to his satellite charts and the few men who understood them.

There were no pleasantries, no attempt to defuse the situation.

"You wanted to see me?" the ambassador said curtly.

"Yes, I did." Lowell Haggard's voice was absolutely neutral. People who disliked him said he was a zero personality with southern manners, a superior computer. He was impenetrable to the lay psychologists who picked away at the Washington elite; he was simply the living embodiment of a policy, and that was the way he wanted it.

"I've received an urgent memo from Dr. Zolti that he wishes me to discuss with you," Haggard continued calmly.

The muscles of the ambassador's jaw tightened visibly. "My instructions come from only two sources. The Secretary of State and the President."

"You don't need to concern yourself about that. I'm sure you're aware that the President is entirely in agreement with Dr. Zolti's policies and plans." Carpenter was indeed aware of that fact.

"You will receive a directive from the President to proceed in accordance with the plan I will outline. My job is to fill you in on some of the preliminary details."

It was precisely moments like this, Tom Carpenter thought fleetingly, that produced the sudden heart attacks and strokes that felled men of power in their prime. To be back-channeled was bad enough; to be humiliated to his face was intolerable. Carpenter was not, however, an insecure man, nor did he take Washington power personally. The thought of Cy Vance came to mind. A real professional, concerned with the survival of the country and the system —he'd met him occasionally over the years—done in by precisely the same kind of politics. But had his honorable resignation been remembered even a week after it happened? It was better to stay in and fight these bastards as long as you could stand it.

"Please proceed," he said quietly to Haggard.

Haggard was relieved. He didn't like having to deal with other people's emotions.

"Dr. Zolti would like you to know first of all that he appreciates your work in getting the new military program on line. He is quite aware that it has intensified and perhaps even disrupted the normal flow of embassy work."

Indeed it had intensified and disrupted the work of the embassy.

123

The staff of the military attaché had been precipitately expanded as military delegations began to flood in. In fact, at the rate things were going, Carpenter had been considering requesting additional office space. It was intolerable for everyone to be so crowded and inconvenienced.

"However," Haggard continued, "I must inform you that the military aspect of the embassy's work will not merely intensify but is now to be given top priority." He paused, looking at Carpenter carefully, but the ambassador's face revealed nothing. "Your military attaché will continue to handle the areas with which he is now working—the joint staff meetings with the Chinese, the new training missions, the increase in equipment transfers. But beginning immediately, I will represent the White House directly in coordinating all military activities here."

Carpenter understood perfectly what Haggard's announcement meant: a definite downgrading of the ambassador's role. They were putting Tom Carpenter on the back burner. Perhaps he would have to consider resigning after all.

"You will receive formal notification regarding all this from the White House soon, but I thought it best to inform you immediately —particularly in light of such matters as your meeting this morning about the strike in Tianbei."

The only indication of Carpenter's interest was his quizzical expression.

"Let me reiterate: Military matters are to be given priority. Concretely, what that means is that problems like strikes are to be considered of secondary importance. Dr. Zolti's instructions are that you should naturally do what you can to cool things down, but that's not where our main energies are to be directed. If it's necessary to shut the zone down and ship the industries out, so be it. We cannot afford, at this time, to become involved in peripheral disputes with the Chinese."

"A two-billion-dollar investment," Carpenter said drily. "Is that Zolti's notion of peripheral?"

They really were striking at his heart. Why else had he taken this absurd job except to implement projects like Tianbei? Carpenter had not been unmindful of the Sino-American military relationship, but for him it was never the raison d'être for the opening to China.

"What I infer from your remarks, Mr. Haggard (Carpenter never used Haggard's military title. As long as the man went creeping around in civilian clothes, he would have to accept being addressed as a civilian.), is that we seem to be going onto a full-scale war-preparedness footing. That's a question of overall policy that I'll take up with the President. In fact, it looks as if I should meet with him soon. I'll give you and the rest of the military staff my full cooperation, as I've always done. But I think we would be ill-advised to neglect the other areas of our relationship with the Chinese, and I must inform you that I don't intend to do so."

"You're aware, Ambassador Carpenter, of the intensification of the war in Baluchistan, and Soviet troop movements in the area. So it would not be inaccurate to say that we're switching onto a full, war-ready relationship with the Chinese. Obviously, Washington expects the worst, and China is our linchpin in this part of the world."

"I'm more than familiar with America's Asia policy. I'm also aware that there are other aspects to it than just the military one. One of our jobs here is to keep an eye on the domestic political situation and let Washington know how that might impact on the military scenario. For example, there's the policy struggle over the border talks with the Soviet Union. There was an article referring to it only this morning in the *People's Daily.*"

Haggard would have preferred simply to cut the ambassador off, but the border talks . . . He couldn't afford to let that slip by. After all, Zolti's worries about the change in the border commission chairmanship had been one of his major reasons for coming to China at this time. And now, what *was* happening on the border? Why was the situation so unnervingly quiet? When he'd left Tang Chen, Haggard had had no doubts that his artful recommendation for a military provocation had been perfectly understood and would be carried out expeditiously. But nothing had happened. Had Tang failed to understand him? That seemed unlikely. He had absolute confidence in his Chinese counterpart's ability to time his moves well. Still, it was disturbing.

"I haven't looked at today's translations from the Chinese press," Haggard said indifferently. "What are they talking about?"

"Just the latest development in the controversy over this new pro-Soviet chairman of the Chinese border-talks team. This morning's article seems to support him." Carpenter hadn't spoken without reflection. It was entirely possible that Haggard might know nothing about the new chairman. It had been difficult enough for him to get the necessary information. There was no reason to believe Haggard had had better luck. His intent was to make explicitly clear that even in the area of military matters, Haggard would be ill-advised to slight the ambassador. It appeared that he'd succeeded, for there was no mistaking the paling of Haggard's already pale face.

"I see," Haggard murmured. "That's rather interesting." But a thrill of excitement ran through his whole body. Zolti's instincts had been right again. A pro-Soviet chairman of the border-talks team! So a military incident on the border would be just as useful for those in power in Peking as it would for Washington! Tang Chen must have known all this at the time of their conversation. What a remarkable coincidence of interests. It was certainly just a matter of time before there would be reports of fighting on the border.

"Well, all the more reason for military preparedness, wouldn't you say?" he commented as he stood up.

Carpenter rose simultaneously. An observer would have found it difficult to determine who had taken the initiative. "And equally so for the political and intelligence analysis that is part of our job here. Thank you for your courtesy in giving me advance notice on all this, Mr. Haggard. I won't interfere with your responsibilities, and I must assume that you won't interfere with mine."

You had to give credit where credit was due, Haggard thought as he walked through the ambassador's outer office. From a position that would have humiliated most men, this one had come out—yes, in all fairness, he had to admit it—on top. A tough fellow. Carpenter would have made a good soldier if he'd been reached early enough. Unfortunate, the shopkeeping mentality of people who'd never known an aristocracy, one of the many pernicious results of the North's conquest, that the best men in the country went into business instead of a man's proper profession, the military.

But Haggard wasted little time on such speculation. He had his duties to perform. There was little reason to question Carpenter's information, but an uncharacteristic curiosity prompted him to pick up the embassy translation of the *People's Daily* article from the usual daily dispatches on his desk. Ordinarily, he wouldn't have bothered. He had his own intelligence network and learned what he needed from it.

He scanned the article quickly. The story of a renowned minister of the Tang period, obscure references to people and events, but the point was quite obvious—that the man's illustrious reputation was based on the fact that he'd achieved peace for several generations by means of reasoned negotiations with an old enemy.

What childishness, Haggard thought, both on the part of those who made policy statements in such a fashion and those who spent their lives untangling them. Still, it was unpleasant to discover a fact of importance—of critical importance—only by accident. He'd been unaware of something that was apparently common knowledge. However, he didn't have the time or inclination for such esoterica. Let those whose job it was to deal with Tang ministers do so. He had more important things to concern himself with.

Haggard loved the challenge of enormously difficult and complex projects, and his present assignment was turning out to be the challenge of his life. As he had informed Ambassador Carpenter, he was the direct representative of the White House in coordinating military operations, but more important, he was the man in charge of implementing the core of the Zolti strategy—the massive secret upgrading of China's nuclear capability against the Russians. It was this aspect of the China card that had never been revealed in the congressional hearings on the Sino-American military relationship. It had not been discussed even in the WASAC meetings that put the present program on line. Though behind all the China military options, it was too explosive an issue for real discussion among any except the few elect chosen by Stefan Zolti.

You either believed in the utilization of nuclear force or you didn't. Zolti and Haggard did. Zolti was extremely impatient with those who argued that there was no guarantee of future Chinese loyalty to the U.S. China's conflict with the Soviet Union was an eternal one. The long border alone made that inevitable, and the fact that both countries had critical need of the disputed Siberian territory. Besides, where else could China turn except the United States? China was in America's pocket. It could be taken for granted, and Stefan Zolti was contemptuous of anyone who did not understand that fact.

But time was short. The President had given Zolti a great deal of power, and he was using it. He had no hesitation about the perfect man to oversee the job—the one man in the country who had impeccable technological and ideological credentials, the military rank, the world view—General Lowell Haggard. He had given him carte blanche.

Haggard had undertaken the monumental task with absolute assurance, but it was soon apparent that the magnitude of the job was far beyond what he'd imagined. The problem for the United States, it seemed, was not simply to upgrade China's nuclear forces, but to create a whole infrastructure for a Chinese capability which did not yet exist. He was horrified at the realities that soon emerged from the stacks of reports on his desk.

The Chinese had no satellite-warning capability, no countertargeting ability whatever. Haggard had come prepared to oversee the installation of missiles aimed at Moscow, but the highly sophisticated mix of satellite, computer, and guidance technology essential for missile accuracy was nonexistent. He shuddered to think of where missiles intended for Moscow might end up. The Chinese were eager to proceed. They were enthusiastic, capable people. However, Haggard's hard analysis, the analysis he hadn't yet brought himself to inform Washington about, was that it would be at least two years before the American teams would be able to produce something the Russians would have to worry about.

Haggard glanced at his watch, the thin gold watch that showed the time in Washington, Moscow, and Peking. His plane would leave in an hour and a half. It was a trip that he looked forward to with great anticipation. He was on his way to the Chinese nuclear complex in Xinjiang. He'd been there before, but this was his first visit since Zolti's intensified program had been put into operation. The reports were basically encouraging.

A new plant producing solid fuel to replace the obsolete Chinese liquid missile fuel was reaching an operational state. The reports on the plant's progress were heartening, but it wasn't going fast enough. There must be some way of speeding the work up. Haggard was confident that if such a way existed, he would find it. He was pleased with the progress reports of the special teams. One was upgrading Chinese warheads. Another was introducing electronic warfare and avionic navigational equipment. With his habitual precision, Haggard had overseen the personnel selection of the teams, and was certain he'd selected the very best.

The C team was his pride and joy. They were working in an area that was of particular professional interest to him, and he read their reports with the devotion with which others might read the sports page. Built into the Soviet missile and aircraft capabilities were passive electronic-suppression systems. The task of the C team was the development of an advanced warning system which would can-

128

cel these out. They were the one group that was ahead of schedule, although it wasn't really of much practical use to have one high-tech capability so far out in front until the rest caught up.

Haggard wouldn't have time to see his own particular pet project in Xinjiang, but just knowing that it had moved along so well gave him cause for optimism. Tactical nuclear warheads stored in South Korea were now in a state of readiness to be transferred to China in four hours. That idea had been Haggard's own brainchild. Zolti had been ecstatic. In that one inspired move, they had potentially cancelled out one of the major Soviet strengths they could never match—Russian tank superiority. Yes, things were coming along well. There was no doubt about that, but time was of the essence.

Haggard's idea about a border incident now seemed to him his crowning coup. The Chinese had managed the 1969 border incident magnificently. It had done what they'd wanted it to do—finished off the political opposition; unified the people behind a dramatic policy shift; maintained antagonism toward the Soviet Union which could be sparked at any time.

Of course, there were always dangers in a military provocation. Everyone understood that. The Chinese had been hit rather hard in '69 when the Russians had come back in regimental strength. However, the Chinese had pulled back, and Haggard was confident that Tang Chen was a good enough strategist to manage things as well this time.

But could the Russian response be guaranteed? What if such an incident provided the very excuse they were looking for? The Chinese wouldn't be ready, couldn't be ready no matter what they did for two years.

Haggard organized his papers neatly and put them inside his briefcase. He couldn't permit himself such idle conjecture. The plans were made, no doubt already in the process of implementation. Like Lee at Gettysburg, Haggard believed in offensive action. Let Pickett charge and fate decide the rest.

129

CHAPTER

10

"I don't know what it is out there that makes all the reporters we send to Peking start thinking they're Edgar Snow." The voice from Washington was far away, the connection poor, but Anne couldn't mistake the sarcasm. So they were killing her story. She waited.

"Anne?"

"I'm still here."

"Look, you know we can't print a story like that. All it is is an interview with people who might or might not be giving it to us straight. It's completely unverified. I'm not even convinced the story's important, but if it is, we've got to have an eyewitness account from someone reliable."

There was no point in arguing more. It had already gone on long enough, and Anne knew that it wasn't a very smart thing to do, particularly with the *Inquirer*'s top editor. Still, she couldn't help saying one thing more.

"There's nobody in the world who could have gotten you an eyewitness account of that strike, Larry. The plant's totally sealed off."

"Okay. If the story's impossible to get, it's impossible. That doesn't justify our running a column of unauthenticated rumor."

"You're the one who makes the decisions," Anne said evenly. "But damn it, Larry, you know that's not what it is. The first stories that came out of Poland weren't eyewitness accounts."

The voice from Washington was brusque. "We'd assumed a little knowledge of geopolitics on your part, but if it's lacking we'll just have to supply it on this end. A Polish strike is in a class by itself. It has very little relationship to what you're trying to blow up into a big story."

Blow up into a big story! . . . Anne was speechless with indignation.

The voice became more conciliatory as growing static made it recede. "Now, don't get your feelings hurt. We have confidence in your work. Your economic stuff has been first-rate. It's been picked up all over the country. Just go back to your typewriter and turn out some more of it. Leave the flashy stuff alone until you can back it up. When you send me a properly substantiated story that there are a million workers out on strike, you'll see that story on the front page. In the meantime, don't try to recreate the Chinese Revolution. Take my word for it, that was over a long time ago."

There wasn't a word of the conversation that Anne didn't recall with absolute accuracy as she lay awake analyzing it, coming up with ever more brilliant rejoinders. She deeply resented Larry's explanations, which seemed to reflect more on her competence than on the content of the story, and which, without a doubt, weren't the real ones. Anne was a strict judge of her own work. She knew when she'd written a good story and when she'd written a poor one. The strike story had been a good one.

There was something in this whole matter that was bringing out Anne's stubborn streak. She couldn't fight it, but Larry's arguments wouldn't work again. Next time, he'd have his eyewitness story.

From the moment Wang Weilai, the rebel leader, had mentioned the possibility of going to Henan Province, Anne had known that was what she had to do. But it wouldn't be easy to arrange. She began with Tan Yulan. Fortunately, Tan Yulan had come to like her new assignment very much. She enjoyed working with statistics, something she was good at but hadn't done for years, and she'd developed a real respect for Anne. She'd observed with approval Anne's long working hours, her meticulousness in checking details, her tirelessness in researching what she didn't know.

Once she felt sure she wasn't neglecting her duties, it was a relief to be able to forget about Anne's outside activities. She'd been informed that Anne was having an affair with the American, Charles Rudd, who had lived in Peking for so many years. Mrs. Tan preferred not to think about the matter. It was disgusting, though somewhat fascinating, the way these foreign women slept with one man one night and another the next; and in addition, that one of them should be old enough to be her father! Of course, there was nothing wrong with a young woman marrying an older man for reasons of security. That was a sensible thing to do. Tan Yulan's own marriage had been in that category. But simply to go to bed with a man in his sixties, with no obligation on his part . . .

It was better not to think too much about the matter. Foreigners were foreigners, quite impossible to understand. They were obsessed with sex. There was no counting the number of times, in her long career working with them, she'd been asked about homosexuality in China, or about premarital sex, or unwanted pregnancies. She'd been frightfully embarrassed when she was younger, but now she regarded such questions as symptomatic of the barbarousness of "outside country" people. She simply smiled pleasantly and informed them that such problems did not exist in China.

Anne had made her request casually: "What do you think the chances might be of my going to some of the neighboring provinces to take a look at the economic situation there? I know that arrangements are being made for me to travel in the early summer, but I'd really like to make a short trip before then. It would be interesting to make some comparisons with what I'm finding here."

Tan Yulan pointed out that there was still a lot to learn here; the weather remained cold; the arrangements for trips were quite complicated. However, she agreed to take the matter up with "the authorities."

When a negative answer came back a few days later, Anne wasn't surprised. It wasn't a literal no—just a non-answer, a wait-and-see. But Anne had learned long ago that in China, when an answer isn't yes, one would be well advised to take it as no. So once again she decided to seek Charlie Rudd's assistance. There were moments when she had twinges of guilt about taking advantage of his protection. The matter of the car that followed her and Xiao Hong was what disturbed her most. There was no avoiding the fact that her activities must in some way implicate him. But Anne forced the problem from her mind. She could not allow herself to be dominated by fear, even for Charlie Rudd.

There was, after all, no one who was more knowledgeable about the ways of the Chinese. Certainly Rudd knew the potential dangers of her "snooping around," as he called it, for he had warned her. He must understand what his relationship with the Chinese would and would not permit. She'd told him from the beginning she wanted to pursue a story that required a cover. It was enough that she had to cope with her own sense of professional integrity in a situation where it seemed there wasn't a single person to support her. Surely Charlie Rudd was able to take care of himself.

Anne awoke late on Saturday morning with a pleasant sense of anticipation. The sun was pouring through her window with the dazzling, unmistakable brilliance of spring. She was glad the week was over, and she had a lively weekend to look forward to—at least what passed for lively in Peking—lunches with the men she enjoyed most, Charlie today and Peter tomorrow. She'd take up the Henan question with Charlie. She felt relieved, as if everything were already successfully settled.

And Peter . . . She realized she'd really come to depend on seeing him. She missed him when too many days went by without at least a phone call. It was true they disagreed about all sorts of things, but that in itself was part of the magnetism—the witticisms about each other's foibles and philosophies, the good-natured teasing, the falling into each other's arms laughing about the ridiculousness of it all. Although Peter often argued with her, at least he knew what she was talking about. There seemed to be nobody here who knew as much as he did about the tangled webs of Chinese politics; who had at his fingertips fascinating bits and pieces of history and poetry; who loved to explore the city as much as she did.

They did all the usual tourist things, staked out their own walking tours in the old quarters of the city, went to Peking operas—they saw *The Monkey King* three times—found a traditional circus in the southern part of the city, and they made love—in the afternoon, in the evening, sometimes on an uneventful Saturday morning like this one. It was always lovely, it was always too brief, and they always disentwined themselves reluctantly. In fact, the relationship was taking on a life of its own that Anne found somewhat disconcerting. Could you fall in love with a man you didn't agree with, or even quite approve of? Perhaps, she thought wryly, she just hadn't adjusted to being unmarried. But why analyze the relationship to death? Nobody was asking her to make any decisions. Maybe it would look completely different to her in Washington, or New York, but for now, in Peking, it was what it was—a surprisingly important part of her life.

There was something very luxurious about relaxing in a pool of early springtime sunshine, Anne thought as she curled up in the armchair near the window, smoking her first cigarette of the day. The prospect of getting dressed and going down to that depressing dining room seemed quite out of harmony with her mood. She'd never ordered breakfast in her room. It was out of the question on the days when Tan Yulan arrived at nine, and on every other weekend, she'd had early appointments or schedules to meet. But why not?

The room attendant who took her order was the same young man who'd transmitted the notes. Though he often came in and out of her room, performing his routine tasks, there had never been anything in his manner beyond the usual conventional politeness. Once or twice, Anne had tried to catch his eye, but he hadn't responded. This morning, however, Anne was positive that she sensed something strained in his manner. His smile, his words were the same as usual, but he was somehow ill at ease. Perhaps it was nothing but the Chinese disapproval of eating breakfast in your nightclothes.

But when the attendant returned promptly with her tray, he was more than usually solicitous in pouring the coffee. He straightened the curtains, placed the books and newspapers on the glass-topped table in a neat pile, watered her plant. Anne watched him curiously. How long was he going to stay? When there were no more small tasks with which he could occupy himself, he spoke at last.

"Don't worry about having your messages delivered. They still will be. But your friend . . ." He stopped. His expression was darkly somber.

"What?"

"Your friend has been arrested."

Xiao Hong . . . and the car. Of course. The beautiful face in the crowd in Tiananmen; in the upstairs room at the restaurant passionately reading the manifesto; in the dim, stark apartment listening to the strikers.

Anne's place in the circle of sunshine was still warm and soothing, but she suddenly felt sick, the same sinking in the pit of the stomach she'd felt inside Charlie Rudd's high protective wall when she heard the car start up. The depression of the past week swept over her

134

again. Xiao Hong in jail; the car; Charlie Rudd inside his walls, but watched nevertheless—and in Washington, Larry Metcalf at his desk, putting her story in a pile of discards. What of the other people who'd been at the meeting? It was as if they and the strike they'd talked about had never existed.

"When?" Anne asked suddenly.

"On Thursday."

"And the strike? What's happened to the strike?"

The young man, usually so cheerful, and now so serious, shook his head. "The leaders have been arrested. The other workers have been sent to the countryside."

My God, she was angry. Angry about the young workers, so earnest and straightforward, arrested for raising demands that were nothing more than ordinary union rights. Angry about her story, the most important story she'd written since she arrived here, censored because some fool in Washington thought it was more important to maintain a superficial impression of harmony than for people to know what was actually happening. She would get to Henan and bring back an eyewitness account no matter what she had to do to get there.

The attendant had started toward the door.

"Wait. Wait, please," Anne said. "Don't you have anything else to tell me?"

"No," he replied gravely. "That's all." He put the thermos on the floor and walked toward a corner of the room. "I want to show you something, though." He pulled back the old-fashioned, moss-green drapes that hung along the wall. They hid a small alcove—an odd arrangement found in a number of old Chinese hotels where the child and perhaps nursemaid of the room's occupants had slept in times long gone. Anne had put her suitcases there and kept the curtains drawn. The young man pulled out an antique bell cord, another accoutrement of the colonial past—not a bell pull, but a pushbutton at the end of a long cord.

"When you called me today, you used the buzzer by the door."

"Yes. That's what I always use."

"People don't think this old bell cord works. You probably didn't even see that it was here."

She shook her head. "I didn't pay any attention to it. It looked like part of the old drapes."

"It works. If anything happens, if you should ever need to call me

135

or the other room comrades quickly, very quickly or for something very important, use it. But don't use it for any other reason." He picked up the thermos. "And don't tell your secretary about it." He closed the door quietly behind him and was gone.

Anne sank back into the overstuffed chair and poured herself another cup of coffee. She looked out the window at the busy Peking street. It appeared entirely benign. A child, as if affected by the contagion of the sunbeams, broke loose from his parents' hands and skipped a few steps, unhampered by the padded clothes of winter. Others held long sticks of small candied apples that are a Peking child's special treat. Even the pace of the passersby appeared slowed by the luxuriousness of the sunshine.

She sat by her window. It was hers in this now familiar room, becoming every day more her home as she accumulated treasures— the graceful reproduction of a Tang dancer that she'd bought in the shop on Liulichang Street; the strangely beautiful potted chrysanthemum with feathery green flowers from the flower shop behind the old market; the four scrolls of bold calligraphy. Yet now, even this room, her home, had become a place of danger, a place in which it might become necessary to call quickly for help.

Anne stacked her breakfast dishes noisily on the tray and half slammed it on the floor in the hall outside her room. She marched into the bathroom and turned on the shower. As usual, it sprayed all over the room. That seemed to be part of the architectural plan, for there was a drain in the floor. Anne sat down on the small wooden stool, holding a towel to her face. The golden mood in which she'd awakened had vanished, and she was on the verge of furious, hysterical tears.

It was fortunate for her state of mind that Anne had a luncheon date with Charlie Rudd. No sooner had she stepped over the threshold of the second red gate into the symmetrical quiet of the inner courtyard than she felt the air of reserve and disciplined calm. Was it the architecture itself—the security and distance created by the illusion of a world within walls? Or was it the asceticism of a garden disdaining the frivolity of flower beds? Even before Charlie Rudd greeted her at the door, Anne felt the turbulence of her emotions subsiding.

Tea was waiting on the low, highly polished table, Lao Li hovering protectively behind the steaming pot. Anne sat in one of the severely beautiful rosewood chairs, leaning her head against its high back.

"Oh my," she sighed comfortably. "This is like coming home."

"I'm glad to hear it." Rudd handed her the hot cup of tea. "But why are you sitting in that difficult chair? Its whole function is to force you to sit up very straight so you can preside over the gathering with the proper dignity and authority."

"That's just what I need, some external force to keep me from splintering into undignified fragments."

"You do look tired." Charlie Rudd's brown eyes were keen as always. "What are you doing, trying out all the Peking night spots? I didn't know there were that many open after ten."

"There aren't. And I even slept late this morning. It's just occupational stress."

Rudd's wry, crooked grin lit up his lined face. "In that case, you have no one to blame but yourself. This is the calmest capital in the world for a reporter, unless you insist on smashing your head against stone walls. I assume that's your personality and you'd be doing it wherever you were."

"No doubt you're right. I'm not entirely neurotic, however. The ambiance of your Chinese sanctum always calms me down."

They began to chat as usual about the events of the past week. He told her the history of some of the places in Peking she and Peter had visited recently, and they examined the symbolism of the Ming *wuzai* covered box on the table. By the time lunch was served, Anne was feeling positively cheerful.

As Charlie carefully selected morsels from the beautifully arranged chicken salad and put them on her plate, she said, "I want to take a little trip, and my official guardians aren't inclined to arrange one before summer. You've said that you take periodic trips to different parts of the country . . ." Anne stopped, vaguely embarrassed. She'd intended to do this more subtly.

But Charlie rescued her quickly. "Actually, I've been itchy to get away myself. This long wait for spring begins to get to you after a while. Where were you thinking of going?"

Anne's serious face radiated her relief. "To Henan."

"Well, well." Rudd patted her arm affectionately with his bony, freckled hand. "You're turning out to be a much less troublesome

137

responsibility than I'd feared. Or maybe you just have good instincts."

"What do you mean?"

"That happens to be the most manageable trip you could have suggested. In fact, if you'd asked me where I might go on my first trip of the season, I would have told you Henan."

The anger and depression of the morning, of the week, began to lift, and Anne looked at him with undisguised delight.

"As you probably know, the area around the modern city of Zhengzhou was one of the major centers of ancient Chinese civilization. It has a history of three thousand years. It was the site of the Shang dynasty city of Ao."

The Shang. Creators of the powerful, confident zoomorphic bronzes that typified one of the world's earliest great civilizations. Anne thought of her favorite piece in the San Francisco Brundage collection, the rhinoceros. Delicately green with the patina of the centuries, for her it embodied the forceful, dynamic elegance characteristic of the Shang artists.

Rudd looked with pleasure at her lovely, eager face. He'd never felt lonely in his study of Chinese art. He was used to being alone, even preferred it that way. The art itself was his companion. But the joy of a protégé was something he'd never experienced. There was a note of excitement in his customarily dry, drawling voice.

"The city of Ao was one of the greatest archeological finds during the first decade after liberation. It's been clearly established as Early and Middle Shang, predating the Ayang Shang culture. Now, east of Zhengzhou, not too far from Kaifeng, a city has been discovered that seems earlier than Ao. Historical tradition has it that the tenth Shang king moved his capital to Ao from an earlier location farther to the east. It's always been assumed that it was quite far to the east, probably Shandong. But now it looks as if this could be that city. The artifacts are not just from Early Shang, but from an even earlier stage, Proto Shang. It's very exciting. Not only might this be the largest, earliest Shang city known, but it could finally provide the key to one of the great mysteries of Shang culture."

"What's that?" Anne was leaning forward, holding her empty teacup in her hand. Charlie's story had driven everything else from her mind.

"As you know, the mastery of technique displayed in the Shang

138

bronzes has never been surpassed. It's comparable to that of the Late Bronze Age of the Mediterranean. There, we have irrefutable evidence of a gradual development from the Early Bronze Age. But in China, there are great gaps. Before the humble predecessors of the great late Shang bronzes were found at Ao, some scholars through the technique must have been introduced from the West. The Ao bronzes just about settled that controversy. Most experts are now certain that the skills of bronze metallurgy did develop independently in China, but archeological evidence of the earlier steps has been missing.

"The first artifacts have been brought out of this new site just in the last few months, and the historians are hinting that the evidence of a primitive bronze technology has turned up at last. If that's so, these are the missing links that will prove definitively the indigenous development of Chinese bronze metallurgy. The Chinese have been asking me to go down, have a look, and write a big article for *Modern China*. I couldn't bring myself to go to Henan in the winter. Terrible climate. The damp from those Yellow River mists seems to eat right into your bones. But now could be about the right time. It'll still be cold, but not impossible, and within a month it'll be so hot you can't stand it."

"Imagine," Anne said, "being the first foreigner invited to see an archeological find like that."

"That's the other side of staying out of the way when the Chinese want foreigners out of the way and keeping your mouth shut when you should. The Chinese have always known that you can't rule by punishment alone. They give out rewards if you're good, and they have a genius for knowing who's susceptible to what. They know they can get to me with a first crack at the Proto Shang bronzes. I just have the feeling they might look favorably on having an American journalist write it up, particularly if she's under the wing of an old China hand who'll give some guidance on how it should all be presented. One of their big PR tacks is their role as protectors of culture, and after the incredible reception the bronze exhibit got in America, yes, I think they might like to have the news appear first in a Washington paper."

Anne had felt confident that Charlie Rudd would help her, but she was, nevertheless, overwhelmed. Not only would she get to Henan, but to one of the archeological finds of the century! Still, nothing was settled in China until you were actually on your way, or even more realistically, until you'd arrived. She mustn't celebrate too soon.

Lao Li had cleared the table. "Now," Charlie said, looking at his watch, "it's nap time, and as you know, nothing is allowed to interfere with that.

"If you have things to do, just go ahead and leave, but if you're not otherwise occupied, you might like to wait to find out about the phone call I'm going to make when I get up. You've seen my etchings, but you haven't really looked at my library. I have all sorts of strange old books—both Chinese and English—and even a few in Italian and Portuguese. For example, I like to reread the diaries of Adam Schall from time to time. Helps give one a little perspective on residence in China."

"At precisely four o'clock, to make sure that I don't interrupt *his* nap, I'll phone my old friend Li Zemin, and we'll see if we can't get this matter settled rather expeditiously."

"Li Zemin? The Minister of Culture?"

"The very one. I did him a favor many years ago—hid him in my house in Shanghai when it was important for him to be hidden. The Chinese don't forget things like that."

The afternoon passed quickly. It was wonderful to be all alone in Rudd's beautiful library. He was, she decided, a man of unerring taste. There were no more mistakes in his collection of books than in his collection of paintings, porcelains, and furniture.

The books were tempting, but looking at them would be the occupation of weeks, not hours. Instead, Anne spent her solitary time wandering about the room, picking up an oxblood vase here, a jade brush holder over there. Picking up, that was the delight of it. To hold a perfectly modeled shape, to feel the cool sensuous texture of these lovely objects. Pale afternoon sunshine filtered through tall narrow windows, added by some twentieth-century resident, and cast a subtle light on the exquisite colors.

She was pleasantly startled when Lao Li appeared in the doorway to ask if she would like coffee this afternoon after Mr. Rudd had completed his phone call. By the time Rudd appeared, smiling, coffee and biscuits in an English tin were already in place.

"How efficient are you at getting ready for a trip?" he asked as he settled himself in his usual armchair.

140

"Very efficient. I could leave in an hour if that's what you had in mind."

Rudd laughed. "We're not quite so uncivilized as all that, you know. I had in mind something more like Monday morning at nine."

"That's the simplest thing imaginable. You mean we really can go? I really can go?

"Yes, you really can go. Li Zemin agreed immediately. He understood perfectly the advantages of having this important art news appear first in a big Washington paper. And he trusts me. If I say you're the one to do the story, he'll go along with that."

For just a second, Anne felt a pang of uneasiness. In her excitement, she'd actually forgotten her real reason for arranging this trip. But the die was cast. Her little plan had already turned into something much bigger. You couldn't get the okay of the Minister of Culture to do a story like this one and then change your mind.

"Monday morning at nine," she replied firmly.

"Excellent. Now take what you need in the way of clothes, typewriters, hair dryers—whatever it is that lady reporters take when they travel. The important thing, though, is for you to do some background reading before we go. Do you have time for a little studying this weekend?"

Anne nodded.

"All right. We'll gather together a bit of necessary research material for you." Charlie Rudd began to work his way methodically along the wall of shelves, pulling out volume after volume. He was totally immersed now in the Shang. Nothing in the world could have dissuaded him from taking this trip. It was the nicest thing that had happened in years.

CHAPTER

11

By the time Peter came by to pick her up late Sunday morning, Anne too was lost in Shang history. The city whose remains she would see was taking shape in her mind. During those centuries from 1500 to 1000 B.C., the earth was still tilled with a foot plow, and the peasants lived in subterranean dwellings or loess caves. But the Shang were city builders, and those cities must have been bustling, complex centers, home to craftsmen in pottery, ivory, and wood as well as metal, turning out goods for a powerful, luxurious court constantly preparing for the wars that supplied its wealth or protected it from envious outside tribes.

Anne had stayed up until three, surrounded by piles of Charlie Rudd's well-selected, yellowing books. It was like being a student again. She could almost forget about the news of the moment—the war in Baluchistan, the strike in Tianbei, even Xiao Hong.

However, she hadn't neglected to give a note to the room attendant, informing whoever read such things with Xiao Hong gone that she would be leaving for Kaifeng at nine o'clock on Monday morning. She was pleased that her precision fit the most exacting Chinese standards. But the young attendant's face was once again expressionless, even when she requested a reply within twenty-four hours if possible. It was as if she'd imagined the instructions about the old bell cord.

Peter arrived—handsome, tweedy, and animated. He caught

Anne in a strong hug as he got in the car next to her and gave her an emphatic kiss.

"You look absolutely dazzling," he said.

It was true. She did look dazzling. In her excitement over the trip, her black mood of only yesterday morning seemed to have disappeared. She felt herself all smiles, her eyes shining, her skin luminous, and she was wearing a wonderful new jacket, a truly self-indulgent purchase. Red, bright red, such as only children, foreigners, and a few daringly westernized young Chinese women wore in this austere city, an opaque brocade lined with white Mongolian lamb's wool that curled appealingly over the top of the Chinese collar.

"It's the jacket," she said, pushing him away affectionately. "Everyone looks dazzling in red. That's probably why the Chinese reserve it for weddings. Too dangerous the rest of the time."

"It's fantastic. You must have decided as long as you're going to stop traffic anyway, you might as well stop it dead." That was exactly what Anne *had* decided. As tall and blond as she was, she couldn't avoid being stared at; so, she'd reasoned, she might as well wear what she liked. Not everywhere, of course, but at least when she was clearly cast in the role of foreigner.

"But that's not why you look dazzling. It's just you, whatever it is in that wild spirit of yours that keeps you from gradually turning gray like the rest of us here." Peter held her face close to his. "Is going out to lunch really what we want to do today? I have a few thoughts in my head."

Anne smiled. "I think lunch is a good way to begin. You committed yourself, you know, and on that basis I didn't eat breakfast. Besides, you can't just reorganize the plans before you've even told me where we're going."

Peter put his arm comfortably around her shoulder. It was hard for him to imagine that until a few weeks ago Anne Campbell hadn't existed in his life.

"You win, because as always you operate from impeccable logic. Food first. Other matters can be negotiated at the appropriate time."

Leaving the wide streets of central Peking, they passed onto the narrower, less traveled road that led through the western suburbs of the city out into the countryside. Carefully tended fields began to appear, their furrows clearly marked, plants still hidden beneath the inhospitable-looking soil.

"Where are you taking me? It looks like we're on our way to a picnic."

"I'm afraid it's a little chilly for that, and foreigners don't have picnics on the hard, cold ground. They take leisurely walks, then eat inside proper restaurants. And that's what we're going to do, walk around the Summer Palace Lake and lunch at the Tingliguan restaurant there."

"Oh, that's the one that's in an old theater, isn't it? Famous for fish."

"My friend who always does her homework. Whatever you want to know: the identity of the new border-talks chairman or the speciality of the restaurant. Yes, that's the one."

Annoyingly, his own offhand remark reminded Peter of the matter he'd put in the back of his mind—Carpenter's request that he talk to Anne about the strike story. Just the exhilaration of being with Anne had driven it away for the first time in days. Fortunately, the inevitable unpleasantness was again delayed.

"Guess where I'm going tomorrow morning." Anne burst out.

"God only knows. Probably someplace that's impossible to go to."

"Not impossible, but difficult, I think. To Henan Province. I'm going to do a story on the archeological find of the century—an Early Shang site, maybe an entire city."

Peter was overwhelmed with relief. So she'd finally gotten herself on the right track, a track both the American and Chinese governments could live happily with. Now he could relax about what to do with Carpenter's little warning. It no longer had such censorious implications. The latest big archeological find. It was certainly a story worthy of the talents of Anne Campbell, and Peter was pleased to hear that the trip had been arranged with the direct approval of the Chinese Minister of Culture. That would be a positive thing to report back to Tom Carpenter.

The car stopped in the parking area behind the Eastern Palace Gate. Walking hand in hand through the bridgelike entryway of the red-pillared building, Anne and Peter found themselves at the entrance of the covered passageway that ran along one side of the lake. A fanciful corridor, a diversion for rulers, its scarlet wooden col-

144

umns were interspersed with decorative lattice work and painted with flowers, fish, birds, and mythological scenes in charming greens, blues, and pinks. It was almost like a chain of linked gazebos, the ceiling of each painted with a different scene. The Hangzhou landscapes had been a birthday present from the eighteenth-century emperor Qian Long to his mother.

Anne and Peter wandered along slowly, their eyes on the paintings, stopping every now and then to talk about them. The weather was cool, the sky radiantly blue. They passed young Chinese families, adults peeping furtively at the strange foreigners, babies staring wide-eyed. Covies of children, girls in one group, boys in another, walked arm in arm through the corridor. It was all strangely comforting.

As long-legged Americans, even their leisurely pace was much faster than a Chinese walk. Soon they left the other Sunday strollers far behind. The corridor was theirs as the landscapes unfolded serenely around them. But not for long.

Perhaps the artificially lovely surroundings magnified the sudden harsh laughter to a peculiar dissonance, but it was frightening. And so were the five young men who blocked their way, huddled together, laughing, shouting wildly, swearing, their attention riveted on something in the center of their circle. Their laughter had nothing to do with humor. It was palpably cruel, and when one of them turned suddenly toward Peter and Anne, the hostility in his eyes was chilling.

There was no way of avoiding them. Anne and Peter were far beyond the customary short promenade, encroaching on a private domain. Their eyes met briefly, and, almost instinctively, they both moved a few steps backwards, but there could be no running away. There was no one else in sight, and the narrow corridor was the worst kind of trap.

As another of the men wheeled about to look at them, there was a momentary gap in their circle. Anne gasped. On the ground a gyrating, frenzied ball of flame, like a pinwheel, but unmistakably a small living creature with four feet still functioning under a burning body. She clutched Peter's hand. The circle closed again.

"What? . . ." he murmured. He hadn't seen, and she couldn't answer. Vomit rose in her throat as she stood paralyzed. She closed her eyes. Now in the darkness the sound was different, a slapping, banging, a gutteral shouting. "Good God," she heard Peter say. She opened her eyes. The tortured creature was now a smoldering pile of black remains only a few feet from where they stood.

"Rat," someone muttered in Chinese. "Filthy rat."

"Good God," Peter murmured again. He gently disentangled his fingers from Anne's frozen grip and put his arm tightly around her.

The men stood facing them behind their charred victim, their bodies a solid wall across the passageway. They glared sullenly, cigarettes hanging insolently from their lips. Suddenly, one of them smiled awkwardly and in slow, careful English said, "Hello, foreign friends. Are you Americans?"

Peter nodded. Anne whispered, "I cannot believe this . . . cannot believe it." She felt his arm tighten around her waist, but from the sound of his voice, it seemed that Peter was absolutely composed. "How's it going?" he responded coolly in English.

The five broke into guffaws of laughter and shuffled about uneasily. Anne was quite familiar with the Chinese habit of laughing during moments of embarrassment, but somehow, now, it was unspeakably awful.

Peter repeated the greeting in Chinese. The wary faces softened into expressions of relief.

"I'm trying to learn English from the lessons on the radio," the thin man who had greeted them said in Chinese. "But I don't have a chance to practice with foreigners. You speak so fast I can't understand you. Would you please repeat what you just said?"

Peter's tone was absolutely even; not friendly, but not unfriendly either. You had to hand it to him, Anne thought—a fine diplomat.

"You probably don't know the expression I used. Kind of an idiom, like 'How are you?' but less formal." As he repeated it, they had all moved forward in a cluster, watching his lips carefully. They'd removed their dangling cigarettes from their mouths, and in a loud, triumphant chorus repeated, "How's it going?"

"That's what we want to learn," the speaker of English said solemnly. "Informal English like American young people use, so we can speak like them." There was a murmur of agreement.

Anne had recovered her composure. She sounded calm, even professional. "Why do you say that?"

Another of the group spoke up. He was short, square, his black hair trained into a careful, archaic ducktail.

"Everything comes from America—everything. You have the

146

most modern system in the world, the most advanced technology, styles, jeans, rock music, movies, TV—it all comes from America. We have to learn everything from you as fast as we can, so we can be a superpower by the year 2000."

As he spoke, Anne realized what it was about their clothes, in spite of the ubiquitous dark blue, that was special. It was their jackets, tentative attempts at the old bomber-pilot style, and especially their pants, rather strange jeans, quite homemade looking in fact, but definitely jeans.

Her eyes met Peter's. He nodded almost imperceptibly. Anne took out her pack of Marlboros and offered them around. Each young man took one with a display of sophisticated unconcern, but with obvious respect. She took one herself, and there was a blaze of wooden matches as five hands reached forward to light it for her.

"I feel like Rita Hayworth," she murmured to Peter.

"You don't smoke?" one of them asked Peter in surprise and definite disapproval.

"No. Causes cancer you know. Not very useful in building a superpower by the year 2000."

There was an embarrassed stirring. How was one to understand these foreigners? In the few old American movies they'd seen and in the movie-magazine pictures that various friends and cousins brought in from Hongkong, all fashionable foreigners smoked.

"What do you all do?" Peter asked. "Sunday must be your day off."

There was an abashed silence. All eyes were drawn magnetically to the remains of the rat on the ground. Finally, the man with the ducktail spoke.

"We're all on waiting lists for factory jobs, but we've already waited a long time. It's very hard to get a job in Peking if your parents don't have connections."

"Why don't you go somewhere else where it might be easier to get a job?" Anne asked.

"It's hard to get good jobs anywhere, and anyway we don't want to go anywhere else. We were all sent to the countryside once. It was very hard to get back then. You can't take a chance. You might never make it back to Peking."

"There's more going on here. The new things come to the big cities. That's what we're interested in." The speaker was a sullen, long-faced fellow who hadn't spoken before. "And besides, our

147

families can help us out here. At least they can give us a place to sleep."

"So how do you make it? What do you do with yourselves?" Peter asked.

"We have a little co-op," the first speaker said, gesturing toward the group. "That's what the government wants unemployed youth to do. We repair things. Radios mostly, sometimes sewing machines or TV sets, but we really don't know much about TV work."

"Can five of you make a living doing that?" Anne asked.

The laughter was unquestionably harsh.

"Not a living. Of course not. We make a few *yuan*, enough to help the family with food and buy ourselves cigarettes, that's about all. Everybody else is doing what we're doing. There are too many repair shops like ours."

"We do a good job, but it doesn't matter," the sullen-faced man interrupted resentfully. "The editorials in the *People's Daily* say that competition is good for business, that it makes people efficient and hardworking, but they don't say that if there are too many of us, it doesn't make any difference."

"So how do you see the future?" Peter asked quietly.

"China has to modernize faster, much faster." A small young man who had been listening spoke up. "Our lives are going by. We have to have good jobs soon. There are lots of things we want to have —a color TV, a motorcycle, maybe even a car. Everyone in China should have a car like everyone in America does. Modernization. Faster, faster. That's the only answer." There was a murmur of agreement.

Peter and Anne, both anxious to end the conversation, glanced at one another. Anne handed the remaining pack of Marlboros to the first man who had spoken, and he accepted them in a business-like way.

Then the inevitable question, "Do you have any jeans you're not using?"

Peter shook his head and, taking Anne's arm firmly, said a brusque good-bye. There was an anxious chorus of good-byes in English and Chinese. Someone hastily kicked the charred remains of the rat off to one side, clearing the way for the visitors to pass, and Anne and Peter went hastily forward, looking straight ahead.

Anne walked rapidly, oblivious to the incongruously idyllic scenery all around her. The fear was gone, but a sense of nausea lingered, and something else. The depression was back. She could feel it, right there, almost like an object inside her. She glanced at Peter. His mouth was shut in a hard line.

"God . . . awful," he said angrily, as if in response to her thoughts.

"So what's the answer?"

"Who knows? What the guy said, I suppose. Modernize, modernize; faster, faster. Rising expectations. Who knows what the answer is."

"And the faster they introduce new technology, the more people they put out of work."

"Have you got any other ideas?" Peter snapped out the question.

"They had some ideas a few years ago about taking a slower non-Western route, but it's not considered in good taste to mention that these days." Anne's voice was suddenly as hard as his.

"Good God, Anne. Everybody knows what happened with all that. It was a disaster pure and simple."

They walked on in silence. Before them lay a placid blue-green body of water surrounded by brown hills, and everywhere were scattered the fantastic pagodas and pavilions of the Summer Palace. Built by the last Empress Dowager, Cixi, this was her playground, her Versailles.

They had walked a long way from the restaurant and for a much longer time than Peter had intended. "Do you want to head back and have lunch now?" he asked unenthusiastically.

Anne had forgotten about lunch. "The very thought of a Chinese banquet makes me sick, to tell you the truth."

Peter felt relieved. Better just to scratch this entire Sunday. There was no way he could have eaten lunch here without thinking about that gang—and probably others like them—lounging a few hundred yards away, burning up more rats or whatever the hell other kinds of activities they used to pass an idle, angry hour.

He suddenly remembered Carpenter's message. Just what he didn't need. He'd intended to pass on some mild version of it tactfully in the course of a congenial meal and consider his duty done. Now here he was. There was no way he could put it off much longer. And their afternoon in bed . . . Very strange, it wasn't something one would care to probe too deeply, but his desire for sex had not been obliterated by the threat of violence, the sight of the rat, or even his own barely suppressed anger. Quite the contrary.

As if by unspoken agreement, they both walked toward a carved

149

marble bench on a slight promontory facing the lake, and sat down. Peter took Anne's hand. "I'm sorry today turned out so badly. But you do have a lot of guts. I just want you to know that I respect that." This was the moment. The only possible one. He could feel it. "I know about your Tianbei strike story being killed," he said as gently as he could. "You've really taken it well. I can imagine how upset you must have been."

It seemed like a long time before she responded. "Well, everything is quite predictable, isn't it? I'm the new Paul Engleberg. Washington kills whatever doesn't fit into some strategist's game plan of the moment, and the American embassy in Peking—represented this time by Peter Matthewson—has a polite chat with the offending reporter." Her voice wasn't angry, only extremely flat.

Peter felt his face become flushed, something that never happened to him. What had he expected? Probably that Anne would become hysterically angry and he'd be gracious and soothing.

"Forget it," she said, already starting to stand up. "We all have our roles to play. We do what our script requires. You were obviously asked to have a word with me about the story, and probably caution me about doing others. Okay, you've fulfilled your responsibility and I'd just as soon not discuss the matter any further. You can just tell whoever's interested that you've done your duty. Anne Campbell has been duly reprimanded and warned."

Anne's self-possessed manner masked a strange turmoil of feelings. She was angry, really very angry. Not just at the inevitable polite reprimand, but at the idiocy of the whole situation. How could she have gotten herself involved, more than involved, with the very man who would be the natural choice to carry out a task like this. She was angry that Peter had been put in the position of doing something he certainly hadn't wanted to do, and that he'd done it anyway. She was angry at the stupidity of the games everyone played about the glories of the press and the lofty obligations of geopolitics. And she was infuriated that she still found Peter desirable.

Good God, what did she expect! She had to stop reacting like a romantic adolescent. Everything was proceeding precisely on course. The real problem was her inability to get the relationship in a proper perspective. Peter was a splendid lover—a talent in which he took some pride. He was also an entertaining companion and restaurant guide. Someday he might even turn out to be a valuable

150

source of information for the *Inquirer.* Period. He was not a potential husband or even a long-term lover. This Peking romance was in the nature of all vacation romances. It was not *Tristan und Isolde.* It would end when one of them left. But there was really no need for it to end sooner than that. She laughed. Peter looked startled.

"Well, here we are," she said. "The California Yankees in the Empress Dowager's Court, all because, in some burst of undergraduate enthusiasm, each of us decided to take a quarter of Chinese."

"And here we are," Peter added, "sitting on a park bench, holding hands like those desperate virginal couples all over China." He laughed too. If she was ready to put the unpleasantness of the morning behind her, then most emphatically so was he. "How about my original suggestion of the day? Let's replay the afternoon scenario."

Anne looked at him very levelly, very steadily, and smiled. Apparently they understood each other perfectly. "Why not? It would seem a shame not to have a proper good-bye before I go off on my archeological excursion."

The afternoon scenario had been Peter's idea. When Anne had told him about Tan Yulan's little slap on the wrist, he had been more angry than amused. But then he'd figured out how to exploit the ingenuousness of it all. One Saturday, as they'd been finishing lunch, he'd murmured, "That's it. The afternoon."

"That's what?"

"Love in the afternoon, that's what."

"People don't make love in the afternoon in China. They take naps, and a Chinese nap—a *xiuxi*—isn't a siesta."

"Exactly my point, dear lady. And what the Chinese don't do doesn't exist. What you do is inform the desk that Mr. Peter Matthewson of the American embassy will be working with you in your room all afternoon and instruct them that we are not to be disturbed under any circumstances. Our activities will thus be legitimated and all will be well."

And he had been right. The room clerk had paid careful, serious attention, taken down Anne's instructions, and had Peter print and then write his name on a lined registration log in which she'd also written Anne's name, the date, time, and her room number. There was to be no hot water or teacups—and there wasn't. So began the afternoon scenario.

Technically, one might say, this particular afternoon was as successful as all the rest—perfect bodies, perfect timing, and all the cultivated embellishments. However, something was wrong—not with Peter's performance, but afterwards. There was an uncharacteristically hostile tilt to his naked shoulders as he sat on the edge of the bed, his back to Anne. She ran her fingers lightly from his neck to the base of his spine. Startlingly, he pulled away and began to put on his shorts.

"What's the matter, the aftereffects of this morning?"

"Maybe." He jerked his T-shirt over his head and sat down in the chair facing her. There seemed to be some sort of symbolism in the fact that he was chaste in white underwear, while Anne was still lying naked on the bed.

"Why are we doing this?" he burst out harshly.

"Why are we doing this!" Anne was wounded, outraged. That he should attack her only minutes after leaving the warmth of her body was unimaginable, indecent.

"Why are we doing this!" She sat up. She was shouting. "You are absolutely unbelievable. That you should suggest it and then say such a thing . . ." She was breathless with anger.

"I know you're furious about my delivering Carpenter's message. So why are you covering it up? Why don't you say what you really think? You're the one who makes a big thing out of saying what you think." Peter's voice rose as hers had. "You're totally cynical about this relationship. For you, it's a good lay, nothing more."

Anne gasped. She could hardly speak. "*I'm* being cynical! What are you, some kind of exploited sexual object?" But even as she spoke, she realized she had hit the mark too precisely. His words confirmed her shocked comprehension.

His voice was very hard, distant. "I'm flattered that I meet your high standards as a lover, but if that's all it is, we should forget it."

Anne groaned as she fell back on the pillows. "Peter, my God, you know . . ." But obviously he didn't know, and she realized she had no idea what she wanted to tell him. Just when she'd made a sensible separation between her murky snarl of emotions and the simpler, more straightforward pleasures of the flesh, here he was, hurt, filled with the rage of an injured lover, an old-fashioned,

152

romantic, injured lover. And along with her own anger and pain there was something else, too. But whatever it was, it was much too complicated to work out now. Still, she couldn't leave him this way. It was just too brutal. Neither of them was that cynical. Why not say what she really thought? She'd have to make the overture, if one was to be made, for she knew he'd made it impossible for himself.

She went over to him and sat on his lap. His strongly muscled legs were hard and unyielding against her body. She put her arms lightly around his neck, and bringing her face close to his said quietly, "Peter, I'm not sure what this is all about either. But it's not what you just said. Today was terrible. It was just too heavy for either of us to handle. We've got to wait until I get back from Henan to get all this straightened out, but I think we both meant what we were saying to each other half an hour ago." As she said it, she half felt she meant it.

Peter put his hand on her smooth thigh. It was a slight gesture of conciliation, nothing more. However, it was clear that he had no wish to storm out the door, saying good-bye forever. He put his arms around her silky body, drew her close, and kissed her.

It was, Anne thought, a very ambivalent kiss. She was reminded of the first time he'd touched her, putting on her coat that morning they'd met at the Embassy. Or perhaps she was only projecting from her own ambivalent response.

CHAPTER

12

The Peking Railway Station was a far cry from the world of the Summer Palace Lake, the Peking Hotel, and Charlie Rudd's exquisite island of civilized antiquity. The dark-blue crowd in the station was overwhelming, crushing. There was none of the atmosphere of deference to which foreigners were accustomed. This seemed to be an arena where the survival of the fittest would prevail. The faces were frowning, intent, concentrating on the difficult and tenuous goal of getting a ticket, getting to the right track on time, and most difficult of all for the unprivileged masses, getting one of the hard seats in the ordinary-class carriages.

Foreigners were so totally separated from the hard, day-to-day struggle of the Chinese people, as separated by money and entitlement as they'd ever been in the old colonial days, that one seldom thought about it.

But here in this crowd, as Anne got pushed and jostled by hurrying bodies, the reality of China was inexorably manifest. It was the reality of a billion people, now fed, to be sure, with clothes on their backs and roofs over their heads, but with a frighteningly narrow margin of safety between their very modest existence and none at all. Would the draconian measures designed to lower the birthrate really work in a country still four-fifths rural? Would the gods of the weather show just a little mercy in China's eternal cycle of drought and flood? Would the United States go on growing enough grain to sell some to China, or would the winds of politics shift and once again waft America's largesse elsewhere?

The swarming race in the Peking Railway Station had something in common with the scene in a gigantic train station or airport anywhere in the world—including the fact that such crowds were, in the last analysis, a conglomeration of vulnerable individuals, and the Chinese, for all their dignity and resilience, did look vulnerable here. Perhaps it was the meagerness of their possessions, their string bags holding a few precious articles—an enamel cup, a sweater, an extra pair of socks, a steamed bun to eat on the train. Perhaps it was the lack of a technology that now moved passengers in the Western world so smoothly along on their journeys—the computers that stored in their fabulous memories millions of reservations, timetables, pieces of luggage, charge-card numbers, dinner menus. Like death, the arduousness of travel had been forced below the Western surface, almost forgotten except in the rarefied moments of hijackings, or plane crashes. Here, traveling still required courage and tenacity.

Charlie Rudd gripped Anne's arm firmly as he steered her through the press of padded bodies. She found herself staring into the startled eyes of children peering over protective shoulders as men and women milled about her. She was enveloped in the close smell of musty winter clothes, worn for many months; of the garlic adored in Peking and eaten by the clove. She was carrying nothing but her leather shoulder bag, clutched tightly. Her luggage and Charlie's had vanished mysteriously and conveniently, as the encumbrances of foreigners always did here.

However, when they arrived at their first-class carriage, they were immediately returned to their comfortable cocoon. Two attendants, a man and a woman, ushered them through the car obviously reserved for special passengers. Most of them, Anne noticed, looking as discreetly as she could into the compartments they passed, were PLA officers, their rank clearly identifiable by their age and corpulence. Military men of high rank were really a class unto themselves. It was startling how much they looked alike no matter what their nationality.

The woman attendant ushered the two of them into their own curtained cubicle. With relief, Anne and Charlie sank down on the facing, stiff-backed velour seats. For several minutes they were silent

155

as they caught their breath, then Anne said, "I know what you think about ingenuous Americans who want everybody in the world to put on a show of democracy, but there are times here . . . What do you really think those harried people out there feel about the fact that we and these fat officers take up all this space when they're so crowded?"

Rudd frowned slightly. "You know what I think, as your preamble indicates. However, your concern isn't misplaced. It's easy to become calloused, to take all this preposterous privilege for granted. Most Americans who come here react the way you do at first. I know I did, but there's really no way out of it. I've sometimes thought there's a kind of diabolic intent to the whole thing, a self-fulfilling logic. By forcing foreigners into a privileged position, 'they,' whoever 'they' may be, know that resentment and even xenophobia will be created, which then justifies separating the foreigners from the dangerous masses."

He was staring out the window. "If you dwell on it too long, though, it becomes impossible to live with. When I came to terms with the idea of spending my life in China, I just decided to take the system as it came."

He grimaced, his thin mouth crooked in his angular face. "You rationalize it, as you do the negative aspects of any culture in which you want to survive psychologically. But it's good you brought it up. It doesn't hurt to have your conscience pricked every now and then. There's nothing you can say to justify it, except to marshal all the old arguments about the intractability of cultures. You're familiar with those, I'm sure so I won't bore you with them."

Anne was moved. What a strange man, such a peculiar combination of honor and opportunism. She was glad now she'd said what was on her mind. The atmosphere between them was serene. It was certainly going to be possible to be frank with him on this trip—up to a point.

The morning passed quickly as they rolled, hour after hour, through the landscape of the North China Plain. It was a harsh, inhospitable scene. Scattered about the barren fields or huddled together in tiny communities were stamped-earth cottages, products of the unyielding gray-brown earth. How unlike the lushly romantic landscapes of South China, where the squares of the rice fields formed a patchwork quilt of varying succulent shades of green,

156

while muted violet mountains rose dramatically in the background, a landscape-painting version of Chinese reality. This was a starkly different world, a remarkably neat countryside, every inch of the precious soil carefully tended, but a world in which nature had not been generous. One long look at this Chinese earth was worth more than the mountains of statistics that Tan Yulan had been gathering.

They rode for many miles in silence. Charlie read a monograph on bronze alloys in ancient China and left Anne to her thoughts. How nice to be at peace with yourself and your place in the world, she thought as she looked at him. No doubt, though, that was an attribute of being in your sixties rather than your thirties. Charlie Rudd at thirty-two had probably lived in a stormier emotional world than she did. Still, her life was in a ridiculous mess. Her attempt to calm things down with Peter hadn't resolved anything. Maybe it had even made matters worse, papering over all the stormy, conflicting feelings. Once again she was going to have to go through all that soul-searching to sort out her relationship with him. That in itself was irritating. He was doing what men always did, forcing her to make a yes or no decision. That's what it always came down to. It was some vestigial imperative of the double standard that defied all attempts at sexual freedom. He would never put up with having the same demand imposed on him.

Now she would be gone for who knew how long before they could even talk about it. It would be festering in the back of her mind, and certainly his too. God only knew how they'd feel and what they'd say and how they'd ever get through their first meeting after she got back.

And now that the rush of preparation for the trip was over and she was actually on her way, she was acutely aware that she had never received an answer to the note she'd given to the room attendant. She hadn't even seen him, and she'd practically begged for a response.

Was it possible she might be on her way to Henan only to write about an archeological site? Interesting, to be sure, but not something that she would have taken this trip for. Not now. Particularly now. Admittedly, the strike in Tienbei had been put down, the leaders arrested, but it was hard to imagine that that was the end of the matter. It was more than likely that there would be some sort of repercussions, and the place where one would hear about that

157

would be Peking, not Kaifeng. Anne slumped down gloomily in her seat. Was she going to be done in by a self-inflicted injury, the result of her own headstrong will?

The train attendant had stopped by several times and exchanged a few words with Charlie, but Anne paid no attention. Finally, she realized she was very hungry, a rare occurrence in this country, where the feeding of foreigners was a matter of national pride.

"What do we do about lunch?"

Charlie put down his journal. "There's a delay in the dining car. Apparently they added on a few extra cars and there's an exceptionally large crowd to feed today. The attendant has been apologizing for the wait." He took out his cigarettes and offered her one. "The usual dining arrangement on Chinese trains is related to what we were talking about a while ago. The crowds of ordinary passengers are herded in first. They always seem to be having a wonderful time —sometimes I've managed to maneuver myself in then and I've invariably enjoyed it greatly. But generally, foreigners are held until last, and then the tablecloths are spread and the special treatment turned on."

Anne looked at her watch. It was 1:30. The officers had been leaving and returning for some time. "I've really gotten spoiled. At home, I often didn't get around to lunch until 2:30, if at all."

"Well, I'll give you a little lecture on the Shang calendar. Maybe it'll take your mind off your hunger pangs."

It was all very interesting, the kind of Charlie Rudd lecture Anne usually loved, but it did seem like a long time until lunch was finally announced.

The attendant led them briskly through a chain of cars, looking neither left nor right, behaving as if everything was quite normal. Charlie, with his years of training, did the same. But Anne was astonished. Theirs was not the only car full of army men. She hadn't thought to count, but they must have gone through at least eight— all literally packed with soldiers, overflowing the hard wooden seats, standing shoulder to shoulder in the aisles, and in the cramped passageways between cars. They were young, rosy-cheeked, round-eyed at the sight of the foreigners. They gawked with unaffected fascination. The Chinese peasant army. Of course, Anne had seen the soldiers of the PLA everywhere—soldiers just like these did guard duty in front of the Peking Hotel—but she'd never seen the Chinese army massed in the hundreds and armed. Their guns were

158

stacked on the overhead racks, next to the windows, and the passageways bristled with a profusion of weapons and ammunition.

The dining car itself was a distinct shock. Several attendants were still clearing up the chaos from hundreds of lunches—the bowls and chopsticks and also the bones and eggshells that the Chinese left on the table. In the midst of it all, there was one table, covered with a white tablecloth, newly set with both chopsticks and forks, plates and bowls, as well as glasses for their beer. Not even the generals and colonels were present to share their splendid isolation.

Anne ignored the menu in front of her. "What are we doing on a troop train?" she asked.

Charlie was considering the menu thoughtfully. "I'm sure I don't know any more about it than you do." He looked at her rather sternly from across the table. "I also don't intend to ask. I'd recommend the same strategy to you if you really want to get to Kaifeng more than you want to satisfy your consuming curiosity."

Anne was annoyed. It wasn't necessary for him to take such a patriarchal tone.

"You must admit this seems a bit unusual."

"Not necessarily. Foreigners don't understand the role of the PLA. They're not just a military force. They're involved in all kinds of civilian projects—big construction jobs, that kind of thing. I don't know why these men are on this particular train, but I'd suggest that you not jump to conclusions based only on your very American assumptions about the military." He continued to study the menu.

"Quite a few guns for a construction job."

He pointedly ignored her. "Food on trains in China is usually excellent, as it is in most countries. Let's concentrate on ordering. It's almost three o'clock. No doubt a good lunch will help everyone's temper."

Temper! If that's the way he wanted to interpret a perfectly reasonable observation . . .

The lunch was wonderful, especially the smoked tea duck. They talked about the scenery and the food. Neither mentioned the soldiers again. However, they had to get back to their car by the same route. There was less staring this time. Perhaps the young soldiers had been given a little briefing. That's how things were done, Anne knew. But now that she wasn't so paralyzed by the embarrassment of having hundreds of eyes focusing on her, she was more sensitive to the mood around her. There was an air of intensity, of controlled

159

excitement, but no laughter and few smiles. These men were not on their way to an event they looked forward to, of that she was certain. Like all soldiers, they were going where they were ordered. But there was an undeniable uneasiness in the crowded cars. She walked as slowly as she could and strained to catch bits of their talk, but the attendant in front of her and Charlie in back determined the rapid pace. And as if by signal, as soon as they drew near, the soldiers' voices fell.

By the time they were in their seats, Anne felt thoroughly frustrated. She took out one of the books she had borrowed from Charlie and turned to the chapter on Shang war chariots. Appropriate. But it was impossible to concentrate. There must be a way to hear what the soldiers were saying. Finally, Anne laid the book facedown on the seat.

"Are we going to stop anywhere between here and Zhengzhou? I'm going stir-crazy. Can't we get out in the air and walk around for a few minutes?"

Charlie just looked at his watch. "It seems to me there's just one last stop before Zhengzhou. It's been several years since I've made this trip, but I think it should be coming up in about fifteen minutes."

It had started to rain. The dreary gray-brown landscape was dissolving into a depressing monochrome highlighted only by the blurred spots that were houses and people. There was something hypnotic about it, Anne thought, as she stared out the window. But Charlie seemed not to find it so. He'd gone back to his book, as tranquil as if he were sitting in his own beautiful living room.

The shrill female voice that was standard on loudspeakers and radios announced the name of the next town, and the length of time for the stop—twenty minutes—plenty of time to walk around. The train slowed down. They were approaching Xinxiang.

Charlie watched Anne as she reached overhead for her puffy American down jacket. "For a reporter who's interested in prowling around discreetly, you don't give much thought to being inconspicuous," he observed drily. He reached up to the overhead rack and took down his own coat—an ordinary Chinese overcoat, blue cotton, hooded, lined with synthetic brown pile. It was the commonplace Peking coat. Everyone had one. Charlie stood up and without a word helped her put it on.

Anne suddenly felt very foolish. "You're a dear," she murmured

160

self-consciously. "It's a platitude, but I couldn't get along here without you. You know that." Impulsively, she kissed him on the cheek, slightly surprised at herself.

He looked directly into her eyes. "And you've really transformed my monotonous life. I'm going to find it very difficult to get along without you when you finally leave this place."

There was a great rumbling vibration beneath them as the huge wheels of the train jolted to a stop. Anne was thrown back into her seat, momentarily stunned. Her face must have revealed her dismay, or perhaps it was just that Charlie Rudd was a very civilized man. He simply proceeded with the matter of the camouflage.

"If you reach in the pocket, you'll find a couple of those face masks the Chinese wear. They're new, clean ones. I don't put much stock in the idea myself, keeping the dust out and your own cold germs in, but Lao Li is an old Peking man and swears by them. He won't let me out of the house from November through April without one." He smiled in his deprecating way. "It's like when your mother made you wear rubbers to school. I just ditch them when I'm out of sight of the house, but it might be useful for you to wear one today."

When Anne stepped onto the station platform, her own charcoal-gray, straight-cut pants and her American boots were quite inconspicuous topped by Charlie's Chinese coat. The hood, well up and forward, covered her blond hair almost completely. The lower half of her face was covered by the gauze mask. Only her height revealed her foreignness, but the late afternoon was dark and wet, and she took care to walk with her head down. What a fine disguise! She remembered Mao had used the same one (or so one Cultural Revolution story had it, anyway): Feeling isolated, as indeed he was, and with the difficulty that all leaders have in learning what people think, he'd gone among the crowds to read the wall posters, his familiar moon face hidden behind just such a face mask.

The station seemed to be situated in the middle of nowhere. The only building in sight was the stucco station building itself. But Anne had no intention of straying beyond the platform. She was in the middle of a packed crowd of soldiers—precisely where she wanted to be. Vendors of steamed buns, tea, beer, and the flat orange soda that was China's ubiquitous soft drink hawked their wares, shouting the names of their refreshments above the roaring hum of the crowd. A haze of cigarette smoke floated overhead. Padded

161

khaki backs, shoulders, arms pressed against her. Canvas-shod feet stepped on her leather boots.

Anne headed toward a pillar. She'd have to stay in one place if she wanted to hear anything, for in the press of bodies moving forward, backward, she could pick up only words and phrases. Some were predictable—"Zhengzhou," "another hour," "eat something now," but others made her catch her breath—"railroad workers," "big strike," "weapons."

She leaned against the pillar. It was an excellent spot, shadowy, but near an open area where clusters of soldiers were gathering to eat and drink. She resisted the temptation to light up a cigarette. She was standing close enough to a tight little group to touch the shoulder of the nearest soldier.

"Of course, I'm proud to be in the PLA," he was saying heatedly. "I never said I wasn't." There were some low mutterings. "That's not what I said." Someone laughed. Anne leaned forward in tense concentration.

"The leaders know. A soldier does what the motherland needs us to do." It was a different voice. There was a clamor of interruptions. Anne picked out only a few bits—"fire on our own people," "counterrevolutionaries," and again "strike." The voices were rising, becoming angry, the tone accusatory.

"Do our duty . . ."

"Serve the people . . ." There was scattered laughter.

"The people . . ."

"Soviet agents . . . hurting production . . ." and again "counterrevolutionaries." The thrust of the crowd pushed the group forward, and though Anne strained to hear, their voices were swallowed up in the din.

Her attention was now drawn to two platoons of soldiers lining up at the end of the station platform. Their two separate formations consisted of double rows of six soldiers standing stiffly at attention with bayoneted rifles held in a ready position. Two officers stood in front of each platoon. In response to rapidly barked orders, each group swung around in a smoothly choreographed exercise which transformed the two lines into a spiral-shaped formation with bayonets thrust out. It was like the sudden opening of a Chinese fan. She suddenly realized that the whole exercise was a crowd control device—hypnotic, beautiful, menacing, and very Chinese.

162

Then, a man next to her, leaning, as she was, against the pillar, began speaking in the clear Peking dialect that, unlike the regional dialects bombarding her ears, was easy for her to understand.

"I know that's what the leaders talk about, but that's not what's happened. We've ended up with neither. You know we're not a people's army anymore. And we're certainly not a modern army." The voice on his other side apparently assented. It was hard to tell, but there was no tone of argument.

"You talk to your family; I talk to mine. They tell us what people think. Wait until we put down a few more strikes. My own brother's a railroad worker. Not in Zhengzhou, in Shanghai."

The other voice responded. She couldn't catch it.

"No more guerrilla wars, of course, that's true. But a modern army, it's all just talk. China can't afford those weapons. Where are these wonderful new weapons? It's the same old army, but with no respect now."

The sharp sound of whistles pierced the air. The khaki-colored crowd pushed its way slowly, steadily back to the train. The station platform was covered, but the rain, now pouring down, was visible on the open sides. It pounded heavily on the roof, adding a yet louder dimension to the rumble of hundreds of voices. Anne saw Charlie peering anxiously out the window. She ran up the steps.

"I don't know why I worried about you," he said, as she took off his coat. "Probably the safest place a foreign woman could be in this country is in a crowd of PLA men. But that looked like a terrible crush and—am I right?—not a very cheerful crowd."

Anne sat down. Though she had spent most of the twenty minutes standing in one spot, she felt breathless.

"I'm not sure I have it completely straight. It was impossible to hear a coherent conversation, but I think there must be a railroad strike in Zhengzhou." She leaned against the stiff back of her seat, bracing herself unconsciously as the train started up. "These soldiers are being sent in to put it down. At least I think that's what's happening."

Charlie nodded, his deeply lined face grave. "It fits. While you were gone, the attendant came in to tell me that instead of changing trains at Zhengzhou, which is what you normally do to get to Kaifeng, we'd be picked up by car and driven there.

"She was very upset to discover you'd gotten out at the last

163

station, though that's also perfectly normal procedure, and said to remain in our compartment at the Zhengzhou stop until she notified us that it was okay to leave."

The train was speeding smoothly now, and the world outside, almost lost in darkness and rain, unrolled like a strip of film negative. Charlie had turned on the lights some hours ago. Anne pulled down the shade. It was pleasanter with the gloom blotted out.

"You know I like to be where the news is breaking. Did you have all this planned?"

"I doubt very much that anyone had it planned, or I don't think we'd be on this train. We seem to be the only foreigners. You're probably benefiting from bureaucratic status. Somehow the organization that was responsible for putting us on this train and the one responsible for these soldiers didn't coordinate their signals."

"Do you think they'll send us back?"

"I don't know. Maybe. It all depends on what the situation is. At this point, it might be harder to get us back to Peking than to get us to Kaifeng. And of course, there are other considerations."

"Such as? . . ."

"Well, if I were in charge of this little operation, I might think it was smarter to cool off an American reporter among the Shang bronzes for a while, rather than letting her go dashing right back to Peking with a red-hot story." There was an unmistakable smile in Rudd's brown eyes.

Anne laughed. There really was very little that Charlie Rudd didn't understand. "That's your Chinese bureaucratic view. What's your personal view?"

"My personal view is that fate has thrown us into an event. It may be a large one or a small one. When you've spent as many years in Asia as I have, you won't think that every strike or troop movement indicates the apocalypse or the beginning of a new revolution. Bits of history are occurring all the time, but there's no question that some very large pieces of history are being brought out of the ground near Kaifeng. That's the reason we're on this train. I'd like very much to carry out our plan. We may have no free will in the matter, but generally, the Chinese make some allowance for what they call 'the right attitude.' I think the choice is up to you. I can always get there later on."

"You know I want to go to Kaifeng!" she said emphatically. "Do you think I should close my eyes when we get to Zhengzhou?"

164

"It's best to keep your eyes open as long as you can stand it in this world. No, the problem is only what you do with what you see."

The conversation was ended by the arrival of two attendants carrying trays. It was their supper—sandwiches and fruit.

"Did you order this?" Anne asked.

"No. They must've decided it would be a mistake to send us back to the dining car again." As they ate, Anne noticed that the officers were coming and going.

It wasn't far to Zhengzhou, but to Anne it seemed to take forever. She found herself looking at her watch every few minutes. Charlie read steadily, ignoring her restlessness. Everyone else seemed occupied—the attendants now hurrying up and down the aisle; the PLA officers no longer relaxing over their card games and gossip, but in twos and threes, talking intently together, studying papers. Never before had she felt so acutely the irrelevance of the foreign position here. She pulled up the shade and pressed her face against the dark window, straining to see.

When the train pulled into the station, there wasn't even the routine announcement of the name of the city. What had happened to the shrill-voiced woman? In the distance Anne could hear powerful male voices barking out orders. After the foreboding darkness of the passing landscape, the Zhengzhou station seemed to blaze with light. Overhead spots illuminated a solid mass of people, mostly men, on the platform. Unlike the other crowds of today, however, these people were not moving. They made up a gigantic, powerful, stationary bloc, firmly in place, holding their ground, waiting for this train to arrive. They greeted it with a massive, angry roar, a thousand fists raised in the air in a storm of thundering voices. Anne stared out the window, hypnotized, only the glass between her and this aggregation of strength and anger.

Charlie's hard hands on her shoulders pulled her roughly away from the window.

"Use your head. Don't you realize the effect that the face of a foreign woman looking out the window might have in a situation as explosive as this one?"

He was right, of course, but he was watching the turbulent scene as closely as she was. He was sitting back in his seat at a prudent distance, where he could see but only his shadowy outline could be seen. Anne did the same.

165

There was a great rush of khaki-colored bodies, as wave after wave of soldiers poured off the train. The tightly massed workers, packed shoulder to shoulder, swayed forward to meet them, the bellow of their voices shaking the wooden structure of the station. The soldiers formed a compact line of steel along the length of the train, their bayonets a deadly barricade. They awaited with set faces the thundering legions of men in work clothes moving slowly but unhesitatingly forward. Massive force surged toward massive force. Suddenly, there was the boom of an explosion, then another and another. A cloud of yellow smoke enveloped the crowd, and the great moving body dissolved into individual bodies, moving backward and forward, stumbling, twisting in all directions.

"Tear gas," Charlie muttered.

The two attendants rushed into their compartment. The woman snapped the window shade down fiercely. She grabbed Anne by the arm, the man grabbed Charlie, and they hustled them unceremoniously down the aisle to a windowless linen storeroom. Their bags were lined up neatly on the floor waiting for them. The woman gestured to two wooden stools.

"Wait here. You'll be escorted to your car as soon as everything is ready."

The attendants disappeared. Anne and Charlie stared at each other in silence. The noise, now muffled, was still tremendous. The sounds of shouting, roaring, the booming of—what? Explosives, guns?

"This is what it must be like to be in jail when there's a war going on outside," Anne said grimly. "It's awful, isn't it?"

Charlie reached over and patted her hand. "You're the one who likes excitement."

"I didn't mean that. I meant being locked up like a child in a closet so you can't see what's happening. I feel totally helpless."

"No doubt that's the idea."

But they weren't locked in their closet for long. It was only a matter of minutes before the attendants were back, this time with a small squad of soldiers—eight, Anne counted quickly. The attendants picked up their bags, and the soldiers locked themselves into an unassailable wall around Anne and Charlie.

"We will escort you to your car, which is waiting just outside the end of the train. We'll have to go through one empty carriage and then out. Please be absolutely silent and walk at the pace we set.

166

We'll move fast as soon as we get off the train." The soldier who spoke was very young. He didn't look more than twenty, Anne thought, but his aura of authority was almost frightening. He had been given the responsibility for escorting these two strange-looking foreigners safely off this embattled train, and he would fulfill his responsibility. His face was emotionless.

They moved quickly and silently out of their first-class carriage, through the swaying passage between the cars, doors opening, shutting, invisibly, quietly. Anne was surrounded by four soldiers, one on either side, one directly in front of her, one behind. Charlie's gray head was visible above his own khaki-capped escort. When they reached the end of the last car, the leader turned around and looked at them, his severe expression communicating everything they needed to know.

At the top of the train steps, Anne was suddenly gripped under the arms, from both sides as if by signal, and lifted off her feet. Within seconds, her feet touched the concrete station floor, and she was propelled forward by the force of her tight, powerful convoy. She was conscious only of the crush of bodies, those next to hers holding off as if by their own strength the thousands beyond them. The sound was deafening—concatenation of wood, metal, concrete, flesh, and voices. She was conscious of a car door opening and of being pushed inside. The motor was running. Charlie was there too, the car already moving slowly but steadily through the human mass. Their driver, from the back a broad figure with a thick, powerful neck, also wore the uniform of the PLA.

Now Anne heard a new sound above the confusing crash of noise. The car windows were tightly closed, and she had to concentrate to separate it from the rest of the din, but she was sure she wasn't mistaken. The volume of a powerful loudspeaker dominated the air. The word that had caught her attention was "Tianbei." Would they repeat it? She strained to hear.

"The Tianbei workers . . . solidarity . . . the Anshan miners . . . our brothers the Hankou railway workers . . . Down with the red bourgeoisie. . . ."

"Did you hear that?" Anne whispered to Charlie. He only nodded.

The sound diminished in the distance. The mass of blue and khaki had disappeared outside the windows. They were no longer in the station, but on a narrow two-lane road. It was very dark and they were going very fast. The road was poorly lit, the night was moonless, but the rain had stopped. After the station, the stillness of the countryside was stunning.

When a decent interval had passed, Charlie spoke to the driver. His tone was pleasant, conversational, nothing out of the ordinary.

"Looks as if the rain has stopped."

"Yes, it's been raining all day. The farmers will be glad. It's been very bad here, drought conditions. Maybe things will start to get better." The driver didn't change his position. His deep, pleasing voice simply emerged from the space in the front of the car. The weather: the subject of conversation between drivers and passengers everywhere in the world, Anne thought. The weather and the crops, our universal biological fate, the common core of human life, the energy of the sun transformed into the food of our survival. Anne closed her eyes, and the two men's voices faded into a soothing rhythm: the price of rice . . . the rainfall . . . the acidity of the soil . . . maize . . . nothing but cabbage . . . one pig and a few chickens. She was half dozing, close to sleep, when a shift in the conversation jarred her into consciousness.

"Yours was the last train to come into Zhengzhou," the driver was saying. "One of the major railway junctions in Central China and it's completely shut down. All of a sudden, these strikes are all over. It's very serious, bad for production schedules. China has its responsibility to the foreign investors. The Four Modernizations have to come before anything else." Anne forced herself to concentrate.

"Are you from around here?" Charlie asked.

"No, from Shanxi. I've been stationed here for a year, though. The people in this area are having a hard time—the drought—and the land's always been poor. There's a lot of problems in the provincial government, big economic problems."

"That must have something to do with the railway workers' strike," Charlie said in his casual, unexcited tone.

"Yes. But it doesn't do any good to strike, especially the railway workers. Production is hurt everywhere then. We all suffer. Everybody has to sacrifice for China's modernization."

Charlie, master of proprieties, didn't push the matter. The conversation went back to the statistics of the area, the size of the towns and the communes, the crops, the weather . . . Anne dozed off.

She awoke to a pat on her knee and Charlie's voice in her ear.

168

"We've arrived. Can you wake up?"

The car door was opened and a sudden draft of chill air swept in. A strong hand reached in to help her out, and when she emerged into the cold dark night Anne found herself facing their soldier-driver. They were parked in a circular driveway directly before a large building, ghostly white in the surrounding blackness.

"Our Kaifeng hotel," Charlie said. He and the soldier were carrying their bags. A white-jacketed figure was holding open the large front door.

They were expected. They were escorted down a wide, dim hallway. Anne, half asleep, was aware of nothing except the geometric path of the flowers on the carpet under her feet. The key in the lock of her door made a loud click as the white figure opened it, followed by another click as the overhead light was turned on.

"Good night," Charlie said. "I'm next door. Knock if you need anything. Otherwise I'll knock at seven to wake you up."

The door closed. Anne sat down on the bed, still bundled up in her puffy jacket. A spare white room like her room in the Peking Hotel—another isolated, protected island. But the roar of the Zhengzhou station still resounded in her head: shouts, explosions, the ear-splitting volume of the loudspeaker, the thud of bodies falling. The last train into Zhengzhou.

CHAPTER

13

"It's in an area similar to the one where the '69 border incident broke out. Here, do you see this little spot on the Amur River?" Stefan Zolti pressed his finger down on it as if he were squashing a bug. "The closest Chinese town on the map is this one, Aihui; the nearest Russian one, over here, Poyarkovo."

Zolti's finger traced the line of Heilongjiang Province, descending from its northernmost point along the curve of its hump to the place where Russian territory bit into China. He tilted the standing globe so Haggard could look directly at the area without moving from the striped damask wing chair. Tastefully antique in style, the mocha brown globe was absolutely up-to-date in content, but the space that Zolti pointed to was quite blank except for the wandering line of the river.

"This time, though, the Russians haven't wasted a second. Our reconnaissance reports fighting on a company level already, and the Soviets are mobilizing three divisions in the vicinity. They're moving quite decisively."

A small, glowing fire burned in the grate of the eighteenth-century marble fireplace. Lowell Haggard leaned back and surveyed Zolti's study approvingly. The rich masculinity of the Chippendale chests and desk mingled in gracious affinity with the cabriole-legged Queen Anne chairs. When Zolti sat—which was seldom—he perched on a long, tufted English leather sofa. Imari bowls were filled with red tulips from the formal garden just visible beyond the French windows.

It was only a matter of hours since Haggard had left the Chinese capital. He'd received Zolti's coded "read and destroy" dispatch in the late afternoon and had prepared to depart for Washington immediately, as instructed. Tang had come through. At last, the border incident was under way. The fighting, picked up by satellite, was still top secret. Zolti had summoned him so they could work out the details of the U.S. response before the Russians and the Chinese started releasing their own communiqués.

Zolti's Secret Service man, familiar to Haggard from past missions, stepped forward from the crowd as he emerged from the first-class cabin of the plane. The adviser's chauffeured Mercedes awaited them. He was to go directly to Zolti's home in Virginia and stay there for the period of his visit. As far as official Washington, or the U.S. embassy in Peking was concerned, Lowell Haggard was simply off on undisclosed business for which he had top clearance and which no one else had sufficient authority to question.

The car purred smoothly over the freeway, sweeping past the silhouette of the city as if it were no more than a stage set, the great dome of the Capitol as irrelevant as cardboard scenery. There was no conversation. There need be no pretense as to the function of this particular chauffeur, this Secret Service man, and Haggard had important matters on his mind. Despite the closeness of their working relationship, Haggard had never been to Stefan Zolti's home. As the gray 280S left the freeway for the cross-fenced roads of Virginia's estate country and then slipped through the iron gates onto the Zoltis' private road, Lowell Haggard understood that he had at last been chosen for service in the privy chamber. He knew Zolti must be truly pleased with the way he was carrying out the China assignment.

The idea of the border incident had been his. Of course he had understood, in an oblique sort of way, that Zolti would approve of a military incident in order to speed up the implementation of the China card strategy. However, the approach, the game plan, the utilization of his old relationship with Tang Chen—these were his own contributions. Haggard felt sure now that Zolti would approve of his little coup.

The house, when it came into sight, was equally comforting. A Georgian brick mansion, it wasn't quite Mississippi, but it was the South. A soft-spoken black butler carried his bag to a spacious white room dominated by a rare and beautiful Philadelphia highboy and an enormous four-poster bed. From his window, he could survey acres of grassy meadows where Arabian horses grazed. A Hungarian émigré, a Yale political science professor—Haggard wondered briefly where all the money had come from. Then he recalled hearing that Zolti's wife was a very wealthy woman. Was it uranium? It didn't matter. The house was no doubt hers, but it did say something about Stefan Zolti as well.

From the moment Lowell Haggard seated himself in the wing chair by the fire, Stefan Zolti radiated the energy of a dynamo.

"There's been a lot of analysis, you know, that shows the '69 incident wasn't as serious as it looked. At the time, everybody was running scared, saying that it could be the beginning of World War III, but there seemed to be an understanding on both sides about how far they wanted to push it. We'll probably never know who really started it, but the evidence indicates it was the Chinese. They got the most out of it, both domestically and in terms of their top-level policy struggles."

"Yes, it definitely looks that way to me, too," Haggard said emphatically. He was a calm, even phlegmatic man, but the impatient energy emanating from his small host was quite contagious. He found himself being drawn into Zolti's magnetic orbit. He'd wait a little longer, just to be sure, but it appeared that he'd be able to explain his own role quite fully.

"Now, the problem is that the Russians are crazy," Zolti continued. "They've had this experience with the Chinese before. They should know better than to take it seriously, but you never know with them. They seem to be getting their backs up about the whole Chinese business all over again. We've just had news from Geneva. In fact, it's probably in the papers already."

"Did they break off the arms-control talks?" Haggard asked.

"Yes. Of course they're an absolute waste of time, but the impor-

172

tant thing is the reason the Soviets gave—that the U.S. is playing the China card. There was no way to keep our upgrading of the Chinese military a secret, but I expected we'd have a little more time before they started to get excited about it." Zolti went to his desk to pick up a few papers.

"Nevertheless, I think this is a crisis that offers great possibilities. Most crises do if they're handled intelligently. Now let's forget about Geneva for the moment and concentrate on the China situation. I've followed all your reports on the military upgrading program and you're basically doing a first-rate job. It should be moving faster, but I assume you're doing the best you can."

His tone was unmistakably patronizing. Lowell Haggard had never, in his entire military career, been spoken to in such a way. For one thing, it hadn't been necessary. His assignments had not only always been completed on time, but often well ahead of schedule. If it were entirely in his hands! . . . He had a flash of hatred for China and the Chinese.

Zolti wasn't troubled by Haggard's discomfort, if he even noticed it. Reprimanding powerful people was one of the singular pleasures of his position. "Naturally, this is top secret, but the President has already been on the hot line to the Russians. He assured them that although it's no secret we're helping the Chinese upgrade their defensive capabilities, we're not giving them any operational stuff —nuclear, in particular."

Haggard was impressed. So this was the function of the hot line —merely a glorified version of the telephone, an instrument so useful in delicate situations, as yet happily untelevised: the man calling his wife from another woman's bed to reassure her that the business conference was lasting longer than expected, and all of the other variations of deception right up to the communications of the two superpowers.

"What was the response?"

"You know the Russians. You never know what the response is until they act. But they listened."

"Was anything said about the border fighting?"

"No. We gave no indication that we knew about it, and obviously they're not ready to go public yet."

Zolti turned back to his globe. He pointed to the spot where the border fighting was taking place. "Here is our opportunity. We must see to it—*you* must see to it—that the Chinese withdraw when

173

the proper time comes. But that time musn't come too soon. This little war is going to be our means for squeezing the appropriations we need out of the House."

"Yes, yes, I see," Haggard murmured. And he did see. Stefan Zolti was indeed the genius he was credited with being. The President and the new administration had taken office with a promise of increased military spending and had rushed ahead with their mandate. As expected, they had cut every social program that wasn't protected by legislative fiat. Once the door was open, however, the rush was overwhelming. Every sector of the gigantic military bureaucracy demanded its share: more ships for the Navy, more planes for the Air Force, more high technology all around, lots of fuel at escalating prices for testing the new toys, and, indubitably, more money across the board for everyone from retired rear admirals to the dependents of corporals. Even the Senate was beginning to realize that they were really running out of money.

The problem with the China card from the beginning had been that playing it required a degree of subtlety. Even to comprehend it seemed to require a rather recondite cast of mind apparently lacking in most legislators. The same politicians seemed perfectly capable of understanding other secret operations: the CIA's covert intelligence operations, for example. All these secret programs were expensive—enormously so. Anyone should be able to understand that, but not everyone did. It turned out you couldn't just say, "We're playing the China card against the Russians. It's a very expensive gamble, because although the Chinese can contribute soldiers, they can't contribute much in the way of cash. And it's going to take a great deal of cash."

Up until this moment, most of the appropriations for the China option had been concealed in other military expenditure packages. That had worked out fairly well. Those budgets were always so bloated anyway that millions of dollars worth of hardware could easily be slipped through. But there was a limit, and it had been reached. The intensification of the program would require billions, not millions.

However, the one thing legislators and their constituents seemed capable of understanding was the demands of a real shooting war. The Soviet invasion of Afghanistan had been a godsend. Appropriations unimagined even weeks earlier had been rushed through. Overnight it was acceptable, even mandatory, to up the defense

174

budget. The border war would have the same effect. At last it would be possible to get the money that this expensive card game required.

"We *must* wait for the Russians or the Chinese to break the news." Zolti gesticulated excitedly as he spoke. "It's important to see what kind of line they're going to adopt. We musn't appear to be preempting the information for our needs. Let matters develop of their own accord. But I have no doubt we're talking about hours, not days. I've already arranged for the President to hold a special press conference, and I'm going on *Face the Nation* next Sunday."

His restive eyes suddenly focused sharply on Haggard's face.

"You're in close touch with key military people in China," he said curtly. "Are we going to be in a position to get the Chinese to pull back when the right time comes?"

"Yes, sir. I anticipate no problems," Lowell Haggard replied confidently. The whole matter had come out even better than he'd hoped. His motive for suggesting the border incident to Tang Chen had been mainly to tip the Chinese domestic political balance. What had happened in that regard he still didn't know, but surely Tang wouldn't have gone through with the idea if he hadn't been certain of its success. Haggard had also been aware of the appropriations problems, but the fact that Zolti had zeroed in on the whole matter so rapidly, that he was so pleased with the opportunities it presented . . . There was no reason not to tell him the whole story.

"We have a good ally in the Chinese power structure," he began. "I originally met him when I went to China with Nixon in '72 . . ."

For the first time, Stefan Zolti leaned back against the firm, smooth leather surface of the sofa. He smiled expectantly and folded his hands. The fire burned gently, and sunshine poured in through the brilliantly shined windowpanes. He hadn't really noticed until now that the fruit trees were in blossom.

The power struggle in China was intensifying. As always, the press was one of the primary arenas in which the battles were fought out. Keeping up with the allusive editorials had turned into a full-time job for Peter. Once you were familiar with the historical framework and had a line on which contemporary political figure was represented by which historical one, the interpretation appeared to be a fairly straightforward procedure. But it was easy to be seduced by that apparent simplicity. There were strange inconsistencies, which Peter thought could be explained only by switches in or struggles for editorial control.

After those brief few days in which Peking's *People's Daily* had bestowed its blessings on the accommodating minister who had made peace with an old enemy, it had returned to the standard praise of powerful alliances to offset the predatory tendencies of northern neighbors. But the Tang minister had his defenders. Once again, as in the past, Shanghai had taken up the cudgels. Day by day, the newspapers of the two great Chinese cities exchanged blows of innuendo, insinuation, and implication. On the streets, every edition of either paper sold out within minutes. In his office, Peter spent his time buried in a growing pile of translations, notes, dictionaries, and historical texts.

Then suddenly it was all over. Black characters four inches high formed a headline visible a block away—"Soviets Attack China's Territory"—and the crowds that had been discussing and arguing over the controversy seemed instantaneously united, unanimously angry, a people ready to do battle against the enemy rather than one another.

The spell of nationalism, the alchemy of war, Peter thought, depressed. The clash had occurred on the Amur River, the thin line that separated the vast lands of the north—China's Heilongjiang Province, once Manchuria—from Soviet Siberia. Like the Zhenpao Island affair of '69, it had something to do with an obscure altercation between fishermen. But this affair had either moved far more rapidly into large-scale fighting or the Chinese were choosing to report that fact earlier than they had done previously.

In the lower corner of page 8 was the inevitable diplomatic obituary—just a few lines, all that was necessary. The border talks had been suspended indefinitely. So much for the meteoric rise of the mysterious Zhang Zhaolin, at least for the moment. Just as Peter was about to make an appointment with Tom Carpenter, the phone rang. It was the ambassador's secretary relaying a request for an immediate conference.

Seated behind his polished desk, Tom Carpenter appeared very much the general at his command post. No matter how many dispatches and memos appeared on his desk, it was always impeccably neat, everything organized in relevant piles. But the last few days

176

had brought a veritable avalanche of memos. There were strikes breaking out all over the country. As they'd feared, Tianbei had been the trigger. It was shut down tight, while the men of the multinationals could only watch and wait. At least there, though, Carpenter had a certain jurisdiction. He was in a position to do some negotiating with the Chinese authorities. The other strikes—coal miners, railway workers—were out of his hands, but they affected every foreign firm doing business in China. And now, a military clash on the Sino-Soviet border!

"Are you keeping up with the military situation?" he asked Peter without preliminaries.

Peter frowned. "I know what I read in the *People's Daily*, if that's what you mean. At this point, I can't tell you much more than the man in the street who's reading the same things."

"At least you can stop worrying about the historical analogies for a while. Once the fighting begins, it's all irrelevant. I take it the border talks are suspended, if not killed."

"Yes—page eight."

Carpenter nodded. "Has it occurred to you that this border clash seems to come at a remarkably convenient moment, or am I becoming excessively Chinese in my suspicions?"

"I must admit I was struck by the utility of the instant patriotism just now."

"We'll have to look into it, though I'm sure it'll be hard to untangle. That's always the problem with replaying a scenario that was successful the first time around. Looks suspicious even if it isn't," the ambassador mused. "Can you be ready to go to Washington with me this evening?" he asked abruptly.

Peter was taken totally by surprise. He knew Tom Carpenter placed great importance in the concept of active management, of being in actual, not merely symbolic control of his position. However, he hadn't been to Washington since he'd taken the Peking post.

"Sure, of course. Of course I can," Peter responded hurriedly.

"Sorry to spring this on you. I'm not happy with the responses I'm getting back from State. They seem to assume I've lost my critical faculties. Not surprisingly, it appears to be getting worse since Haggard got here. I've been trying to arrange a meeting with the Vice-President. We've known each other for years. He also knows China and understands what I'm trying to do here. This

177

border incident has given my request top priority, and an emergency meeting has been arranged for tomorrow. I'd like to take you with me, so let me give you an idea of my thinking on the matter."

Carpenter was now standing behind his desk chair, his large hands resting on its back.

"Let's summarize the situation. First, would you agree that there's a struggle for power going on among the Chinese leadership and all this business in the press indicates it's intensifying?"

"No doubt about it."

"All right. Now this is merely speculative, though it would be very important if it turned out to be true—that this military clash could be related to the power struggle as it was in '69." Carpenter looked at Peter sharply. "I don't expect you to confirm or refute that speculation. I'm just giving you my thoughts."

Peter nodded.

"At the same time, there are clear indications of domestic instability. All of these strikes. We don't know how far they're going to go or how widespread they'll be, but we'd be very foolish not to take them seriously."

Although the *People's Daily* said nothing about the strikes, the embassy dispatches that piled up on Peter's desk seemed to report a new one every day. However, he was so involved in the demands of his arcane research that he didn't know much more about them than that they were occurring—with one exception. He'd used all the diplomatic facilities at his command to penetrate the frustratingly scant information on the Zhengzhou railway strike. Despite that, he still knew no more than the exact time Anne's train had left the Peking station last Monday morning. The train and Anne both seemed to have been swallowed up in the provincial hinterlands. Her secretary, Tan Yulan, whom he had finally reached at the Foreign Ministry, was maddeningly vague. Yes, Miss Campbell was in Kaifeng, where she'd gone to write a story on a new archeological site. No, there were no problems. No, she could not give him a telephone number. The railway strike in Zhengzhou? There was silence. "I don't know anything about that, Mr. Matthewson." Then she'd hung up.

Carpenter went on speaking. "It looks to me as if, once again, we've put all our eggs into one basket. This has happened so many times in U.S. foreign-policy formulation that you'd think we'd finally have a handle on the problem. It's not that there aren't

178

people, particularly in State, who have a pretty good idea how to deal with these sorts of events. It's the constant internecine struggles in Washington that undermine things again and again. You're familiar, I'm sure, with Walter Sullivan's position when he was ambassador to Iran."

"Yes, he makes a very convincing case that if he'd had his way there never would have been a hostage problem, and maybe the whole Iran situation would have come out quite differently."

It had seemed to Peter such an eminently sensible strategy. Once it was understood that the fall of the Shah and the triumph of Khomeini were inevitable, to make connections with Khomeini through a sensitive, knowledgeable envoy; to expedite the removal, along with the Shah, of those military officers most closely associated with him, but to leave behind those who could be incorporated into the new military establishment. Above all, to see to it that the military remained intact so that the new government would, in fact, be able to govern. All rather obvious, really, and all sabotaged by powerful advisers to the President.

"It looks as if we may be in a similar kind of situation," Carpenter said seriously. "Not nearly so far advanced as the one in Iran was, that's the hopeful factor. But I think we should consider the possibility of beginning to talk to some people in the Chinese opposition. At this point, we don't even know who they are. The other thing we don't know enough about is the military. Here we are, dumping tons of military hardware into this country, upgrading their military services and God knows what else, a new military expert arriving from the States every day, and we have no real sense of the balance of power in the Chinese military. We don't even know which people are gaining access to all this new stuff or what they might decide to do with it if some kind of struggle broke out."

"What our reports have shown," Peter interjected, "is that there's been lots of dissatisfaction in the military. It can't be pigeonholed under a single label, either. There are angry old generals, some still loyal to the Mao they knew; ordinary soldiers unhappy with the new agricultural policies that make things harder for their families in the countryside; and officers unhappy with their cut of the military budget or even in disagreement over what the role of the military is now. One of the bits of conventional wisdom we hold to is that the military is basically very conservative. The soldiers, and a lot of the officers, too, come from the peasantry. They haven't been

179

particularly enthusiastic about the wholesale introduction of decadent Western ways of doing things."

Carpenter nodded. "Makes sense. At any rate, these are the kinds of questions I want to take up in Washington. We can't afford to sit back and wait to see what's going to come of this unraveling. Nor can we afford, as we did with the Shah, to tie ourselves to one leader or group of leaders. We have to be prepared to go with what happens. There's a basic rule of business that's always seemed to me equally applicable to diplomacy: Never bet the whole company. My own feeling is that if we handle the situation intelligently, there's no reason for a change in the leadership to hurt the relationship with America. The Chinese, objectively, need us for their modernization, and I think all factions recognize that."

The ambassador seated himself at his desk once again. "We're going to work out an agenda. I'll need you to put together some background briefing materials for us to take along." He smiled. A bit ironically, it seemed to Peter. "And in addition to your material, I want you along on this mission to reinforce my hunches with the proper scholarly authority. I have the impression from Washington that I'm suspected of going native or something of the sort. They hear what they want to hear—Zolti particularly—but we have to try to make someone listen before it's too late."

They worked hard on the agenda. The ambassador knew precisely what he wanted and zeroed in on the points one by one. Time pressure was no excuse for not doing things well. This was the way Thomas Carpenter always worked, but for Peter, the intensity of the work was a welcome escape. He really wanted to get Anne out of his mind. The whole thing was such a mess, and whose fault had it been anyway? He'd had to intervene with her for the ambassador. She certainly understood that, but what did she really think? That he was a tractable little bureaucrat, nothing more than a good man to go to bed with? That was exactly what he'd yelled at her in that stupid argument. But if she really thought that, why did she make those overtures afterwards? Maybe she was worried about the same sort of thing, that he regarded her as a batty reporter but a good woman to go to bed with. Anything was possible.

It wasn't right to have left things so unsettled and unpleasant. God knows what must be running through her head at this moment. And where was she anyway? She'd probably laugh at his worries, but he *was* worried. The Chinese usually just barricaded foreigners in a safe hotel when anything out of the ordinary was going on, but how could you be sure? No word of her or Charlie Rudd at all. It was very unnerving.

The work. Concentrate on the work. The prospect of the trip to Washington should be very gratifying. After all, that's why he'd gone into this career in the first place. He just had to stop thinking about Anne.

But then, when they were practically done and Peter was preparing to leave, Carpenter suddenly asked, "How's your friend from the *Washington Inquirer?* I appreciate your talking with her. I assume you managed it well, because that's one of the few problems I haven't heard about from Washington in the last week."

Managed it well. What a joke! Yes, he'd managed it well, but only because she'd decided to take it the way she had. And damn it, he'd hoped Tom Carpenter would never bring the matter up again. Undoubtedly it had already compromised his position, serving as the ambassador's emissary in a "personal" capacity, and he didn't want to continue in that role. Obviously though, Carpenter wasn't going to let him slide away so easily.

Peter was brusque. "She was on one of the last trains into Zhengzhou, and then she disappeared."

Even Tom Carpenter, habitually imperturbable in the face of shocks of all kinds, didn't hide his astonishment. "Amazing! That railway strike in Zhengzhou is probably the most serious one in the country, and the most violent, from everything we can learn. That whole province has been closed to foreigners! How in hell did she manage that?"

"With the blessing of the Chinese Minister of Culture, no less. She was on her way to do a story on Shang archeological sites near Kaifeng."

"Alone?"

"No, with an old American China hand, Charlie Rudd, who's lived here for years."

Carpenter was interested, that was clear. "Oh, yes, I know who he is. I met him at our Thanksgiving reception. He's completely in the Chinese pocket—even a Chinese citizen, if I recall. Well, I have to hand it to your young lady. She's a real pro."

"I'm sure the business of the archaeology story was completely on the up-and-up. She couldn't have had any way of knowing she was going to run right into the Zhengzhou strike," Peter said defensively.

Carpetner laughed. "You don't think so? This is the same reporter who made connections with the Tianbei strike leaders. I imagine she had an idea of what she'd find in Henan."

Peter was silent with embarrassment. It had never occurred to him that Anne's disappearance in the Zhengzhou strike area was anything but coincidental. Was it possible that, in addition to playing games with him, she'd been lying to him as well? The Anne Campbell who made such a big thing of honesty? He caught himself before he could go on. What nonsense! She had no commitment to him, no more obligation than he did to explain everything she was doing. That had been implicitly understood from the beginning. My God, he was reacting like a Victorian husband! But not even to have suspected anything. That was just stupid. Carpenter must think him a complete fool.

However, the ambassador had no interest in humiliating his aide. "You did everything you could, obviously. If the Minister of Culture gives an American reporter permission to do an exclusive story, we're not going to prevent her from going after it." Carpenter was thoughtful for a moment. "As a matter of fact, your friend—what's her name?"

"Anne Campbell."

"Anne Campbell may turn out to be a blessing in disguise. She apparently has contacts with the Chinese opposition that no one else does. She may be the very person we need as this situation continues to develop."

Peter had never told Carpenter where his information finally resolving the mystery of Zhang Zhaolin had come from. There'd been no need to. Carpenter gave him research assignments. It was Peter's job to figure out how to do them. Whether the information came from one of the China research centers around the world, from Peter's own analysis, or from informants was normally of no concern to the ambassador. Now, whatever the ego loss in admitting Anne's role, there was no doubt that he should tell Carpenter the whole story.

It was exactly what he'd wanted not to do, to have his relationship with Anne intrude even more on his professional relationship with the ambassador. He also felt an uneasy sense of disloyalty to Anne in what he was doing. Was he falling into some sort of dubious gray area, exploiting his relationship with Anne for his own benefit? Of course, she'd known, when she told him about Zhang Zhaolin, that the information was going directly into the official hopper. She hadn't asked to remain anonymous.

However, there was something else. As Peter recounted the story, he realized that Carpenter was not only interested but apparently even approving. Anne was smart and spunky, no doubt about it. It was nice to have someone else recognize that. Of course, the best thing that could happen would be for Tom Carpenter to maneuver Anne onto their team, but that was crazy. That just wasn't Anne Campbell. She'd say Carpenter wanted to use her, and she'd be right. Goddamn it, how had he ended up in this classic triangle? Love affairs with reporters were murder, everybody knew that. But he couldn't help it. This particular reporter was no ordinary woman.

Well, nothing to do but get on with it. To Washington. That would be interesting, no matter what. Then back to Peking. Surely Anne would have returned by then and they'd give it another try.

He was so absorbed in his own thoughts as he left Carpenter's office that he was completely startled by the ambassador's parting comment. "Interesting time for Lowell Haggard to have disappeared from our midst, isn't it?"

Although Peter had been in the White House on various ceremonial occasions, he'd never been in the East Wing before. The Vice-President's office was properly dignified and rather severe, like the Vice-President himself. As in many of the White House public rooms, late Federal furniture established conservative decorative limits. The Vice-President, Geoffrey Butler, had none of the macho trophies of sport and war that most political men seemed to find essential to their office images. Only a picture of his family ornamented his desk.

He was a somber man, as terse as his reputation had indicated, uninterested in Peter though punctiliously polite. His pleasure at seeing Tom Carpenter, however, was undisguised. Like Carpenter, he was a corporate man, a millionaire. It was well understood that he was Wall Street's man in the White House.

Geoffrey Butler was a good listener. He asked precise, informed questions, but not too many of them. Carpenter was also precise and well prepared, occasionally referring to Peter for specifics. Butler took notes, again not too many, only when major points were covered. His nods of agreement, his assenting "um-hum's," made it clear that he appreciated Carpenter's analysis, but when it was all over, he was not particularly affirmative.

"I'm very glad you came to me, Tom," he said. "This is important, and your recommendations make sense. I'll be seeing the President tomorrow, and I'll go into it all with him immediately." He shook his head. His expression now was very dour indeed. "But you shouldn't underestimate the difficulties. Zolti has the President's ear. You know that. There's also another problem. The President has absolute faith in his old buddies. He doesn't feel intellectually outflanked by them, and he really believes in all that folksy snake-oil wisdom."

"A penny saved is a penny earned," Carpenter remarked.

"Yes, the voodoo economics, but we could live with that. The real problem is their world view. They simply believe that any problem erupting anywhere was instigated by the Russian bogeyman. The subtleties of making connections with a political opposition, particularly one that might look the slightest bit revolutionary, is quite beyond them. And the ideological linchpin of the whole business, of course, is their virulent anticommunism."

"What about China, then?" Peter asked. He hadn't intended to speak, but he couldn't help himself.

"They, of course, are *our* Communists," the Vice-President responded. "And there lies the difficulty of making an argument that we might be able to work with their opposition."

He stood up and shook Carpenter's hand warmly. "I'll do everything I can. We just can't absorb many more economic blows, since we haven't gotten everything we wanted out of the China connection to begin with. But still, I agree with you that it's basically a healthy relationship. Everybody understands what the potential is, and this border fighting looks like a very bad business."

Peter and the ambassador were silent as they walked together down the long hall and then out the portico door to their waiting car. It was already dark. Carpenter didn't speak until they were inside the black limousine. His voice was resigned and matter-of-fact.

184

"Well, we've done our duty. Now, it's all in the hands of the gods. I'm sorry this has to be such a fast trip—back to Peking early tomorrow morning. It's unpleasantly tantalizing to put your feet down on home soil and pick them right up again. I took the liberty of making dinner reservations for us. I thought we deserved a little reward for such a tough trip. How do you feel about trying out La Pyramide des Beaux-Champs? Have you read about it?"

It would have been rather difficult not to read about it, even in China. What had happened was that one of France's master chefs had replicated a classic French restaurant within convenient driving distance of the American capital.

With much publicity, America's most famous food critics had once again gamely eaten their way through a dozen courses. This time, though, there were fewer indignant letters to the *Times* remarking on the immorality of such behavior in the face of world starvation, for the critics' work had been performed in the course of their proper duties, not as the result of a prize fortuitously won. From the *Times* "Living Section" to the Sunday supplements which appeared in small-town papers around the country, La Pyramide des Beaux-Champs was promptly declared the greatest restaurant in America, and thus probably the world. The only holdout was *The New Yorker*, which maintained that *it* had once again discovered the greatest restaurant in the world, this time in Utah.

And there it was—just a very beautiful, very simple early eighteenth-century farmhouse set down in the Maryland country-side; American on the outside to be sure, but on the inside, entirely decorated in the charming, idiosyncratic style of the great French country restaurants: the round tables covered with flower-sprigged cloths and centered with tall silver candelabra and silver baskets of perfect tea roses; surrounded by large chairs with wooden arms and firm upholstery, chairs for serious dining.

They were awaited, expected, served with such quiet tact and excellence that both men were quickly soothed out of their tension and lack of sleep. The first wine was a mellow old madeira with a double consommé, followed by a terrine of squab accompanying a magnificent 1971 Montrachet. Even as they picked up their heavy silver forks, Peter was aware of a quizzical expression on Carpenter's face. It was obvious that he saw someone he recognized coming in. The ambassador stood up.

"Well, well," he said, his voice touched with amusement. "This

185

is what happens when a restaurant gets so well reviewed. People come halfway around the world to try it out."

Peter looked up and then hastily stood. There were Lowell Haggard, Stefan Zolti, and a very blond woman wrapped in a pale chinchilla coat constructed of curiously cut up little pieces of fur—Mrs. Zolti, it turned out, when introductions were made. Everyone understood that it was necessary to exchange a few words, but only the ambassador seemed entirely relaxed. In fact, he even seemed to be enjoying the encounter. Lowell Haggard very clearly did not.

"Quite a few developments have taken place since we last met, Mr. Haggard," Carpenter said cheerfully. "It looks as if the Sino-Soviet War has begun. You all must have had the same idea I did—that you should eat the best meal you can find before the holocaust begins."

Stefan Zolti's absolute lack of humor was well known in Washington. "I hope, Mr. Carpenter," he said sternly, "that this holocaust talk isn't something that's being bandied about outside circles such as ours. Even among ourselves, it isn't constructive. These border clashes are of little significance. Quite manageable, I assure you."

"I'm certainly glad to hear that. I know you have a great deal of influence in Moscow and Peking. I'm delighted to hear that you're in a position to turn off their wars. Well, Mr. Haggard, I assume we'll meet again soon in Peking. With a shooting war in progress, I don't like the idea of running the embassy with the President's direct military representative absent from his post."

Haggard flushed angrily, and Zolti snapped, "General Haggard is at his post."

"We all are at our posts," Carpenter said, making a slight mock blow. "Good evening, Mrs. Zolti. Good evening, gentlemen. I hope you enjoy your dinner. Perhaps we'll meet on the plane, Mr. Haggard."

The Zolti party, heads high, swept off to their table, which was fortunately located in the far corner of the room. Peter and Tom Carpenter resumed their seats.

"So, at the very moment we were briefing Butler, Haggard was briefing Zolti," Carpenter said in his unruffled way. "The two Washington tracks are being simultaneously activated. The only question that remains is, Who briefs the President?"

They picked up their forks. The terrine was superb.

186

CHAPTER

14

"This is what it must be like to be under house arrest," Anne said impatiently. She and Charlie had just completed five rigorous turns around the bare winter garden of the hotel grounds, and were beginning the sixth. It was four o'clock in the afternoon of their third day, and they were still waiting to hear when their archeological tour would begin. As far as Anne was concerned, they were in Never-Never Land, the big old-fashioned building surrounded only by acres of brown fields as far as the eye could see. But Charlie, who had stayed here before, assured her that they were only a few miles outside Kaifeng.

It was extremely eerie. The first morning they had contemplated the possibility that they were the earliest risers among the hotel guests, for the long drafty dining room was empty. By the time they'd finished breakfast and gone to the equally desolate lobby to inquire about the plans for their tour, it was apparent that they were the only guests in a hotel built to accommodate hundreds. Someone appeared sporadically to make their beds. Someone else stood ready to serve them in the echoing dining room. Occasionally, they ran into a woman sweeping the hallways in desultory fashion. It was as if the hotel existed simply for its own sake.

As for the purpose of their trip, it was impossible to tell whether the impersonal figure behind the counter in the lobby was really waiting to hear from the "authorities" about their viewing of the archeological sites or whether she was just putting them off. With

187

the serious news, however, there was no delay. On that third morning, the grim-faced guardian of the hotel desk snapped out her announcement, her face dark with anger.

"China has been attacked. The Soviet army is firing on our soldiers on the northern border." Her hands were knotted into tight fists on the counter before her.

"Oh my God," Charlie murmured under his breath. "That's all this poor country needs right now." He was speaking to himself more than to Anne.

But Anne was concerned with facts, not emotional responses. "Do you have any details? When did it begin? What does the news on the radio say?"

"It began only a few hours ago," the clerk replied severely. "What I told you is what I heard on the radio myself, just that we've been attacked and there's heavy fighting."

"That's terrible, terrible," Charlie said gloomily. "Where on the northern border?"

"Heilongjiang—somewhere on the Amur River. They didn't say the exact place."

Anne interrupted. "I'd better phone Peking and see what I can find out."

The stern woman behind the counter folded her arms across her chest. Her expression was distinctly hostile, as if foreigners who came to places where they weren't wanted—like this empty hotel near Kaifeng—and foreigners who attacked Chinese soldiers on the border were all cut from the same cloth.

"This is a national emergency. There are no telephone connections between here and Peking now."

Anne gasped with indignation. "But that's ridiculous," she said to Charlie in English. "There's no relationship between telephoning from here and the fact that there's fighting on the border."

He merely shrugged. "There are probably other reasons—the strike for one. There's nothing you can do about it. You have to take it as it comes."

Anne was thoroughly annoyed. But she did understand, even without Charlie's counsel, that this was not the morning to inquire about the plans for their expedition. Clearly, as far as the woman behind the counter was concerned, they were entirely responsible for the inconveniences of their own predicament—and for who knows what else.

Breakfast in the ghostly dining room was grim.

"Do you realize what this means?" Charlie said.

"I'm afraid I do. China isn't Afghanistan, or even Poland. If we're lucky, it'll just peter out like the '69 border incident. If we're not so lucky, we may have the good fortune to be on the spot for the beginning of World War III. Good God, what a time for the correspondent from the *Washington Inquirer* to be stuck out here in the middle of nowhere," she groaned. "They'll be furious with me. A Sino-Soviet war begins and one of the world's leading papers can't locate its correspondent in China. It's awful."

"If I remember correctly, you were the one who wanted to take this trip," Charlie responded laconically.

"I know. I know."

But what for, Anne wondered. Almost three full days and not only was there no word from their official hosts, but none from her rebel contacts either. The evidence of their existence was everywhere. The very fact that the Zhengzhou railway workers' strike had sealed Henan off from the rest of the country was proof in itself. But her own links with the rebels—that was another matter. The whole thing was probably a wild goose chase. God knows how long she and Charlie would be stuck here, isolated from the capital at the very moment when it was critical for her to be there. And now there were a million questions she needed to pursue. What did all this have to do with Zhang Zhaolin, the border-talks chairman Xiao Hong had told her about? How much was known in Peking about the Zhengzhou strike? What were the connections, if any, among all these events?

Charlie had brought a small transistor radio with him, and they'd spent the day listening to it. The Voice of America and the BBC reported the same sparse information—Soviet and Chinese troops fighting along the Amur River, in a virtually unpopulated area. Each side accused the other of instigating the conflict. There were reports of heavy troop movements, particularly on the Soviet side of the river. That was all. The same meager facts commented on, analyzed, but still only those few bits. When it was clear that their rapt listening would produce no further news, they clicked the radio off in disgust and went out for their constitutional.

Back at the entrance of the hotel, they looked disconsolately out at the dreary garden landscape.

189

"Don't you think we've had enough exercise?" Anne asked. "I can't face doing that again."

Charlie looked at his watch. "I suppose so. We won't be pushing the cocktail hour by too much if we go in and have a drink now." He had come well supplied with good Scotch.

But their wait was over. When they entered the lobby, the desk clerk, at her post behind the counter, informed them as if in the routine course of business that a comrade from the Bureau of Archaeology was awaiting them in the sitting room. She was here to make arrangements for their tour.

The ride to the site the following morning was much longer than Anne had expected, over an hour from the time they left the hotel. The representative from the Bureau of Archeology, a slender, genteel woman in her fifties, clearly Western-educated from her excellent English, sat with Anne in the back seat and Charlie with the driver in the front. This Chinese lady, with her refined reserve, was the last person on earth to whom one might complain about the unexplained delay or ask about the border fighting, the railway strike, or the problems of Henan Province. She was extremely knowledgeable in her field, however, and gave them a thorough history of the Shang city.

It wasn't certain, she informed them, whether this city was really the legendary one from which the tenth Shang king had moved his capital to Ao. However, it was definitely of an earlier period—Proto and Early Shang as opposed to Ao's Early and Middle Shang. And yes, it was just as significant as Charlie had surmised. It appeared that the missing links in the development of early Chinese bronze technology were coming to light here. This was all quite bizarre, Anne thought, like attending the first art history seminar on the moon while all around, comets, planets, and stars crashed explosively into each other.

They drove much of the time over narrow unpaved roads, coming nowhere near the town of Kaifeng. At last, they stopped before a newly constructed building. As their companion gave the driver his instructions about the length of the visit, Anne whispered to Charlie, "Did we take a very roundabout route to get here?"

He nodded. "It looks that way. I'd expected to go directly

through Kaifeng. I was looking forward to showing you a few interesting historical spots."

The modest, whitewashed building was a makeshift exhibition hall and a workroom for the archeologists excavating the site. The treasures that were coming out of the ground were displayed on wooden tables with breathtaking casualness. The first table was covered with pottery—shards, but also intact pots, jars, and vessels —ceramics combining the characteristics of both the Gray and the Black Pottery culture which marked the beginning of the Shang.

"Look at the number of *li* tripods," Charlie remarked. "It's a pottery shape unique to ancient China. Strange, isn't it? Seems such a logical shape for a cooking vessel, to have three legs." He gently picked up one of the reddish-brown pieces and ran his fingers over it. Anne touched it gingerly.

"Gray pottery?" she inquired dubiously.

"Its immediate predecessor. This was baked in an oxidizing atmosphere, probably an open fire. The color began to look different once they'd produced a better-controlled kiln." Their guide looked at Charlie with surprise and respect.

"You know a great deal about this," she said approvingly, and realizing that it was possible to discuss the fine points of the artifacts with Charlie, she directed to him her comments about the other early Shang shapes—the *ting* tripod, the *yong* jar, the *jia* warming cup, and the earliest and most primitive form of the *que* cup.

And then she led them triumphantly to the table that was the high point of the exhibit. To Anne, it was nothing spectacular—a few crude metal arrowheads and next to them, also of metal, a *li* and a *que* tripod, both rough and undecorated, shaped like the ones made out of clay.

"From the same stratigraphical layer?" Charlie asked.

"Yes, the earliest one. The archeologists don't want to jump to conclusions. Chemical analysis is still going on, but if it means what we think it does . . ." She gestured eloquently with her hands. "These may be the earliest bronze pieces that have ever been found in China, and most important, bronze vessels from a period when we didn't think they existed."

Charlie turned to Anne. "Well, that may turn out to be your scoop of the century."

"But it's not definite yet."

"No," their Chinese companion said. "You may describe what

191

you've seen and write about the speculations of the archaeologists, but it will be a while before there's anything certain. Perhaps it will be years, even decades. You know how difficult these matters are, particularly with something as significant as this. We must be cautious."

Anne sighed and then laughed. "It may be the scoop of the century, but it will probably be my granddaughter who writes the story about it, not me."

Still, big story or not, there was something thrilling about simply being able to touch or even hold the cooking utensils, weapons, implements used in everyday life millenia ago. They spent the rest of the morning touring the digging sites—pits in the ground with improvised canvas roofs to protect the precious artifacts from twentieth-century weather. These early Shang sites displayed graphic evidence of that fierce ritualistic society: skeletons not only of the honorably buried, but of the servants, the prisoners of war, the retainers who had been sent into the tomb—some dead, some alive—to follow their masters into the afterlife. There were huge pits of skulls and others only of headless skeletons, the corpses of the beheaded sacrificial victims neatly separated and then reorganized. There were the remains of chariots, the skeletons of horses and drivers, the dogs that were always found in Shang burial pits, the sheep, the cattle, the oxen.

"Sometimes it's useful to be rather explicitly reminded of the realities of the past," Charlie remarked. "When you look at those wonderful bronzes elegantly displayed in modern museums, you have a tendency to forget about this sort of thing."

The morning was over too soon. There was something uncanny about leaving behind the world of three thousand years ago. Charlie was immersed in conversation with their companion. The two of them stopped just outside the little museum, absorbed in their talk, and Anne wandered slowly ahead toward the car.

The driver was leaning against the hood staring idly into space and smoking a cigarette. The only other person in sight was an old man sweeping the hard earth path that led to the building. He was stooped and very wrinkled. As Anne approached, he smiled through sparse, discolored teeth and greeted her with a pleasant, "*Ni hao.*" She smiled in surprise. Then as she passed him, he pressed a piece of paper into her hand.

She got hastily into the back seat of the car. Charlie and their guide were walking slowly down the path, talking like old friends. Anne opened the note and scanned it rapidly. "Wait at the side entrance of the hotel tomorrow morning at 1:00 A.M. The door will be unlocked." That was all. She crumpled the paper into a ball and stuffed it into her jacket pocket, holding on to it all the way back to the hotel.

At ten minutes to one the desolation of the hotel was complete. Was it possible that no one was on duty through the night? If she'd been conscious of this nocturnal abandonment before, Anne might have been uneasy. Now, though, she was greatly relieved at the silence and the darkness. Not a single light had been left on to waste precious wattage in a hotel empty except for two foreigners presumed to be docilely sleeping.

Their rooms were on the second floor. As Anne felt her way carefully down the back steps that led to the side entrance, she remembered that she had a tiny pocket flashlight on her key ring. It was perfect, all the light she needed to make her way to the ground floor, where the door was unlocked, just as the message had said it would be.

She stood in the shadow of the doorway and shivered. The night was clear and cold. The only light came from a pale sliver of moon and a sky crowded with a multitude of stars. She was wearing Charlie's coat, which she'd managed casually to borrow late that afternoon.

Before Anne was able to see anything, she heard the sound of her escort—the dull thump of a bicycle over the hard ground. As a shadowy moving shape coalesced slowly out of the darkness, she realized that it was a person walking two bicycles. Closer still, the figure was identifiable as a woman from the head scarf that Chinese women always wore. Even when the figure was standing in front of her, Anne couldn't distinguish her features, but the voice was that of a young woman and the accent that of the Henan peasants.

"Can you ride a bike?" the young woman asked without ceremony.

"Yes."

Strangely, Anne hadn't ridden a bike since she'd come to China, where the entire population rode them, but all her life she'd felt as

193

secure on a bike as on her feet. That was fortunate, for this bike was one of the cumbersome ones that provided transportation for most Chinese. No gear shift, none of the refinements that Western bikers took for granted; just two large wheels and a heavy frame connecting them.

"You ride behind me," the peasant woman said. "It will take us about half an hour to get to our destination. I don't think we'll meet anyone on the way, but if we do, be silent. I'll do the talking."

With those instructions, she turned and got on her bike. Anne followed. One behind the other, they wheeled through the front garden on the circular carriage drive and out the open spiked-iron front gate. For a second, Anne glanced back. The hotel building was totally dark. How strange, even frightening, to think of Charlie asleep in his room, perhaps entirely alone in the mausoleum-like structure.

Anne's eyes gradually became accustomed to the moonlight. Her guide kept steadily to the middle of the narrow road, apparently confident that they would meet no oncoming traffic. The flat countryside was a great, dark void through which the two cyclists cut a thin path, the turning of their wheels the only sound in the night. Anne was conscious of nothing but the figure before her. Her own body functioned automatically, legs circling monotonously, gloved hands gripping the handlebar tightly.

Without warning, her guide turned off the two-lane rural road, and they were riding directly over the bumpy fields. Anne caught her breath as her bike jolted up and down on the uneven ground. She concentrated on the figure in front of her, bouncing precipitously but still moving unhesitatingly forward. She was totally intent on the task of taking the jolts, one after the other, without tipping over. Then her guide extended an arm, waving up and down in a gesture which, in any culture, meant "slow down." The peasant woman pulled her bicycle sharply off to the side and jumped off. Anne's momentum kept her coasting a few yards farther before she was able to ease to a stop. When she got off her bike, she saw they were standing a short distance from a small building, probably a peasant house. The woman started to walk toward it, and Anne fell in next to her.

"There's a meeting here of peasant leaders from this county and the five neighboring ones. It's been going on for several hours, but we didn't think it would be safe to bring you here until this late. I think you'll be able to follow what's happening anyway."

Anne hesitated. "May I ask what the meeting is about?"

There was a short laugh in the darkness.

"Since you've been allowed to attend, of course we want you to know what it's about. We have serious problems in this area. The soil has always been poor. Then last year we had a very bad drought. The government's policy now is that if any economic unit doesn't make a profit, it just goes under. The peasants in these counties are in a desperate state. We've done everything we can to be self-reliant, but we can't be held responsible for natural disasters. People are starving here. When there was nothing else left to do, the six counties affected by the drought appealed to the central government for help. We were turned down. Not a penny. We were told it was a matter of priorities. But for us, it's a catastrophe. We must have help or there will be famine here within a month."

Famine. Anne was stunned. However, there was no opportunity for further questions. They were in front of the house. No light shone through the traditional latticed windows. That was strange, Anne knew, for everywhere in the Chinese countryside, what light there was inside the peasants' homes could be seen through uncurtained windows. The house itself was oddly situated. Chinese peasants seldom lived off in the midst of their fields, but rather clustered together in the protective shelter of villages. Here though, there was nothing in view but the vast darkness.

The wooden door opened, and they were whisked inside the crowded, smoky room. Only for seconds had a glimmer of light been permitted to escape the guarded space of the interior. It was a small room, but every inch of it was occupied. For a few moments, Anne felt dizzy, so rapid was the transition from the fast, cold ride to this dark, crowded cave. She was simultaneously led and pushed, the same firm guidance she'd experienced in all the crowded or dangerous spots she'd been in in the last few weeks.

She found herself seated in a space that was quickly cleared for her on the end of the *kang*, squeezed tightly between bodies padded in worn and well-patched clothes. The *kang*, the platform that was traditional in the homes of northern Chinese peasants, took up about a third of the room. At night, it provided a warm bed for the entire family, lined up in a row in their quilts. In the daytime, it was a cooking stove, furnace, heated seating space, and, with the addition of a low table, an eating area. In this meeting, it afforded a seating area for perhaps several dozen people, sitting cross-legged, backs and shoulders supporting one another, the warmth of each body warming its neighbor.

In the rest of the room people sat jammed side by side on the low stools that Chinese peasants carried with them for such occasions. Other people leaned against the walls. The only light in the room came from a kerosene lamp on the wall behind the man who was speaking. Next to the lantern hung a large poster. Anne squinted and strained to see. Could it be possible? The dim light of the lamp flickered across the familiar but now seldom seen features of Mao.

The lighted tips of cigarettes cast a pale glow on shadowy, weathered faces, men and women of all ages. Perhaps fifty people, a quarter of them women, most young, but a few of them sturdy, broad-faced, middle-aged. Most of the men, Anne guessed, were between thirty-five and fifty, but there were a few elders with wispy white beards and one tight group of thin, intense men in their twenties. She could catch only the outlines and occasional glimpses of the features of those around the room, but she observed the shabbiness of the faded clothing, and their hair, that of both men and women, cut strictly for utility. The sparse facial hair of Chinese men sprouted unshaven on chins and cheeks. They were very different-looking from their Peking cousins, who, though simply dressed and coiffed by Western standards, were distinctly urban and well-to-do in comparison with these peasants.

However, to her surprise, there was a face she knew, a young man. As he became aware of her stare, he nodded courteously, the nod of an acquaintance. The image of another dark room flashed into Anne's mind. It was Wang Weilai. Anne felt a tremor of excitement. Let Larry Metcalf try to tell her now about the need for eyewitness accounts! Through an accident of fate—and yes, her own ability to take that accident as far as it would carry her—she knew, knew with sudden and absolute certainty, that she had penetrated close to the core of this new revolution, whatever it might turn out to be.

She focused all her attention on the speaker. He was a short, squat man, probably in his middle thirties. His voice was harsh. He spat out a series of rough, choppy sentences, punctuated by fierce thrusts of his arms, his hands clenched into hard fists. He had the look,

Anne thought, of those muscular, righteous workers, peasants, and soldiers who used to appear on Chinese posters and billboards calling for an end to U.S. imperialism, Soviet revisionism, and all the other evils of the world. Seldom seen in art these days, they still appeared to exist in life.

"We peasants of these six counties are not beggars," he was saying. "We have struggled with poor land and managed to be self-reliant year after year. We've coped with droughts and floods again and again. Now we're being punished for policies that we're not responsible for. The communes that sustained us during hard times have been undermined. Once again, the ruthless few are managing to get richer, while most of us are becoming poorer and poorer with every year that passes." There was an angry growl of assent throughout the room.

"That's right."

"He speaks the truth."

"That's the way it is."

The speaker raised his voice above the muttering. "And we're being punished for something else, too! We're being punished for having the courage to protest. The government in Peking doesn't believe in education for the children of peasants anymore, but we still believe in it, and we told them so."

The growl in the room grew in volume, although when it reached a certain pitch there was a leveling off that indicated a consciousness of the need for caution. They had selected an isolated house for their meeting. They were keeping the room in near darkness. Noise was a danger to them all.

"It used to be possible for a few of our children to go to universities. There weren't many, but we thought it was the beginning. Now it will never be possible, because none of them, no matter how smart they are or how hard they study, will have the possibility of a good middle-school education."

Although she knew nothing about the protest the speaker had referred to, Anne was well aware of the policy behind it. With the immense demands on the limited funds available for China's modernization, hard choices were being made. One of them was in the field of education: Concentrate on the specialized education of the few rather than the broad education of the many. There were a number of obvious arguments in favor of a poor country making that choice, but Anne knew that, in private, some Chinese officials were now stating the problem in the crudest possible terms. In a situation in which there were already too few desirable jobs for the young educated population, it was asking for trouble to educate more. No point in raising the expectations of hundreds of millions of peasants. The danger in such a policy here was that unlike the situation of other developing countries—Brazil, for example—the peasants were not going from nothing to nothing, but from a tantalizing taste of the possibilities of education to nothing. It was quite a different matter.

"We're not asking for anything more than we have a right to. The grain we grow is turned over to the state. They sell it for the price they set and spend the money as they decide. But we have the right to a very small part, enough to get us through this hard period after the drought and enough to maintain decent schooling for our children. If our government can't give us back that much of what we've earned, what good is it?"

The waves of sound which had subsided in the room rose again.

"Yes, what good is it?"

"We'd be better off keeping everything we grow for ourselves."

The speaker's arms were at his sides. His voice was quieter, very steady. "That's why we must do what we've planned for tomorrow. We must go together to the Party headquarters in town. We must make them see that we all agree on this. We must make them see that we're not divided by factionalism, not fighting among ourselves as they want us to do. We've had our disagreements and we always will, but we all agree on this—that we peasants of the six counties have the right to survive, and the government has the duty to help us when we need help. We're not willing to die just because we had the bad luck to be born in a poor region. Chairman Mao used to say that the workers, peasants, and soldiers were the rulers of China. We're going to remind the government of that." He turned away from his audience, faced the picture of Mao, and solemnly bowed his head before it. There was a reverent silence in the room and a bowing of heads. Anne watched, fascinated.

Three speakers followed, symbolic representatives of the young, the old, the women. Each affirmed support for the plan, a demonstration before the provincial Party headquarters in Kaifeng beginning at noon the following day. (Today, Anne realized, looking at her watch.) At the end of their brief presentations, each of the three speakers faced the picture of Mao and with raised fist pledged unity.

198

Each person in the dark, smoky room, fist in the air, silently joined the pledge. There was an aura of shared power, the same mysterious strength of collective faith that even strangers and nonbelievers feel in religious processions, political demonstrations, and revival meetings. Anne, sitting in the midst of these shabby, quietly passionate people, might have been invisible, absorbed into this collectivity, her feelings merged with theirs—the anger, the resolve, the solemnity.

So there was a moment of shock when she was suddenly returned to her proper place as observer, guest, and "foreign friend." Wang Weilai had taken the speaker's place. He looked very tall, much taller than Anne remembered him.

"You comrades have all spoken very well," he said, gesturing to the previous speakers. "And the meeting has ended well—on a note of unity. Nothing is more important than that. We've been divided into warring factions for the benefit of those in power for too many years. It has taken us a long time to learn that lesson, but now that we've learned it, we'll be able to win. I can't add anything to what's been said about the conditions here and the plans for struggle. You live here. You suffer from the problems. You know the local political and economic conditions far better than I do. I just want to say a few words about our national and international situation. Your own struggle here is your primary concern, but it's important for everyone to understand how your struggles fit into the larger picture."

Wang paused. He was a master of his understated style. To the unpracticed observer he was entirely relaxed, but Anne realized that he waited precisely the right number of seconds to gain the maximum drama and attention. Every face in the room was focused on his. He had an air of beneficence combined with an implicit authority. A natural mandarin, born to rule, Anne thought, as she studied his handsome face, his high cheekbones and heavy eyebrows faintly touched by the flickering light behind him.

"First, though, we welcome a foreign friend among us tonight."

All heads turned toward Anne, but here in the dark, Anne no longer felt self-conscious.

"She's an American friend, a newspaper writer, and she's going to send the news of what you're doing here to the United States. We have friends all over the world who support our struggles, and she's going to tell our friends in America about what's happening here." He applauded lightly, making the gesture more than the sound, and the rest of the people followed him, clapping quietly as

199

they murmured approvingly, "American friend. Foreign friend. Good, good."

It was the same thing Xiao Hong had done! It seemed impossible for them to accept the fact that a journalist might be interested in reporting their struggles, even sympathetically, without necessarily being their advocate. Of course, from their point of view, it was all perfectly logical, because for them, journalism *was* a means of advocacy. No doubt that was why Charlie had gone to such lengths to warn her about the dangers of being used. But how could you report what was happening if you didn't get close to the events? It was very irritating.

But the matter that was of such importance to her was of little significance to Wang Weilai and the peasants here. She'd been introduced, identified, and promptly forgotten. Wang had gone on to more serious matters.

"You've all heard about the battles on our border with the Soviet Union," Wang said. The atmosphere was punctuated with angry mutterings, swearing.

"Filthy Soviet turtles."

"Russian bastards."

"Wait, please." Wang raised his hand admonishingly. "This is not a simple matter. Right now, you have your own struggle here, but you're not alone. The railway workers in Zhengzhou are on strike. You support them and they support you, for you're all fighting for the same things. And there are workers and peasants all over China who are also striking and demonstrating for food, education, better working conditions. Do you all agree with me?"

"We agree."

"That's right. We're all struggling together."

"All right," Wang continued. "Now what would happen to your struggles if you should all suddenly unite together with the Party and government to fight the Soviet Union?"

There was a confused silence in the room. No one seemed sure of how to respond. Finally, a young woman with a long braid down her back said uncertainly, "We would all sacrifice together to fight the Soviet Union."

"That's right. The workers and peasants would all stop their strikes and demonstrations, wouldn't they?"

There was a murmur of assent.

"Now let me suggest to you a terrible idea." Wang Weilai paused dramatically. There was a hushed silence in the small room. "Suppose some people in the government wanted to end the strikes and demonstrations? Suppose they knew that the only thing that would end them would be to unite the people against the Soviet Union? Do you think it is possible that such people might be desperate enough to provoke a fight with the Soviet Union to accomplish that?"

The murmur in the room had turned into a low roar.

"That, comrades, is what has happened." Wang Weilai waved his arm with a flourish and waited for the impact of his statement to take hold. The room was in chaos—as much chaos as these disciplined people would permit themselves. Wang motioned for silence, and now his voice became very quiet. Anne, along with everyone else, leaned forward and strained to hear.

"There is no question this is what's happened. We have the information from our people in the army and in the top echelons in Peking. The border conflict was provoked by a faction on the Chinese side, and some people think by their American henchmen." Wang was composed, entirely in command of the situation. There could be no doubt of his influence with these people.

"The negotiations with the Soviet Union over the border question were going well under our friend, the new chairman, Zhang Zhaolin. Those talks have now been discontinued, but a secret message has been sent to the Soviets explaining the situation and telling them there's widespread sentiment in China for settling the border question. We need peace. Do you all agree? The Chinese people need peace or we'll never be able to win our struggles and solve our problems."

The crowd picked up his theme and started to chant it in a low monotone: "Peace, peace. We need peace."

And that was the end. He had convinced them. The last moments of the meeting were devoted to final arrangements for the demonstration. People gathered briefly in twos and threes to have a few last words, but there wasn't much lingering. Rest was precious. There would be only a few hours of sleep before the day was upon them. Some probably wouldn't sleep at all. One after another they slipped silently through the door and vanished into the night.

Anne looked around at the dozen or so people left in the room and realized that her guide had also disappeared. She got up, stretched, and lit a cigarette. From childhood, everyone around her on the *kang* had been accustomed to sitting cross-legged or squatting, but for her, several hours in such a knotted-up position stretched her leg and back muscles in unpleasant ways. She paced back and forth, trying to pull out the kinks.

"I hope you're not too tired. I'm afraid our meeting was very late for you." It was Wang Weilai standing next to her, his words the prescribed formalities accorded to foreigners. They could have been spoken by any Chinese bureaucrat of any political persuasion. However, his aristocratic courtesy, even courtliness, was disarming, and his classical good looks very winning indeed.

"As you know, reporters keep strange hours," Anne responded, smiling. "So I'm not tired at all. The meeting was fascinating. I'm very grateful to you for letting me come to it."

"It's we who are very grateful to you for coming. We understand that this isn't easy for you."

Anne felt a sudden rush of sympathy for this man before her, his tired face now expressing nothing but concern for her welfare. For her, this was only a story, no matter how important. For him, it might quite literally be a matter of life or death. Impulsively, Anne grasped his hand and pressed it warmly. No doubt he was startled. The Chinese weren't given to physical spontaneity, but he gripped her hand firmly, with no indication of his surprise. It was a very different hand from the rough hands that had led Anne through the darkness of the room—the long sensitive fingers of a Chinese scholar.

"It's good you're not tired. You seem to be a strong woman. That's good too, because I'm afraid we have to send you back to your hotel in a rather rough fashion. It will soon be light, and we think it would be too dangerous for you to be on the roads on a bicycle. The area will be so full of soldiers that it's unlikely that you wouldn't be spotted and stopped."

Wang looked at her closely, as if watching her reaction to each word. Anne returned his gaze steadily, smiling as one learns to do in such tense encounters.

"Whatever you think best. Everything you're doing seems to be very well organized. I certainly got here smoothly enough."

"We're going to put you in a large basket on the back of a pedicab flatbed. It won't be comfortable, but it will certainly be safe. There would be no reason for anyone to be suspicious of a peasant peddling such a load along the roads at daybreak. There are dozens of them, and it won't take long, maybe half an hour or so."

Anne was truly amused. She couldn't help thinking of some startled faces in Washington when she was finally able to tell the story of how she got her scoop in Henan Province.

"It sounds delightful, much more interesting than going by car. How far will it take me?"

"Right up to the side door of the hotel. This kind of vehicle delivers food to the hotel. A second basket on the flatbed will be filled with produce for delivery there. Even if the pedicab is seen by the people who work in the hotel, nothing will seem unusual."

Very impressive, Anne thought. If the rebels handled all their affairs with such careful attention to detail, they were really quite a formidable group. She and Wang Weilai walked together to the waiting pedicab. The gnarled man who would pedal it sat on the flatbed puffing nonchalantly on a traditional long-stemmed small-bowled pipe. Graciously, as if assisting a lady with rustling skirts into a high-seated carriage, Wang Weilai handed Anne up onto the platform where the two huge baskets were loaded.

"Do you think you can climb in?"

"No problem, if you'll just hold the basket steady for a minute."

"I'm going to give you a document to read that I think you'll find interesting," Wang said. "Do whatever you think might be useful with it. Perhaps it'll just help you understand more about the general situation or perhaps you can publish it. You decide what's best."

He held an envelope out to her. Anne hesitated. For the briefest moment, she felt a new flash of irritation. Why hadn't he mentioned this sooner? Why didn't he tell her what was in it? But it was too late. There wasn't time to go into all that. The driver of the pedicab was on his seat, ready to go. Wang was holding the basket for her to step into. Besides, what difference did it make? She did want to see what it was, and then she'd decide, just as Wang had said.

She grabbed the envelope and sank into the bottom of the basket. There was plenty of room. A cloth was placed lightly over the top, and as the awkward but sturdy vehicle began to move bumpily over the rough ground, Anne heard Wang Wei-lai's resonant baritone voice in the distance.

"Good-bye, American friend. The Chinese people thank you for your help."

Anne closed her eyes and tried to adjust her tired body to the rhythmic bumping of the cart. It was all dreamlike, hypnotic, impossible to sort out, but somewhere beneath the fatigue and confusion there was a vague feeling of unease she couldn't shake off. She hadn't committed herself to anything in so many words. But somehow, probably just by observing the meeting, even by agreeing to being transported in such a clandestine fashion, she *had* committed herself, fallen into the very role Charlie Rudd had warned her against, that she'd always so carefully avoided.

The pedicab lurched off the rocky ground onto the road, and as Anne felt its pace become a steady, thumping rhythm, she fell into a semiconscious doze. Everything would have to wait until she'd slept. She couldn't work it out now.

CHAPTER

15

The document was horrifying. There was no other way to describe it, but Anne was also aware, as she read it by the weak light of her bedside lamp at five in the morning, that she was in no state of mind to evaluate anything calmly.

It was a xeroxed copy entitled *Consolidated Guidance—China 10* and was stamped *Security Classification Royal—18 copies.* Under the subtitle *Royal Copy No. 12* was the specification *Joint Chiefs—Navy.* Anne sank back on her pillows. Her head was whirling with a thousand disparate impressions, all Chinese, all arising from the extraordinary night and few days since she'd left Peking; but the paper in her hand was from Washington. With a fierce effort she tried to clear her head. "Royal." What was it? Somebody had told her about it somewhere. But where? She couldn't make herself remember. Something about . . . a classification. "Royal." Under the previous administration. That was it. An attempt to stem the leaks endemic since Watergate. Who had told her? She couldn't remember, but it hardly mattered. "Royal," a new category of classified documents, the most restricted of all. She looked again at the copy in her hand. Access limited to fifteen or twenty top people and this one clearly sent to the naval head of the Joint Chiefs—or more exactly, a photocopy of his copy.

Anne couldn't move. She felt paralyzed with exhaustion. Lying on her back, she simply held the document up to the light and turned hastily to the next page. It was titled "Phase III," followed by a note, "Phases I and II already completed (See *Consolidated Guidance 1* through *9*)." The title of Phase III was *Crisis—Contingency Plans—Wartime Aid,* and there were six section headings in a table of contents.

1. Joint Contingency Planning—U.S./P.R.C.
2. Pre-Positioning Munitions and Equipment
3. U.S. Support Base Structures—Mainland China: Xian, Chengdu, Shenyang, Xinjiang
4. Warhead Transfer—South Korea to Haerbin
5. U.S. Ground Forces—China
6. U.S. Naval and Air Stations in the P.R.C.

In a frightened rush, Anne flipped through the remaining pages. They contained the detailed plans for each of the six sections. She'd thought of a beating heart as a literary conceit, but she was actuely aware of her heart pounding in her chest. Was it her horror that such plans, plans that would certainly begin World War III, actually existed, or that she was holding them in her hands? It must be the latter, for she had always known such plans must exist. All one had to do was read the voluminous testimony of scholars and government officials before the congressional committees to know of their existence.

Her head was pounding and she felt sick to her stomach. A stolen military document planted on her. Yes, that's what it was. She hadn't asked for it. She hadn't even known what it was. And she knew how journalists were used in this way. She'd even been thinking about it after Wang Weilai introduced her at the meeting. She hated him. If he'd walked into the room at that moment, she could have strangled him. How dare he put her in such a dangerous and compromising position! All that garbage about "American friend," and this is what such friends were good for—couriers, emissaries, spies who could move easily across national borders, a naive little pawn in the great international chess game.

So this is what it came down to. You went after information and ended up with intelligence. Damn that handsome, slippery man for doing this to her. And so coolly, so courteously. What did she care what his international connections and intrigues might be. In fact, she absolutely did not want to know. Anne was lying flat on her

206

back, still fully dressed, unable to move. Shivering, she pulled a pile of blankets on top of herself and clutched one of them next to her face. She'd known, she'd really known when he slipped the envelope into her hand that she shouldn't have taken it.

And who could help her now? No one. Absolutely no one. Good old Charlie Rudd had warned her, lectured her, then helped her do what she wanted to do, and here she was alone with him, the last man in the world she could tell. And even after she got back to Peking . . . Peter. There was a question. Would she tell him? Imagine having an affair with a man you might not tell about the most terrifying thing that had ever happened to you in your whole life. She really must have lost her mind. What had she done?

And if she did tell Peter, what then? What would he do? Logically, he would say something like, "You'd better turn it over to the CIA," and arrange it all very expeditiously, and then she *would* be acting like a spy. For whom? Who knows, but spies often didn't know whom they were working for. Oh God, where was her old husband when she needed him? The only man around with brains, guts, and integrity, and she'd thrown him away. She wept from exhaustion and fear and self-pity. The coarse cotton sheet that she mopped her eyes with was soaking wet.

Anne dropped the document on the floor. She had to pull herself together. Should she immediately shred it, flush it down the toilet, burn it? She was too tired to think. Tomorrow she'd read the whole thing, and that would be the end of this kind of business. She'd do her story on the peasant protest in Henan Province, see what the *Inquirer* did with it, and then reevaluate her whole role here. No more of this, no more.

When she awoke, the room was filled with midmorning light. She groped for her watch on the bedside table. Ten o'clock. She sat up abruptly with the ugly feeling of lateness and something forgotten. What had happened? Anne lifted her leaden body out of bed. As her feet touched the floor, she stepped on scattered pages of the document. Gathering them together, she stuffed them back in the envelope and shoved it under a small pile of notebooks at the bottom of her suitcase.

As she walked groggily toward the bathroom she picked up a piece of paper slipped under the door. A note in Charlie's handwriting: "Today's expedition canceled. Hope you had a good sleep. See you in the sitting room when you feel like coming down."

207

A shower helped, and the cup of coffee she made from the jar of instant coffee in her suitcase helped even more. Still, it was after eleven by the time she found Charlie by the long windows of the old-fashioned sitting room, absorbed in his book. He looked entirely contented, as if reading by the window were the very way he would have chosen to spend the day.

"So we're back to square one," Anne said crossly, plopping herself down in the armchair opposite his.

"I'm afraid your linear, rationalist world view hasn't been much affected by your stay in China. It's inconceivable to start back where you were before. The dimension of time alone makes it impossible. Haven't you read your Einstein?"

Anne grimaced, but she was amused. Dear Charlie. He somehow managed with the little games they played together to make it all go away. Here with him, everything seemed safe and familiar and she was the Anne Campbell she recognized. The weeping, frightened woman of last night didn't exist. All those dark, confused, awful nightmares—she'd push them away by playing the game with Charlie.

"Correction accepted. Assuming that we can't discuss where we are in a linear time progression, maybe I should just go back to bed, and you can wake me up when something happens."

Charlie smiled as he put his book down.

"Actually, that *is* the way a lot of people respond to this kind of situation. Probably my long naps are part of the same syndrome, but it doesn't seem in character for you. I'm rather inclined to think you'd crack up a bit more dramatically. That happens too."

How much does he know? Anne wondered. Is he warning me? He must know. He must sense something. At five that morning, she *had* felt as if she were cracking up, as if she were beginning to lose control of what she was doing. It must show now. Why had he said that?

"What's happening on the border?"

"No news. Just routine reports that the fighting continues." Rudd leaned forward and patted her affectionately on the knee. "Come, come, don't look so depressed. I'm afraid you've taken my flippant talk too seriously. In fact, I regard you as one of the steadiest people I've known in a long time. I wouldn't have taken this crazy trip with you if I hadn't thought that. We're just victims of circumstance. There are reports on the provincial radio stations, in indirect language naturally, of peasant demonstrations all over this area. They can hardly be conducting archaeological tours for foreign guests in the middle of that sort of thing."

Anne took out a cigarette and turned her face away from Charlie as she bent forward to light it. "Do they say what the demonstrations are about?"

"The usual terminology—reactionary elements, Gang of Four elements stirring up trouble, that sort of thing. But it isn't hard to guess, is it? They had a drought here. That means famine in this part of the country. It always has."

As if by common instinct, they both looked out the window at the dry brown stems and branches of the hotel garden and the gray, earthen brick wall that was meant to protect them from the miles and miles of hard parched earth beyond.

"If I were you," Charlie said, "I'd organize the notes you got at the site yesterday. I don't have anything definite, but my sense is that our first trip there will be our last. From the manner of the woman at the front desk, I have the feeling that our stay here will soon be terminated."

Anne nodded. Charlie's intuition for the Chinese was seldom off. She suddenly felt terribly depressed. Nothing had come out well. They hadn't seen enough in one day for a decent story on the Shang site, not without pictures, anyway. And her visit to the peasants' meeting . . . a repeat of her meeting with the strikers. At least Larry Metcalf would say so. After all that trouble, he'd still say, "But you didn't actually see anything."

And that frightening document! She hadn't wanted it in the first place. If only she could give it back right now. Metcalf would kill her for being here when the real news was taking place on the border and she couldn't even go back to Washington with the satisfaction of a Paul Engleberg. After all, they hadn't put her piece in print. And Peter, he might really turn her into a spy if she gave him half a chance and . . . Stop it! Anne thought and forced herself to look out the window.

Lunch was announced. They ate in silence. As they got up from the table, Charlie said gently, "I'm a little worried about you, dear companion. I know this has been very disappointing, and my nasty sarcasm was not at all what you needed, but don't take it quite so hard. There'll be other opportunities, you know."

Anne reached for his hand, and they walked out of the dining room looking for all the world like an old married couple. She felt all choked up, and realized with embarrassment that if she spoke, she might burst into tears. It was absurd. He had been nothing but kind and sensitive. Now he was even blaming himself for her depression and she couldn't even be honest with him about what was bothering her. It had been a mistake from the beginning, this whole charade, and now matters had gone too far. There was nothing she could say that would clarify it.

They stopped in the hallway outside their rooms.

"You know I always get up early, no matter what's happening. That's just part of the little structure I've built against the irrationality of circumstances. So I really do have to have my nap. I feel terrible leaving you, but can you entertain yourself for just a couple of hours?"

Anne tried to sound cheerful. "I'm the one who feels terrible, to turn into such a neurotic on you. It really isn't like me at all. Don't worry, though, I'm much better now. Have a peaceful nap. I've got plenty of work to do. We'll take a farewell walk around the garden when you wake up."

But Anne couldn't work. In fact, she couldn't concentrate at all. When she took out yesterday's notes, she scanned them absently and put them back on the table. This was the logical time to read the document. She was sure not to be interrupted. There would even be enough time to memorize it and quietly dispose of it. She looked at her suitcase, neatly closed on the straight chair across the room. But something, some unreasonable fear kept her from opening it. Tonight, she told herself. She would certainly read it tonight.

She shut it firmly out of her mind and let the images of last night's meeting flood in. Now, at this very moment, the peasants she had sat squeezed against were undoubtedly in the thick of a demonstration only a few miles away. Anne jumped up and pulled Charlie's coat off the hanger. It was her last chance, her only chance, to get the story she'd come for. To hell with Larry Metcalf. To hell with Peter. To hell with good old Charlie Rudd. She would see something happen today. She would be the eyewitness, the only one for the whole world. She would make her Henan gamble pay off, once and for all. She would see the demonstration and that would be it, the end of her contacts with the rebels, the end of notes mysteriously delivered, clandestine meetings, travel by strange vehicles to unknown rendezvous, the end of dangerous documents. She would do it and then they would all leave her alone. All of them!

She slipped quietly down the back stairs. It seemed weeks ago that she'd crept out by this same route. The hotel was as quiet now as it had been then. Empty or sleeping, it didn't matter. It would just be a matter of luck. Either there'd be an unlocked bike parked near the kitchen or there wouldn't. She and Charlie had discussed this very matter during one of their many walks around the garden. Yes, Charlie had said, there was a lot of petty theft in China, far more than was realized by all the tourists who'd had the symbolic discard, the torn sock or a used-up ball-point pen, returned to them. Most Chinese locked their bikes as a matter of course, but here, well, perhaps not. There were so few people working in the hotel. They all seemed to know each other well. The whole area was securely closed off. And he was right. There were four bikes parked in the covered passageway at the back of the building; two were locked, two not. Anne selected the unlocked one that appeared to be in better condition. She was wearing Charlie's face mask and had the hood of the coat pulled as far forward over her face as it would go. She knew the general direction of Kaifeng. If stopped, she'd simply say that she was out for a ride and let them deal with that as best they could.

The two-lane country road was almost deserted. Anne passed a few carts, pulled by donkeys or people, several pedicab flatbeds like the one she'd ridden on last night, and half a dozen cyclists. That was all. She pedaled steadily, looking neither left nor right, and no one paid the slightest attention to her. Her old optimism began to return. The sun was shining brightly, and she reached the outskirts of the town in something approaching high spirits. Yes, this time she was going to get the story.

The buildings were closer together now. Walls of crumbling brick provided humble screens from the traffic, but ducks, pigs, and dusty toddlers were not confined by them. The smell of food cooking came from the outdoor stoves in the courtyards. Larger buildings began to appear, workshops or small factories, Anne imagined. She was in a town bustling with the activities of everyday life, yet both buildings and people had an air of grimness, of sparseness and deprivation that was unlike anything she had encountered in Peking. Even with their padded clothes, everyone looked thin, and the

211

children, always the rosiest and best-dressed of the population, appeared wan and serious.

The number of bikes increased. The incessant jingle of their bells filled the air. It was necessary to cycle carefully now. Anne tried to keep her head down, but the demands of maneuvering through the crowds made that difficult. Every now and then she encountered startled eyes, but no one stopped her. She had no idea where she was, except in Kaifeng. However, she wasn't worried. She'd entered the town by a major thoroughfare. Logically, it should lead to the center of town.

Suddenly, she was aware that something odd had happened. A minute before, she'd been tightly packed in a crowd of cyclists. Now, she was biking down a virtually deserted street. She jumped off her bike and walked it down the sidewalk, moving close to the protective walls and overhanging roofs.

It was the sounds, not anything she could see, that told her she'd arrived. All around her there was an eerie silence, totally foreign to a Chinese town, but somewhere very near, perhaps only a few blocks away, was the noise of a battle.

Anne pulled her bike through an arched entry, and then, stepping back into the narrow passageway, she stood listening. It was the sound of the Zhengzhou Railway Station, this time not muffled by the closed windows of a car—a roar of voices, like distant thunder, and above that, a fearsome rumbling and the piercing sound of screams. There were explosions and a thousand unidentifiable crashing, splintering, falling sounds. Anne hesitated only a moment. Finding the most inconspicuous spot at the end of the dim passageway, she leaned the bike against the wall. It seemed like a good hiding place. If it was stolen, she'd just have to deal with that later.

She stretched her mask to cover as much of her face as possible, and moved cautiously back to the deserted street. There was no one in sight. She started toward the exploding mass of sound, feeling frighteningly exposed, staying as close as possible to the gray camouflage of the roofs and walls.

At the corner, she looked across the narrow street and saw that she was in luck. Running parallel to the next block, behind a row of old buildings pushed one against the other, was a *hutong*. She'd be able to get off the main street. She walked quickly.

The *hutong* narrowed into another passageway that ran thinly between two rows of buildings back to back, becoming rougher and

212

more treacherous as she went. She had to concentrate her attention on the ground to keep from stumbling. The fearful sounds were very close now.

Sudden light signaled an opening at the end of the tunnel-like path. She moved the last few yards flattened against the wall of one of the gray buildings to a point where she could see but, she hoped, not be seen. She was on one side of what must be the town square, and it was quite simply a battlefield. Several thousand peasants were packed into the square, their faces dark and weathered, their faded clothes ragged and patched, a swarm of bodies, people of all ages—defiant-looking teenagers, hundreds of young and middle-aged men and women, and even a few gray heads and beards—running, chased by soldiers with bayonets, hit with rifle butts when they fell. And many did, in the pushing, screaming, panicky crowd. With horror Anne saw an old woman knocked off her feet, disappear into the swirl of the tightly packed crowd. Didn't anyone see it? Couldn't anyone help her up? But the thickly entwined crowd pushed, twisted, writhed relentlessly, and the old woman did not reappear.

Screams filled the air: of fear and pain, of people trapped and terrified, fallen or afraid of falling. A thin man ran doubled over, shielding the body of a child carried in his arms. Wide-eyed with shock and fear, two young girls swept by, arms around each other. Gun butts could be heard striking with sickening thuds against skulls, backs, shoulders. Faces, blood pouring down them, appeared over the shoulders of friends struggling to carry them.

It was not, however, a crowd that was submitting easily. As soldiers rushed forward, a solid wall of bodies turned to resist them. Unarmed men and women were using their fists, arms, legs, feet. They pummeled, pounded, threw themselves on top of individual soldiers, and like all unarmed crowds under attack, they were beginning to find weapons. Knives appeared from pockets, bricks from walls, boards from a construction site, stones from the street. Soon soldiers too began to fall into the depths of the crowd, blood streaming down their faces, howls of pain issuing from their mouths. A churning, inexorable sea swallowed up the victims and sometimes threw them above the waves again, to be rescued and carried off wounded by their comrades.

Anne was hypnotized with horror. She'd lost all sense of herself, of where she was standing, of who she was or what she was doing

213

there. Opposite her, half a dozen trucks had been overturned, some of them burning. Several of them looked like army trucks; the others heavy, dusty farm trucks of the kind that had passed her on the road. People crouched on the ground behind them, their backs to her. Others rushed back and forth, bent low. A torso would straighten, hurl a brick toward a group of soldiers concentrated on the broad steps of the building across the square, then disappear. There was a volley of bricks. Then another. Another. Suddenly, a squad of the soldiers rushed down the stairs toward the barricade, their bayonets pointed menacingly. From somewhere there was the popping of tear gas being shot. Cannister after cannister spiraled into the crowd, skittered along the ground, and then were thrown back. In the smoke-filled space, khaki blurred into the black and blue of peasant clothing. It was impossible to see, but above the roar of the crowd she heard a voice, amplified, shout powerfully, "Fire!"

There was the crack of gunfire, not so much a volley as a few isolated shots. From the hazy, tear-gas-choked area of the barricade, Anne heard a terrible scream pierce the roaring wave of sound. Behind the trucks, figures, arms defiantly raised, hurled bricks and vanished. Then, among the phalanx of soldiers massed on the steps, something began to happen. They were running off in all directions, a few throwing down their guns. Two by two, three by three, they were swallowed up in the crowd. But others, bayonets unsheathed, burst toward her side of the square running after peasants and striking them fiercely. Men and women, young and old, grasped sticks and stones to throw at the soldiers, pounding them, gashing them. Everywhere—running, pushing, shouting—soldiers and peasants embraced in mutual fury.

Several soldiers rushed past Anne's hiding place. And then another group, and another. They ran steadily, in formation, as they'd been trained to do, cutting a path through the milling, thrashing crowd. "Regroup!" She heard the shouted order. "South wall!" Then heard it repeated to the next group, and the next. "Regroup. South wall!" Unconscious of anything but the scene before her, Anne moved closer to the spot where the narrow passageway opened into the square. Perhaps only a few feet from the furious melee, she stood frozen, transfixed.

Then the inevitable happened. A face glanced sideways. A soldier's eyes met her eyes, and there was the shock of recognition, the realization that hers were not Chinese eyes. With a suddenness that caused bodies around him to be thrown off balance, to topple forward and backward, he stopped. With one fierce thrust of his arm, he reached into the passageway and pulled Anne out. It happened so violently that she couldn't make her arms or legs move. Nothing was in her mind but an overwhelming wave of fear. She stood rooted to the ground as the soldier roughly shoved back her hood. Anne's long blond hair spilled over the top of Charlie's coat. The soldier's darkly tanned face was blank with incredulity. He and Anne stared into each other's eyes, each incapable of speaking or moving.

The shouts of his comrades roused the soldier.

"A foreigner, a foreign spy!" He spat the words out with a venom that sent waves of terror through Anne, but his words and his expression broke her trance.

"No, no," she gasped. "I'm not a spy. I'm not a spy."

"A foreigner," he snapped at the soldiers clustering around them. "She was hiding in there." He pointed to the passageway. "She was hiding and spying."

Suddenly, Anne's mind functioned with perfect clarity. She couldn't move, couldn't have run, even if he'd let her go, but she could think. She must get them to take her to an authority. She'd be much safer in a police station, a military headquarters, anywhere but here in the hands of soldiers—outnumbered, panicked soldiers.

With great effort, Anne put on what she hoped was an angry and dignified expression. She must not, absolutely must not let her voice tremble. Summoning up every reserve of strength, she swept the mask off her face and said severely,

"Take your hands off me. I have no intention of running away from you. I'm an American journalist, not a foreign spy, a guest here of the Chinese government, of the Minister of Culture, Li Zemin. Take me immediately to the police so we can get this straightened out."

It was as if Anne's voice, the voice of this strange, blond, blue-eyed woman speaking Chinese, had hypnotized the young soldier. The hostility didn't leave his eyes, but his mouth dropped open as he listened to her. He loosened his wrenching grip on her arm.

"You were hiding. Hiding and spying." There was the slightest note of uncertainty in his voice.

"Yes, I was hiding." Anne's confidence flooded back as she saw his weakening. "I came into Kaifeng to do some sightseeing. I had no idea what was going on here. I hid to stay out of all this."

He looked at her steadily. "You're alone. Foreigners don't go sightseeing alone."

There was a sudden clamor of voices as his comrades began to speak.

"That's right. Why is she alone?"

"She had to hide. She might have been killed."

"She's speaking Chinese."

"That doesn't matter. Spies speak Chinese."

Anne spoke loudly, coldly, with as much force as she could muster. "I'm a guest of your government. I want to be taken to someone in authority. I won't discuss anything further with you, with any of you."

Her hands trembled. If only the soldiers were too shocked to notice. If only their fear of the possible power of foreigners over-whelmed their traditional suspicion. Her appeal to authority would ordinarily have automatically guaranteed her safety, but here, order seemed to have broken down.

Unconsciously perhaps, the soldiers had backed her into the shad-owed recess of the narrow passageway, but even through her terror, Anne was aware of the crashing of the battle only yards away. The soldiers were nervous, glancing apprehensively over their shoulders. They looked at each other. Their artless young faces were hard, unyielding, but she knew they were hesitating. She was in danger, but they were too.

She looked slowly around the tight little circle that enclosed her, a circle with the physical force to do whatever it wished with her.

"I demand that you take me to the police. I have all the proper papers to show them, but I won't show them to you."

And then from the back of the group came an assured voice. "She's right. Take her to the police. If she's a spy, they'll find out. If she's a foreign friend, we could get in a lot of trouble. We've got to get rid of her." There was a hurried, whispered conference.

"Come," the same confident voice said curtly. The speaker was a very small, winning boy of perhaps eighteen, but for Anne, there wasn't a flicker of warmth in his sparkling black eyes.

"Turn around and walk back the way you came. We'll follow you."

216

Anne turned, and they marched single file in a grim procession through the narrow passageway. Where it began to widen out, the boyish, decisive soldier and the broad-faced one who'd captured her swung out on either side of her. The two of them stared sternly ahead.

When they reached the intersection where the *hutong* opened out on the street, Anne's captor led the way to one of the army trucks parked there and waved her toward the front. He hesitated briefly, then gave her a hand as she stepped up into the high cab. She slid onto the hard steel seat. He slammed the door and jumped up onto the platform area behind her. The other soldier was in the driver's seat already starting the engine.

The police station wasn't far away. It was housed in a nondescript three-story gray building she'd passed on her way into Kaifeng. Her soldier escorts directed Anne brusquely to a hard bench just inside the front door and disappeared through another door. The bare white room was swarming with people—civilian police in their neat navy-blue and white uniforms, soldiers, peasants, both men and women, several lying on the floor injured. The telephone never stopped ringing. Harsh voices snapped out orders. People rushed frantically in and out of the front door. Interior doors opened and slammed shut.

Anne's presence attracted little more than momentarily shocked glances, but she didn't have to wait long. It was only five or ten minutes before the soldier who had discovered her came to the door and motioned her in. The two soldiers stood watchfully beside a man seated at a desk. He was not a pleasant-looking person, but Anne supposed that was probably true of policemen in powerful positions anywhere in the world. He was fiftyish, broad-shouldered, his dark jowly face frowning. He motioned her to the chair in front of his desk, his manner totally impersonal. It was impossible to guess his intent or attitude.

Her name, nationality, occupation, status in China, reason for being in Kaifeng. To visit the Shang site, she told him, and gave him her letter of authorization from the Ministry of Culture and the name of the hotel where she and Charlie were staying. Her letter, he pointed out, gave her permission to visit the Shang site, but it said nothing about sightseeing alone in Kaifeng.

"I know," Anne replied disingenuously. "I suppose I shouldn't have done that. I just felt like taking a bike ride while everyone else

217

was napping. It was such a nice afternoon, and I thought it would be interesting to see what Kaifeng looked like."

There wasn't a flicker of expression on the man's face. No doubt he was a professional interrogator of some sort. She should not have done that, he said. She must know that foreigners shouldn't go wandering off by themselves. The state was responsible for their lives and welfare while they were in China. How did she happen to go to the town square?

She was attracted by the noise.

He nodded. A scribe in the corner wrote busily.

And how did she happen to be hiding in the passageway?

Anne took her cue from the soldiers' remarks. To protect herself from the dangerous situation, she replied.

How long had she been there before the soldiers found her?

A very short time. It was impossible to say.

He persisted. Would she say ten minutes, half an hour, an hour?

It was impossible to say, but not for long.

He persisted. What did she see? Why did she stay there when she saw it was dangerous? How long had she intended to stay? How did she plan to return to her hotel? Ah yes, and where had the bike come from? She'd borrowed it? Did she have permission to borrow it? Why hadn't she just asked the hotel personnel for a car to come into Kaifeng? The questions went on and on.

Anne was aware that her story didn't sound convincing, and the questions were becoming more difficult to evade.

Had she known about the demonstration before she came into Kaifeng?

She hesitated. She knew from a local radio broadcast that there were demonstrations in the area, she said, then added hastily that she didn't know she'd find what she did in Kaifeng.

It was a partially honest answer, but only partially. A good interrogator would be able to tear it apart in no time. She was frightened now. She was guilty of something she knew the Chinese didn't want —making contact with the rebels and coming to observe a demonstration. But that wasn't a crime. Or was it? A chill of apprehension enveloped her. She'd written stories herself about the fine, at times nonexistent, line between crime and political opposition in China, between seeing what you weren't supposed to and spying. For a troublesome foreigner associated with a Chinese oppositional faction to be labeled a spy would certainly be nothing new. She was

218

not unaware of the fate of foreigners who had chosen the wrong side in the Cultural Revolution.

How was it possible that she was suddenly here, alone and vulnerable, and no one even knew where she was? How long was this going to go on? Were they going to torture her? Lock her up and say they didn't know where she was when the American embassy made its inquiries. *If* the American embassy made its inquiries.

"Look," she said desperately. "You don't have to go through all this to find out who I am. You can check with the American embassy in Peking. You can call Peter Matthewson, the political secretary of the embassy." She could hear her own voice rising in panic. "You can get in touch with the American who traveled here with me. He's lived in China for many years. He's a Chinese citizen. He'll tell you who I am."

"I'm not concerned about who you are. Your passport gives me that information. We're only interested in one thing—what you were doing here in Kaifeng this afternoon."

The voice was noncommittal, but a new wave of fear swept over her, and with it came heightened caution. The situation was just as dangerous as she feared. She tried to breathe deeply. Above all, she mustn't let herself panic. She mustn't do that.

The questioning continued. The same questions in more detail. Related questions arose. Did she know anything about the political situation in the area? No, very little. Had she met any local people? Again, no. She seemed to have lost the ability to analyze the questions. Mechanically, she replied, "No. No." She concentrated on the breathing. She saw nothing but the heavy, oppressive face before her, the white walls of the bare room.

Then, abruptly, the interrogation was over. The policeman pushed a buzzer. A husky young woman came in and escorted Anne down a dimly lit hallway to a tiny room. It was furnished with a cot covered by a thin mattress and a khaki-colored blanket. A chamber pot was on the floor under it. There was one small, high window. That was all. Not precisely a cell, but something very near. Anne sat down on the bed.

"Are you hungry?" the matron asked.

"Yes, very hungry."

Without a word, the woman went out, locking the door behind her, and a few minutes later returned with a large bowl of rice covered with cabbage, a pair of chopsticks, a thermos of hot water, and an enamel cup. She handed the bowl to Anne, placed the cup on the cot and the thermos on the floor. Again, she shut the door behind her, clicked the lock, and walked heavily down the hallway, her steps becoming more and more faint until the sound disappeared entirely.

Anne sat on the edge of the bed and ate the cabbage and rice mechanically, unaware of the movement of chopsticks from bowl to mouth, unconscious of the taste of food. When she looked at the bowl, she was surprised to see that it was empty. She stared at the white wall opposite her, her mind immobilized with only the drumbeat of the questions resounding inside. She couldn't even hear her answers, only the questions again and again. Why were you in Kaifeng? Why were you hiding? Do you know any local people? Why didn't you order a car? Why were you alone?

But Anne's normal fortitude finally overcame the paralysis of panic. Reporters did end up in jail every now and then. Look at poor Anthony Gray of the London *Times* who'd been a prisoner during the Cultural Revolution. He'd been a scapegoat, pure and simple, probably guilty of fewer "crimes" from the Chinese point of view than Anne was right now. He was still alive and sane and had written a book about his experience. That was probably the very worst that could happen to her. People became the victims of history, hostages to events for all kinds of reasons, many entirely circumstantial. At least she had gone consciously into a dangerous situation. And she wasn't yet in prison. Not exactly, anyway. This room must be some kind of holding area.

She must do what she knew prisoners had to do. She looked at her watch. They hadn't even taken that away. It was eight o'clock. Less than twenty-four hours ago she'd left the hotel for the peasants' meeting. At only five this morning she'd sat reading the stolen document. It was one this afternoon when she'd started off on the stolen bike. If at any point she'd broken the chain of circumstance, had refused to take the next logical step . . . but she mustn't think of that.

Anne stood in the middle of the small room and began touching her toes, counting systematically. So the night passed. She did calisthenics, gave herself a Chinese lesson, writing invisible characters with her finger to cover the vocabulary of the day—police, soldier, interrogation, demonstration. But what was the character for "tear gas"? Her bag, of course, had been confiscated, and everything from her pockets. She was painfully aware of how important a pen was for her, and a piece of paper, and how much she took them for granted. If they kept her here for long, she'd ask for a Chinese dictionary. Surely they'd agree to that.

She groaned and sank back on the hard, flat cot. She couldn't sleep, her anxiety focusing on the harsh glare of the bulb that hung from the ceiling. She got up and searched everywhere in the room for a switch to turn it off. There wasn't one. She stood on the bed and unscrewed the bulb from the socket. The room became impenetrably black. It was terrifying. She screwed the bulb back in, paced across the small space one hundred times exactly, and fell back on the cot, where she continued to toss fitfully. She was awakened by the sound of the door being unlocked.

"Come with me," the same young woman said. Anne followed obediently. At the end of the hallway, just outside the door that led into the reception room, Charlie was sitting on a bench, wearing his brown silk padded jacket and a fur hat. Odd, Anne thought, she'd never seen him dressed like that. Then she remembered she had his coat. He was staring at the ceiling and didn't seem to notice Anne until she was directly in front of him. His face was expressionless, but at that moment it didn't matter. Anne took hold of both his hands.

"Oh, Charlie, I'm so glad to see you. I'm so glad you're here." She was overwhelmed with relief.

Charlie didn't reply. The matron had disappeared. Apparently they were releasing her. With no explanation, nothing. Her bag was lying right there on the bench next to Charlie. He got up and opened a door for her. It led directly outside. The car from the hotel, the same one that had taken them to the Shang site, was waiting.

The car wove in and out of the narrow streets. Anne stole an occasional glance at Charlie to see if he was ready to break the oppressive stillness. He was looking out the window on his side of the car. He appeared absorbed in the passing scenery. She wanted to ask him a dozen questions. What had the police told him? When had they notified him? What had he heard about yesterday's demonstration? Most of all, she wanted to thank him. If he hadn't been around, if she'd been here alone, God only knows what would have happened.

Anne opened her bag and carefully checked the contents—her passport, official papers, and notebooks, which fortunately contained nothing but her notes on the Shang site. The peasants' meeting existed only in her memory. Not a scrap of paper was missing. Everything else—the pens, cigarettes, matches, money—was neatly in place; if anything, more neatly than before. She took out her comb and, with a feeling of immeasurable contentment, combed the tangles out of her hair. Maybe it was going to be all right. But Charlie. She glanced at him again. Had she lost Charlie?

And the bike, what had happened to it? Well, that at least she could replace with money.

"Well, take a good look." Charlie's voice was dry as always. "That's all you may ever see of Kaifeng, at least for a long, long time."

"You mean your hunch was right? We're leaving?"

"We're leaving, but not quite the way I anticipated. You're being expelled from the province. And I, as your assumed guardian, have been asked to escort you back to Peking. You're going to have just enough time to pack your suitcase and eat a sandwich. They're shipping us out at noon from a military airport."

Now that she was here, Anne's fear was subsiding. Who the hell did these people think they were, putting her in jail for watching a riot, and then expelling her! "Expelled from the province! . . . I suppose that'll mean expelled from the country as well."

Charlie's voice was distant. "No doubt you know more about that sort of thing than I do. You seem to have been conducting yourself by your own set of rules. I'm sure you must know how these games are played." There was no mistaking the hurt in his voice.

"Oh, Charlie," Anne said softly. "I'm sorry to have involved you. It's true, I've been playing by my own rules, and if it weren't for you I wouldn't feel there was anything wrong with that. But I'm truly sorry to have gotten you mixed up in this."

He didn't respond.

"But don't you know what's going on here?" she rushed on. "Those protests you heard about on the radio are huge. They're uprisings, not demonstrations. People have a right to know about what's happening here."

"There are no abstract rights in this world. The government of China also has the 'right,' if that's the word you choose to use, to prevent foreigners from seeing the things they don't want seen or reported."

Charlie spoke forcefully but directly at the back of the driver's

222

head. "However, I'm not interested in debating questions of cultural relativity with you. You made your own decisions. That's your right. But from now on, you're on you're own."

The silence between them was terrible. They each stared out at the bleak Henan landscape.

Suddenly Charlie grabbed Anne's hand. "Don't look, don't look!" he ordered, and she fell back against the seat as he thrust his other hand over her eyes. "Hurry! Drive faster!" he shouted at the driver.

Anne shoved his hand away. "What are you doing?" she asked angrily. "Are you out of your mind?"

What was it he'd tried to prevent her from seeing? She looked out the rear window. A few hundred yards from the road, in a bare brown field—a line of figures, a blur of blue and black, but with brown sacks over their heads. Even farther away another row— khaki-colored men, soldiers, with their guns pointed. As the car speeded up and the figures receded, there was a volley of shots and the small black and brown figures crumpled like leaves in the wind, folding onto the harsh earth.

Charlie hadn't turned around. He still held her hand in his, but his grasp was gentle now, his old kindly grasp. Anne stared at him, her dark blue eyes wide with horror.

"An execution. Was that really an execution?" Her voice cracked.

"Counterrevolutionaries get executed," he answered quietly. "And people who kill PLA soldiers are counterrevolutionaries."

Anne closed her eyes. Which of the people she'd sat near the night before last? . . .

"That's mass murder," she murmured.

"No, it's selective punishment. That's the way it's been done here for centuries. 'Kill one, frighten ten thousand.' " Charlie's voice was grave but dispassionate.

When they arrived at the hotel, they walked through the empty lobby and up to their rooms without exchanging a word. There was nothing left to say. As they parted by their respective doors, Charlie mentioned only matters of business—food, departure time, the trip to the airport. Anne responded in monosyllables, and closed the door behind her with relief.

She took clothes off hangers and folded them mechanically. She lifted the lid of her suitcase and began to place them inside. At the bottom of the suitcase were her envelopes of clippings, notebooks, and of course, the document. It was unbelievable, but she'd actually forgotten it. Now, they were sure to search the bags at the Peking airport, if not here in Kaifeng. She'd been a fool and a lousy reporter. Where had her instincts gone to? She'd blown the last chance to read it slowly and concentrate on remembering the details. She'd have to rush through it in fifteen or twenty minutes and dispose of it. She reached in and pulled out all the notebooks. She separated them, and then sifted through them one by one, but where was it? She sifted through them again, more carefully, then felt in the pockets of the suitcase. She turned the suitcase upside down and shook it onto the floor, then pulled open every drawer in the room. All empty. She rushed frantically around the room, digging into pockets, shaking out the sheets of the bed, going through the wastebasket. But it was, as she knew it would be, useless. The document was gone.

CHAPTER

16

Haggard arrived back in Peking in a very upbeat state of mind. His talks with Zolti and with the President had gone splendidly. Although he wasn't a man who depended on praise to do his job well, it had been pleasant to be so highly complimented by the two most powerful men in Washington. Of course, like all assignments, this one had had its unpleasant moments. The encounter with Carpenter and his young toady had certainly been one of them, but life in the embassy proceeded just as before. There was no reference to the fact that either he or Carpenter had been to Washington. Both went their separate ways and had as little to do with each other as possible.

However, no sooner did Haggard resume work than snags began to surface. As he checked systematically on the many-faceted aspects of the military upgrading program, he ran into one problem after another. To his dismay, he discovered that virtually every project seemed to be at a dead standstill. Was it really necessary for him to be in Peking one hundred percent of the time and personally oversee everything! Absolutely nothing had moved forward during his absence. With time so critical it was unbelievable.

Only when he could move decisively into Phase III, the transfer of tactical nuclear warheads from storage in South Korea to the border areas of China, would he begin to feel at ease. The plans had been laid out for a whole network of transfer landing strips from which he would then position the nukes. Once that occurred, two million Russian troops wouldn't be able to cope with what he had in store for them.

One by one, he called in the military experts in charge of the various projects and subjected them to imperious cross-examinations. For years, Haggard had been legendary in the Army for the icy rage with which he cut down subordinates who failed to fulfill his orders not just satisfactorily, but perfectly. Men with years of military experience, with considerable power themselves, went to work for Lowell Haggard with fear and trembling. He'd had the pick of the country for his China assignments, though, and he'd chosen the very best. As he turned the captains, colonels, even a one-star general slowly over the spit, it became clearer and clearer that not one of them was at fault, not even minimally.

It didn't hurt to put the fear of God into one's staff every now and then, but Haggard wasn't one to confuse an exercise in discipline with the solving of problems—and the problem was entirely on the Chinese side of the equation. Strikes, everywhere in the country. The fragile, barely adequate industrial infrastructure was simply folding up. Top-security military flights were landing somewhere in the vast reaches of China almost every day. High-technology equipment was pouring in from America. However, such complex and advanced technology was dependent on a very large and constant supply of energy, on a steady stream of reliable transport rolling day and night over road and rail.

Haggard was enraged. The coal miners were on strike. That meant sporadic power shortages around the country. How could the Chinese allow this to happen! He'd had countless discussions with Chinese officials, trying to explain that advanced computers were not like radios that could be switched on and off with no harm to the equipment. It was obvious that some of them simply hadn't understood what he was talking about. They had given him all sorts of inane excuses. They had told him that if the military computers were never to suffer a lack of power, something else would. They had insisted that although the Chinese people were disciplined, obedient, and quite accustomed to doing what the government told them to do, there were limits to how much electricity could be diverted from their modest household needs. Patience, they'd said. Time. He was a very patient man, he'd told them, but if they wanted an advanced military technology, they'd better be prepared to pay the price. Obviously they hadn't been prepared!

226

Just as serious was the railway workers' strike in Central China. One of the major rail intersections in the country, Zhengzhou they called it, shut down. Virtually everything that moved by rail in that part of the country halted. So far, thank God, that strike hadn't spread to other major rail centers, but there were rumblings and small flare-ups that didn't bode well. What was the matter with these people in the government who were supposed to be keeping everything under control?

He'd followed the dispatches on the first strike in the Tianbei zone very carefully and had been much impressed. There'd been no hesitation. The Army had been sent in quickly and in sufficient force, the strike leaders arrested immediately, the strikers fired, and the factories restaffed within hours. Naturally, the productivity problems had been terrible. You didn't make soldiers into electronics workers overnight, but that wasn't the major worry. The most important thing was a proper show of force, an example that demonstrated where the power was. Everything had seemed to be going well then. What had happened?

A visit to Tang Chen had been on Haggard's agenda, but he'd hoped to wait until Tang contacted him. That hadn't happened, and although Haggard felt quite at ease with the relationship, it irritated him a bit that he was the one who always had to request a meeting. Chinese of power did have a tendency to make you go to them so that they were always the ones holding court and graciously receiving you. As the representative of the country that was doing the giving, it could be interpreted as rather humiliating. Haggard had never been able to decide whether it really should be taken that way or not, and anyway the big problems were too critical to waste time over such niggling matters. Haggard buzzed his secretary and told her to make an appointment with Tang Chen immediately.

In the cool delicate air, tender leaves quivered lightly on the branches of the rows of poplars. As the car left the crowded city for the suburbs, there were touches of green everywhere. Pink and white canopies of blossoms suddenly appeared above ever present gray walls, and from the bare branches of tulip trees, magnolia-like purple and white flowers shot out in bold display.

North China was not normally beautiful, Haggard thought as he

227

watched the scenery go by, but it did have its moments, and certainly these few fleeting weeks of spring were among them. Perhaps he was even getting to like the place. If the Chinese leaders could only keep their people under control, China would be a very congenial place to work. But keeping people under control . . . Haggard sighed. That was the problem everywhere.

Everything was the same as it had been last time: Tang Chen greeting him at the door; the same meeting room, the same sofa; the daughter pouring tea from the same celadon teapot; the same opening formalities. It was very reassuring.

Haggard's report on his trip to Washington obviously pleased Tang. It also provided Haggard with an opportunity to compliment Tang Chen in a properly oblique fashion on the success of the border operation, whose status his intelligence reports indicated was as it should be—quiet. There were, however, disquieting reports about Soviet troop buildups in the area.

"I'd be interested to know your opinion about the present status of the fighting," he said. "We have the impression that everything's under control."

Tang's face was expressionless. "Perhaps you know that our troops have pulled back fifty miles all along the combat zone."

"I knew you'd pulled back, yes, but not the precise distance. And the Soviets?"

"The Soviets are an imperialist power, a war power. They've pulled back for the moment, but they're moving large numbers of troops into the area."

"Large numbers?" The American spy-satellite reports indicated something like 80,000. It would be interesting to hear Tang's estimate.

"Perhaps two hundred thousand."

"Two hundred thousand!" Ten divisions! Surely Tang must be wrong. The Russians had been keeping their main force facing west ever since Poland. And now there was Baluchistan, too. They couldn't have 200,000 troops to shift around like that. Perhaps Tang had his own reasons for wanting to alarm him. He must be wary. "And what's your estimate of what they intend to do with them?"

"General Haggard, you know the Russians as well as I do. No one's ever positive the Russians are going to strike until they do so. I personally think they have enough problems without risking a war with China. After all, we're both aware that the Baluchistan revolt

228

is spreading. The Russians may soon have to take it directly in hand if they want to control it, and then they'll be faced with another Afghanistan. I feel confident that if we Chinese handle the border war correctly, there's no reason for it to get out of control. And of course, if you and we continue to work closely together."

Tang Chen had spoken confidently. His analysis was an intelligent one, but for some reason Haggard felt uneasy, more so than before the conversation had begun. He hadn't been worried about the border war when he arrived. Now he was. Why? It had something to do with Tang's last remark, "If we Chinese handle the border war correctly. . . ." Where was the guarantee for that? A month ago he would have taken it for granted, but today, with his entire program stalemated. . . .

"Yes," Haggard replied. "Working closely together. That's the most important thing. We've made excellent progress together on the military upgrading program. That was one of the things I reported on in Washington that particularly pleased the President, and I'm afraid that's what has me rather worried since I've come back to Peking."

Tang Chen raised his eyebrows questioningly, almost disingenuously, Haggard thought. It was utterly clear that Tang didn't intend to give him a bit of help with this unpleasant subject.

"These strikes . . . They're causing very serious delays in our work—power shortages, deliveries of material particularly. You're aware of the deadline that we're up against. We're just not going to be able to meet it if these matters aren't brought under control quickly. And if there are two hundred thousand Soviet troops being brought up to the border before we're ready . . ." Horrified at the picture he was presenting, Haggard didn't finish. The border incident had been a calculated risk. It had certainly accomplished what he needed—the release of funds by Congress to make the completion of his project possible. However, if the fighting expanded into a larger confrontation before the project was finished . . . He'd relied on Tang Chen's perfect understanding of the variables of the Chinese political and military situation. Could he have misjudged his man?

As if reading Haggard's thoughts, Tang Chen's bony face had become quite rigid, his narrow eyes almost closed slits. "General Haggard," he said very slowly, "in our last conversation, you may recall that we talked about the problems both our countries have had

229

from time to time in dealing with enemies within the system. The strikes you're referring to are a manifestation of that problem. There are those who for reasons of their own personal and political ambitions wish to disrupt our modernization plan. They've incited hysteria among the masses in order to further their own careers, but we know who they are, and their performance on the political stage will not last long."

Tang paused dramatically. The tension in the room was overpowering. "We will take care of our enemies," he stated finally, "But . . . " His commanding voice had lowered to a growl.

Haggard sat apprehensively, his muscles taut. What was all this about?

"But what we will not tolerate is interference in our internal affairs by spies and provocateurs." Tang took a folded stack of papers from the table next to him and handed them to Haggard. "You might find it interesting to look at this."

Haggard unfolded the little bundle and began to read. *Consolidated Guidance—China 10. Security Classification Royal—18 copies. Royal Copy No. 12. Joint Chiefs—Navy.* Slowly, methodically, he turned the pages. CG 10. Yes, it was the real document, the whole thing, the one he'd spent months working on. No fakery here. Without any doubt a stolen copy.

Haggard was cold with fury. How was it possible, with all his care in working out airtight security arrangements, that such a thing could have happened? What good did it do to make brilliant plans to defeat the Russians when everything was unraveled by incompetence and subversion?

He placed the document on the coffee table with great deliberateness.

"Would you judge it to be authentic?" Tang asked coolly.

"There's no question about it. I wrote it myself."

Tang merely nodded. "Would you assume that finding such a document in someone's possession would be evidence of spying?"

"It would be hard to draw any other conclusion, wouldn't it." The question did not really interest Haggard. The Chinese could deal with their own spies, as far as he was concerned. The only important question was who'd been responsible for stealing the document in Washington. That was an investigation he would set up himself.

230

"It was found in the possession of an American journalist—a woman—in her suitcase." Tang waited calmly to see the impact of his statement.

Haggard was sitting stiffly in his most severe military posture. His voice quivering with half-controlled rage he asked, "Do you mean here? In China?"

"Yes, in a town not far from Zhengzhou, the center of the railway strike." Tang paused significantly. The implication of his statement was not lost on Haggard.

"Do you know where she got it?"

"Yes, we know everything." Tang's expression seemed to Haggard unnecessarily supercilious, but there was nothing to be done. The Chinese had the information. They'd uncovered the spy. It was their victory. At least Haggard knew he wouldn't have to beg for the facts. Tang was undoubtedly anxious to tell him about the matter.

"She was given the document by a notorious Chinese rebel leader, an enemy counterrevolutionary, very much involved in instigating the strikes and demonstrations that you're concerned about. We know everything we need to know about him and will arrest him soon. Once he and a few others like him are gone, you'll see a quick change in the problems that are worrying you."

Haggard suddenly felt almost ashamed of his momentary doubts about Tang Chen. Yes, he was an excellent judge of men and didn't make many mistakes. Thank God there was one man in the world he could trust to deal with problems as they should be dealt with.

"Do you know where he got it?"

"It came from the Russians, funneled by them through the recent chairman of the border-talks team who has since been removed and will also be arrested soon."

"And the Russians—how did they get it? You understand, I'm sure, that I'm particularly concerned with how this document got out of Washington in the first place."

Tang shrugged indifferently. "I personally can't tell you much about that. I'll arrange for you to talk to some of our intelligence people if you like. As I recall, I believe I was told a Russian agent simply purchased it from some employee of your government. We hear that it's extremely easy for them to get information that way." The note of contempt in his voice was unmistakable.

231

But Haggard was not so easily intimidated. He didn't regard himself as personally responsible for the corruptibility of his fellow Americans.

"You see what's happening," Tang went on. "The Russians are linking up with counterrevolutionary forces here in China. Their plan is to disrupt the country through strikes and riots. As you can see by the transferral of this document, their aim is to disrupt our mutual military arrangements, overthrow the government, and set up a puppet Soviet state in China. That, quite simply, is the explanation for the problems you've been talking about today. They're not simply strikes which are delaying deliveries and disrupting power supplies, General Haggard. They are part of a comprehensive plan for Soviet subversion of China."

Haggard was impressed. He was in the presence of a man who had his finger on everything, who understood both the general problem and the minutest details. It wasn't difficult to understand how Tang Chen had survived one bloody power struggle after another, while rising steadily to the top. He operated in the shadows, but had sources of information everywhere.

"What's the connection of the journalist with this plan?" Haggard asked.

"She's a Russian agent, working for the KGB. She's here in China as a correspondent for one of your big Washington papers. The *Inquirer*, I think it's called? We've been watching her carefully, and she's been engaged in spying activities ever since she got here."

So, a KGB agent working for the *Inquirer*. It confirmed what Haggard had always suspected about the press in general and the *Inquirer* in particular. All the ballyhoo about First Amendment rights, when the First Amendment itself was a very dubious piece of work at best, opening the way for fanatics and misfits of all kinds to disrupt the state. It was precisely the First Amendment that had led to the national unraveling of the past two decades, and the very security leaks that had allowed the theft of this document in the first place. Spying and investigative reporting—he'd always known they were all of a piece, and here was proof positive.

"I suppose you've arrested her."

Tang looked rather surprised. "No, we didn't. That didn't seem to us a wise way of dealing with the problem. We're not interested in having an international incident regarding your freedom of the press."

232

Haggard felt slightly chagrined. What did you do with spies? Presumably either arrest them or shoot them, although he couldn't recall the latter happening in a long time. In fact, the whole question of spies made him rather uncomfortable. As a technocratic man, Haggard had more confidence in electronic spying. Still, he knew there were times and situations when nothing replaced the old-fashioned human spy.

From a personal point of view, though, he found the whole subject distasteful. He much preferred direct, face-to-face military confrontation. It seemed to him the gentleman's way, although he was well aware that there was something in the northern gentleman's code of honor that found spying a felicitous and congenial occupation. And the British! For them, it was not just a suitable profession but the sport of aristocrats, a veritable art form. No doubt it was all a question of culture. The Chinese? He didn't recall having heard of a Chinese Philby or McLean. Certainly, Tang had already made his own plans for the disposition of this particular spy, but he would be a fool to ask him directly.

"Why do you suppose the Russians are using her at this stage of the operation?" Haggard asked. "After all, the document was in their hands in Washington." Really, the whole business did seem a bit peculiar to him. A singularly roundabout way of doing things.

"As I mentioned, one of the objectives of the Chinese counter-revolutionaries is to disrupt our military plans. That's one of the reasons they find a document like this useful, to whip up hatred of the United States among the people. The role of the American newspaperwoman is very much the same, but with the American people. She is intended to play the same role as that man—what was his name?—who disrupted your government's plans for the Vietnam war by giving the Pentagon Papers to the New York Times."

Haggard nodded. Now it was quite clear. There was no question the Chinese were geniuses at figuring this sort of thing out. If only he had a Tang Chen or two on his security staff, everything would have been shipshape.

"Daniel Ellsberg is the man you mean."

"Ellsberg, yes. Of course, it's difficult for us to understand why a strong government like yours permits such things to happen, but . . ." He waved his hand in a gesture of indifference.

Haggard felt himself growing more and more tense. It was bad enough that such a theft had taken place. Things like that just didn't occur in well-run institutions. But now he was being subjected to another, quite gratuitous humiliation, the Chinese contempt for American liberalism, as if he were somehow a representative of the very things he despised! The whole business was disgusting. Nothing was too strong a remedy for such treachery.

"It's no problem for us to remove this person from China," he said. "Consider that done."

Tang nodded. "We assumed that you'd be able to take care of that without difficulty. However . . ." He looked off into space as if deep in thought. Haggard waited him out.

"However, she knows entirely too much. She's the only foreigner to have made contact with a number of rebel leaders. She met with the leaders of the Tianbei strike soon after she arrived in China. As part of her spying assignment, she was caught secretly watching a battle between the Army and a bunch of rabble in Kaifeng, a city near Zhengzhou. She was turned over to the local police, but it was decided to let her go until a higher-level decision was made on what to do with her. As you can see, from the beginning she's been involved in the very developments that are undermining our military arrangements. She knows too much. With her information, she'd be a great danger to both of us once she was back in the United States in a position to write and talk freely."

Tang had evidently completed his statement, for he offered Haggard a cigarette and took one himself. It seemed to Haggard that Tang's words could have only one meaning. The Chinese weren't going to arrest this woman, but neither did they intend that she simply be thrown out of China.

Haggard proceeded carefully. He had no intention of making a diplomatic faux pas. "She should disappear," he said.

"That would seem wise." Tang waited a moment, then added, "Naturally, it must be permanent."

"Naturally," Haggard said flatly.

He didn't like the way this was proceeding. Tang's recommendation was, of course, the correct one. The realities of the world struggle had harsh imperatives. However, men of breeding didn't personally soil their hands with such matters. That was the reason the CIA had started using the Mafia years ago. Why hadn't the Chinese, who uncovered all this, taken care of it themselves? Unfortunately, he already knew the answer. They were much too smart. American woman disappears in China. What an uproar that would

234

have caused. Every reporter in China and who knows what other crackpots would have devoted the next decade to uncovering the mystery. It would have been as bad as the Kennedy assassination. Nevertheless, he said with as much indifference as he could muster, "Since it occurred in China, don't you regard this matter as being in your jurisdiction?"

Tang almost imperceptibly shook his head. "She's your national. You know best how to deal with your own people, and it's our policy never to interfere in the internal affairs of other nations."

"Of course," Haggard responded calmly, although he was furious. He was not accustomed to being backed up against the wall, and there was no doubt that that's what had happened. His mind raced ahead. The Chinese always took pride in having the patience to play the last card, but this time Haggard was determined that they wouldn't have that pleasure. They could lay this unpleasant duty in his lap, but he would see to it that it was carried out by Chinese assassins. If it were ever uncovered, the Chinese government, not the American, would be implicated; if it were not, at least Tang Chen would understand that Lowell Haggard was the master of this game.

The matter was settled, but Haggard's mood, as he got into his car, with Tang standing by to wave him off in correct Chinese fashion, was distinctly sour.

When he got back to his office in the embassy, he got on the problem immediately. Using his own special scrambler line to Washington, he began the process of taking care of the spy from the *Inquirer*. He'd decided on a stage-by-stage procedure. First, to preclude any further Chinese contacts, a suspension of her assignment. Only then her dismissal as the *Inquirer*'s correspondent. During this time, arrangements would be properly made for her assassination.

It would appear to be a suicide. That was the classic scheme, and in such matters, Haggard was convinced, traditional ways were usually best. Her job severance was essential. That would be the motive for the suicide. On the other hand, it must not happen so rapidly that she would just jump on the first plane and escape. The deed must be done in Peking. That was Haggard's little card, his delicate revenge for having been forced into this disagreeable role.

He felt quite satisfied with his strategy. The details would be left to people who specialized in that sort of thing. He knew such people must exist in China. No country with its tradition of ferocious

235

political infighting could lack them. If the clan culture of Italy had spawned a Mafia, the clan culture of old China had produced something analogous, the organization that had done so much useful work for him in the past—in Saigon, Djakarta, Manila, all over Southeast Asia. Surely they would have a Peking connection. Feeling pleased with the way he was working things out, Haggard dialed a Hongkong number that he hadn't had occasion to use for several years.

Anne felt enormously relieved as soon as the plane began circling Peking's airport. The end of the Henan trip had been a hideous jumble of events. Even their flight out on the small military plane had been as distasteful as possible. Everything in her possession had been searched, something that had never happened to her before, and all in a nastily suspicious way that made her feel contemptible. No one said they suspected her of being a spy, but everything they did and the way they did it produced precisely that effect. There was even a body search, demeaning and humiliating, conducted by another of those tough-looking police matrons.

Her suitcase and her shoulder bag were literally turned inside out. Even the linings were carefully cut away. Every scrap of written material in her possession was confiscated, including her notes on the Shang site and, unfortunately, notes she'd written in the hotel about the Zhengzhou Railway Station battle, as well as her Chinese vocabulary lists that included such new words as "riot," "tear gas," and "interrogation." They even took the books on Shang history. They were Charlie's books, but Anne decided it would be better not to say anything about that. No point in causing him any more trouble. His own luggage was politely passed through without even a glance.

Then, the plane itself. It was hardly necessary to make the point. In the midst of unbelievable upheavals, a military plane had been especially allocated for the frivolous task of removing two troublesome foreigners from an area where they had no business being in the first place. Charlie did nothing to mitigate the unpleasantness of the situation. He'd become a distant acquaintance, nothing more. They both spent the flight reading. He supplied Anne with books and magazines, since she now had none of her own. But the cozy companionship of their train trip to Zhengzhou was gone, probably forever, Anne thought despondently.

Only when she saw the sprawling city of Peking below did something like her old buoyancy begin to resurface. The trip to Kaifeng had been a gamble, and, in a way, she'd done quite well. Certainly, no foreigner in China knew more than she did at this moment, and her luck had even held. After all, the Kaifeng police could have made much more out of her arrest than they had.

As for the document—well, there was no way to put a good light on that, but no point in getting into a panic over it either. For all she knew, she might never even hear of it again. That was the way the Chinese conducted their political struggles against each other. There was always tons of incriminating evidence on everyone, but most of it stayed in the archives, and was only taken out if a shift in the political balance made it suddenly useful to one faction or another. It must be the same for foreign journalists. She'd just have to be prepared for it to reappear at some unexpected point. It was ironic, but her main problem at the moment wasn't in China at all. It was to convince those fools in Washington that they should run the stories she was going to send them.

The plane taxied to a stop at the main Peking airport in a special area at the far end of the regular landing field. There were soldiers everywhere. The pilot preceded Anne and Charlie across the airfield, and when inside the gate, said a few indistinguishable words to a thin young man in black civilian clothes.

"I'm Lin Yaoping, your secretary-interpreter," the man then said to Anne. His tone was unfriendly.

Anne was shocked but not flustered. "I already have a secretary. I have no need for another one, thank you."

"Tan Yulan was needed at the Foreign Ministry to do other work. I will take her place."

Anne made no attempt to hide her displeasure. "I'm sorry to hear that. I was very pleased with the way our work together was going."

"I hope I'll be able to assist you just as well," the black-suited man said flatly.

It wasn't his fault, of course. He was on assignment, just as Mrs. Tan had been, but Anne detested him, detested everything he represented. If they insisted, he could sit at his desk all day doing his

237

spying job as well as he was able, but as for the secretary role, she'd have none of it. She'd played her polite part in this game, but she wasn't going to do it any longer.

The ride into town seemed interminable. Anne had nothing to say. Charlie, as always, maintained the amenities, chatting with Lin about the usual polite topics—the weather in Peking, where he was from, and what the weather was like there. Anne was disgusted with the whole business. There should be a limit to one's capacity for hypocrisy. Somehow, it seemed to take the edge off the pain she'd been feeling about losing Charlie.

However, when the car stopped before the revolving front door of the hotel and she jumped out, the good-bye was not so simple. Before Anne could speak, the irritating secretary was already standing on the sidewalk. "Don't get out," she said to Charlie. "I can manage my suitcase. Good-bye."

She spoke briskly, but when she looked at him, she was suddenly choked up with tears. His face, which she'd so often seen lighted up with enthusiasm, humor, and—yes, affection, now looked tired and old. His brown eyes, usually sparkling with amusement and interest, were quite lifeless.

"Good-bye, Anne. Good luck," was all he said, but the "good luck" was devastating, not the sort of thing one said except in a final farewell. She turned away quickly to hide her tears and grabbed her suitcase out of Lin's hands.

"I'm not going to work today. I need to rest. I don't need your help."

His composure was not easily rattled. "Mrs. Tan told me she started work with you every morning at nine o'clock. I'll arrive tomorrow morning at nine."

"If you insist," Anne said shortly. As she entered the lobby, Anne heard the car drive away.

It was a great relief to be alone in her old room, and she was anxious to start writing her Henan pieces. With that hideous young man hovering about, she'd have to use every solitary moment well. She'd also have to think of some sort of project to keep him busy.

But first there were two phone calls to be made—one to Peter, the other to the *Inquirer*. It was really incredible, after their awful, awkward leave-taking, how much she looked forward to talking to Peter. Everything that had burst out so furiously that last time seemed beside the point now. It was what they shared that mattered.

238

He cared about what happened to her. Though he would think she'd been crazy to get herself into such a situation, he'd be angry and sympathetic. She needed him.

The warmth in his voice was apparent even over the phone. "I've been going out of my mind trying to find out about you. You realize, don't you, that you just dropped off the face of the earth when you got on the last train to leave Peking for Zhengzhou. The whole province is sealed off tighter than a drum. Even the ambassador hasn't been able to get a phone call through. I thought you were O.B.E."

"O.B.E.? What on earth does that mean?"

"Overtaken by events—intelligence term. That's what they send over the wires when the whole operation's been done in. I've been going crazy worrying about you. I think I must be in love with you."

For the first time in days, Anne laughed.

"I was overtaken by events, in more ways than one," Anne said, suddenly aware of the exhaustion running through her body. For a moment, she felt an overwhelming desire to tell Peter everything and be done with it, but something—maybe simple paranoia about the phone, stopped her.

Fortunately, Peter cut into her thoughts. "I've got to see you, Anne. Would you like to go out to dinner right now?"

She glanced at her watch. It was 3:30 in the afternoon. She wanted to laugh again, this time at his uncharacteristic enthusiasm. "I'm absolutely exhausted, and, yes, I do feel like going out to dinner right now."

"Great. Shall we try out a new place or one of the old ones?"

"I don't know. I don't care. I'd just like to see you, that's all."

"How about our oldest one; the Blue Door, or am I getting sentimental in my old age?"

"That sounds fine."

"I'll pick you up in twenty minutes. We can have that incredible carp."

This time she really laughed. Nothing interfered with Peter's devotion to the art of good eating.

Speaking to Peter made her feel truly better. Their leave-taking seemed too long ago to matter. So when she made her second phone call, she was strangely confident, ready to take on Larry Metcalf and a few others like him if necessary. She knew exactly what she had to offer and exactly what she wanted to say. This time there'd be no runaround about eyewitness stories. He might still say no. That was entirely possible, and she was prepared for it. But at least he'd have to be straightforward about it and then she could consider her options.

But it all turned out to be completely disconcerting. An impersonal secretarial voice informed her that Mr. Metcalf wasn't able to accept phone calls at this time and—oh yes, Anne Campbell in Peking. She had instructions to transfer Ms. Campbell's calls to Mr. Cogswell. Mr. who? Anne asked. Mr. Benjamin Cogswell, the associate editor. Anne was startled. Benjamin Cogswell? She'd never even heard of him. Clearly, though, she'd have to talk to him.

Mr. Cogswell's voice was heavy with the weight of authority—even at a distance of 8,000 miles. "Ah yes, Ms. Campbell. So you've returned to your post in Peking. You put us in quite an embarrassing position when the border fighting broke out. We thought we had a China correspondent of our own to handle that news. Unfortunately, we had to rely on the wire services. We've since worked out a satisfactory temporary arrangement with the *Times*'s man in Peking, who's taking care of things for us."

Anne felt her face becoming hot. She sat down and tried to make her voice as strong as she could.

"There are some extremely important domestic developments here, Mr. Cogswell. I was given the opportunity to go to the area where they're taking place and I took it. I'm the only Western correspondent with an eyewitness account of the Zhengzhou railway strike and a peasant uprising in Central China. I think you'll find them valuable."

The assured voice came back without a second's hesitation. "I'm afraid, Ms. Campbell, that you've taken upon yourself the task of determining editorial policy. That's our job here, not yours. We have a pretty definite idea of what we want you to be doing there, and I believe we've communicated it clearly to you. One of the things we want is for our China correspondent to be in the capital when a war breaks out. That's rather a minimal requirement, I'd say."

She faltered. No response came to mind. "Would you like me to send you the stories I got in Henan Province?" was all she said, and in a meek voice that she hated the second it came out.

"No, I don't think you need to file anything further. Please just

240

wait until you receive notification from us about your assignment and your contract."

That was the end of the conversation. Was she fired? He hadn't said so, but surely that's what it amounted to. Or were they putting her on ice? And what was this business of turning her over to someone she'd never worked with and didn't even know? In one day, she'd acquired a strange new secretary and a strange new editor. It was like being banished into darkness. And what about her precious stories that she'd risked so much for? She'd lost what notes she had, but everything was still fresh in her mind.

Anne sat down at her desk and opened her typewriter case. She was going to write the stories. She'd wait until she heard from the *Inquirer* again. But if they fired her, she'd sell the stories to someone else. It wasn't quite as easy to kill reality as these people seemed to think.

CHAPTER

17

Charlie expected the visit. He didn't even count the first one from the local police in Kaifeng. It had been brief and curt. He'd simply been informed of Anne's activities—that she'd gone to a secret meeting of peasant counterrevolutionaries and been arrested at the riot they'd instigated. He'd been given orders to leave the province and told he could pick Anne up at the police station, but they'd asked him no questions. He knew that was only the beginning. There would certainly be a visit of more consequence.

He was angry with himself. Especially after he had avoided the flames of Chinese factional politics for so many years. As he'd told Anne, he had no taste for martyrdom, and was entirely aware of the price presumptuous foreigners could pay for their transgressions. Sometimes it was safe to be curious and sometimes it wasn't. One never knew when the winds would change, and when they did, anyone was fair game. It would be difficult to convince the Chinese authorities that he was unaware of what he was doing when he provided his respectable guardianship as a cover for Anne's activities. In fact, he would never have believed it himself. The Department of Public Security would have every reason to assume that his role had been a conscious one.

It must have been old age, or the price in poor judgment one finally paid for too much loneliness, or simply his own weakness for the company of attractive women. But those women had always been a part of his life on his terms, not he on theirs. That was one of the reasons he'd favored the beautiful Asians he'd picked up and then dropped all over the Far East. Perhaps, too, his attraction to Anne had involved nostalgia for the foreign correspondent's life that he'd left behind so many years ago.

He was not an unperceptive man. He had simply not permitted himself to think about what Anne was doing under the protection of his established position and good name. But he *had* known. Angry as he was with Anne, he had to admit it. She'd been fairly honest about the whole business. Even Henan. No, he could never plead naiveté. Nor would the Chinese believe him if he did, a man of his experience and years in China. He could only plead culpability to the attractions of a young woman engaged in the profession that he too had loved, an enthusiastic art history protégé, a lively, charming companion for his isolated life, and he had too much dignity to plead that. The Chinese had contempt for culpability.

Thinking all this, Charlie had arrived home from Kaifeng very tired, depressed at the prospect of resuming his hermitry—and more than a little frightened. What form would the visit and the interrogation take? If they chose to put him in jail while he contemplated his crimes, there was nothing to stop them. He knew that Anne had been relieved and surprised at being released so quickly, but for him, that quick and unexpected release boded something worse for the future. He doubted that she would get away with a reprimand. For himself, it was almost impossible.

Lao Li was awaiting his arrival. The rocky garden and the cloistered rooms of the house were quiet with the deep tranquillity of time and history, but instead of bringing him his usual sense of peace, the silent spaces filled Charlie with a great disquiet. He refused Lao Li's anxious offers of tea or lunch and fell into the comforting familiarity of his own bed. The bed was a hard one, Chinese style, with a thin mattress, and was piled high with goose-down comforters covered in the charming, gaudy cloth traditionally used for such purposes—bright red with riotous pinks and greens forming giant chrysanthemums and long-tailed mythological birds. There was no need for comforters on a balmy spring afternoon, but sprawled beneath them, he felt warmly secure and hidden.

Charlie slept deeply and felt much better when he arose from his nap. After all, he'd lived alone for many years and now he'd simply be alone again. Perhaps Lao Li could serve dinner in the garden. If he ate early, it would be rather nice to sit outdoors and contemplate

243

the symmetry of the rocks and the first shoots of the bursting plants, then finish off the evening with light reading and a few drinks.

The one thing he hadn't expected was that the visit would come so soon. As if they knew his schedule perfectly, the visitors arrived at the precise moment when he was up, dressed, and refreshed by his first cup of late-afternoon tea. There was no need for them to identify themselves. Their appearance was a sufficient badge of identification. Although he'd kept his distance from such types for years, Charlie knew instinctively what they would look like, for they were the same the world over.

There were two of them, men of young middle age, their tunic suits black rather than the more common and benign gray or dark blue. One was quite tall, the other of average height and thickset, but their dour faces were startlingly similar, and bereft of feeling. Without a doubt, Charlie thought with a shudder, they were faces that would remain entirely unchanged as your fingernails were being pulled out.

Where did such people come from—the police interrogators, the torturers, the prison guards of the world? What was it in every society that produced them, as if from the same mold? There was no talking with such men, no reasoning. You just hoped that some interest of theirs, which you couldn't possibly know, would let you slip through. That was the only hope. So Charlie waited, silently.

The two security men sat stiffly in the Ming chairs. The inconspicuous Lao Li had discreetly poured tea for the sinister guests, but the cups remained untouched. The tall man, perhaps a bit senior in age as well as rank, opened the proceedings.

"You were informed in Kaifeng of the activities of the American Anne Campbell."

"Yes."

"You're aware that in addition to spying on the riot there, she went in the middle of the night to a meeting of the counterrevolutionaries who were planning the riot. That was how she knew precisely when and where it would take place."

The tall man was simply stating the charges. Charlie was well aware that his own interrogation was beginning, and the way he responded to these charges against Anne would determine his guilt.

"I was told she'd gone to a meeting in the middle of the night that was somehow involved with the riot. I wasn't aware of how precise her information was."

244

The stocky man was writing rapidly on a pad of paper. It seemed to Charlie that he must be putting down more than was actually being said, for he wrote a great deal.

"Were you aware that at the meeting she had a rendezvous with the notorious rebel counterrevolutionary, Wang Weilai?"

"No, I wasn't." Rudd shook his head. Could this really be true? There was no way for him to know whether the interrogator snapping the questions off at him was telling the truth, but the charge was frightening. How could Anne ever have made contact with such a man, an almost legendary figure in China, a bandit-intellectual living underground, turning up mysteriously to lead first one riot and then another. No one in the country was more hated and perhaps feared by the men in power, a fear manifested in the editorials that had begun to appear in the *People's Daily* warning against the dangers of "criminals" and "'Soviet agents" who were attempting to seduce the young with ideas of rebellion and anarchy.

Charlie sat rigidly, conscious that his hands were wet with sweat. It didn't really matter whether Anne had made contact with the man or not. The fact that she was charged with doing so was enough. Nor, after all his years in China, did Rudd believe that the Chinese simply invented charges. There was usually an element of truth in the "facts." It was the way the facts were put together and the associations made that left something to be desired from the Western legal point of view.

The interrogator proceeded methodically. "She first established contact with him at a secret meeting in the southern suburbs of Peking on the night of March 24. She left from your house and returned here. She was escorted by another counterrevolutionary leader, the woman Li Yifang, who was arrested shortly after that meeting."

Charlie sank weakly against the back of the sofa, unable to respond. The evidence was overwhelming, damning.

"The other people at the meeting that night were leaders of the illegal strike at Tianbei." The flat voice went on pitilessly. "They also were arrested shortly after that meeting, but they are responsible for fomenting the wave of strikes that have devastated the country since then."

Charlie was now truly terrified, more so than he'd ever been, but his mind hadn't stopped working. He was aware that the last statement had been a perfect example of the sophistic way the Chinese tied things together. Obviously, the nationwide wave of strikes arose from something more serious than the "fomenting" of trouble by a few leaders in a closed-off foreign-trade zone in Shandong Province. Fortunately, they couldn't read his mind.

"Was it Anne Campbell's idea to go to Kaifeng or was it yours?"

The suddenness of the question caught him off guard. "Both of us," his answer tumbled out. "We both were interested in going to the archeological site there."

"But Anne Campbell, did she express interest in going there for any other reason?"

"I don't know," Charlie whispered hoarsely. Why was he protecting her? Of course she'd asked him to go.

"And you made the request to the Minister of Culture?"

Charlie knew he must pull himself together. He must not let his emotions determine his answers. Obviously they knew everything.

"Yes, I did. The Minister of Culture is an old friend of mine and is aware of my long interest in Chinese art and archeology." He gestured authoritatively about the room. His statement was written down.

"It would have been impossible for Anne Campbell to go to Henan Province without your assistance." It was rhetorical, declarative, but it seemed best to assume that for every contribution from the interrogator, one was expected from him. He paused thoughtfully.

"I really don't know about that. She's a correspondent for a very powerful and influential newspaper. I'm sure she must have access to many people and places. I have no way of judging that. I'd had an invitation from *Modern China* for many months to write an article on the newly opened archaeological sites. She was interested in seeing them also and writing about them for her paper."

The interrogator glanced for the first time at the note taker, but nothing was said. He returned to his questioning.

"Why did you decide to go at this particular time?"

"I didn't want to go to Kaifeng until spring came. The winter climate there is very hard on my arthritis." Flip as it sounded, even to him, it was true.

There was only the scratching of the pen in the quiet room.

"We have incontrovertible evidence that Anne Campbell was in regular contact with various people in the underground. It is no accident that she went to Henan at the time she did."

246

A chill of fear engulfed Charlie. The best they could assume from his statement was that he was a gullible fool. More likely, they'd assume he was lying.

"The authorities have suspected from shortly after her arrival that Anne Campbell was a spy. She has systematically made contact with counterrevolutionary leaders at critical moments in their plan to undermine the stability of China and overthrow the government. However, there is now definite proof."

In the deathly stillness of his beautiful living room, Charlie could hear the gentle rustle of the plum tree branches just outside the slightly opened window. He was their prisoner. They were simply informing him of their right to do whatever they wanted with him. His carefully constructed life, judiciously aloof from the pendulum swings of Chinese political upheaval, would be torn apart, and he would join the heaps of victims of those struggles. His "treachery" would be used for whatever someone could manage to make out of it, and he would then be discarded into "the dust bin of history," as the Chinese loved to put it.

"She had in her possession in the Kaifeng hotel where you both were staying a secret Sino-American military document stolen in Washington by Russian spies. We now know without a doubt that she's part of a KGB network."

The whispering of the leaves outside the window was amplified grotesquely by the contrasting hush of the room. Charlie was whipped, crushed. He crumpled visibly. Even though Anne had deceived him, he couldn't believe for a minute that this was why she'd done it. He knew too much about the passion for investigative reporting, and though he'd known Anne for such a short time, he was sure he understood her.

Anne Campbell a KGB agent! If such an accusation had been made in a less ominous context, they would both have found it a great joke. But it didn't matter. This was not a court of law. If it had been officially decided that she was a KGB agent, she was, and there was nothing he or anyone else could do about it. The consequences for the man who had provided such a KGB agent with a cover . . . there were no limits to the punishment that could be meted out to him except for those that death would impose. He was finished. Everything in his slumped body, his sunken face, his frightened eyes displayed his helplessness, his inability to resist.

The stony-faced, black-suited men watched him almost clinically.

The note taker spoke. "You've lived in China for many years."

What did that mean, Charlie wondered? It could mean anything. "Yes," he responded softly. "It's my home."

If he had intuitively felt that the sacred word "home" would have a softening effect, he appeared to have been wrong. The sinister faces were, if anything, more unyielding.

"The Party and the Chinese people placed great trust in you, a foreigner, to allow you to become a Chinese citizen."

"I know." Rudd's voice was almost inaudible.

"You have violated that trust."

Charlie Rudd could no longer speak. His thin body was bent over pathetically, his head in his hands. Waves of nausea swept over him. A single memory drove everything else from his mind—one of his oldest friends, another foreigner who was also thought, during the Cultural Revolution, to have violated China's great trust. Five years in jail, in solitary confinement. After he was released, the regime in power explained it as a crime of the previous regime. That was the usual arrangement, perfected over centuries. A public apology, political "rehabilitation," but the man himself . . . One has only a single life, a single body, and lives and bodies once broken are broken. He now moved with the fragile steps of the very old and said yes to everything. Charlie's hands were wet with his own tears, tears for his friend and himself.

"You have endangered state security," the voice intoned. Charlie didn't raise his head. It was coming, it was all coming down. There could be no worse charge than that of endangering state security.

"You have made a very great error in protecting this spy." From out of the fog of terror, the words "very great error" emerged with stunning clarity. Was it possible that he was being charged with an "error," not a crime or a counterrevolutionary act? There was a vast difference. He knew, now, that the most important thing, his only chance, was confession. Whether you were guilty or not, you didn't have a chance unless you confessed. But he must be careful, careful not to confess to more than he'd been accused of.

"Yes, yes," he blurted out. "I did. I made a very grave error. I was very foolish not to know about this woman's activities while she was under my protection and in my house. It was an error, a very grave error." Shaking with fear, he was still able to muster sufficient self-control to repeat the term they'd used. He must admit to it— and he had to be sure they'd meant what they'd said.

248

When he glanced up hopefully, both of the black-suited men looked as menacing as before. There was nothing to indicate that they were pleased with his performance.

"Did Anne Campbell talk to you about any of the meetings she went to, any of the people she met?"

"No, no she didn't," Charlie muttered. Maybe he'd been wrong. Maybe grave error didn't mean what he'd hoped it meant.

"Think again. Are you absolutely sure? Didn't she tell you anything about what she'd seen when you picked her up at the Kaifeng police headquarters?"

The tall man's voice sounded angry. Was he impatient with the lack of cooperation?

The words poured out of Charlie's mouth. "Yes, yes, that time yes. I'm sorry. I was confused. Yes, she told me what the battle looked like. She told me what the police asked her."

The note taker was writing busily again. The tall man seemed to have become taller. His presence filled the room, blotted everything else from sight. He waited. It wasn't necessary for him to instruct Charlie about what to do. Charlie stuttered out everything he could remember. There wasn't much. Anne had told him very little. He culled his memory desperately. There was the train trip.

"She got off at Xinxiang. She listened to the conversations of the soldiers in the station. She learned why they were being sent to Zhengzhou."

The two security men exchanged a glance. "A good spy," the note taker said. Charlie nodded. There was a heavy silence in the room while the two men gave him time. Charlie shook his head. "There's nothing else. There's really nothing else." They did not look pleased.

Finally, the tall interrogator spoke. "It would be advisable for you to think about all this for a while. You'll probably be able to remember a few more details. Meanwhile, you'll want to write out your self-criticism." Charlie nodded numbly. Write out his self-criticism. The forced confession. It must be done, and with great care, for his method of stating what these men now knew would determine his sentence.

The two men looked at each other. The interrogator nodded. His cohort folded up his notebook. The interrogation was over, their mission satisfactorily accomplished. Charlie Rudd would live out his life in Peking a docile and obedient aging man. There would never be a problem with him again.

When Lao Li had closed the door softly behind them, Charlie walked slowly over to the low teak sideboard that was his liquor cabinet. He took out a glass and a bottle of Scotch, poured the glass full, and set the bottle next to it on the coffee table. It was over. Done. Finished. His beautiful home was now his prison, into which he would never again bring guests from the outside world. A KGB agent . . . There was no doubt that Anne was in acute danger. God knows how they would handle this, but that it would be terrible, he had no doubt. And there was nothing he could do—even a hand-delivered note of warning would be discovered.

He drank to the bottom of the glass and poured out more. What was that statement of E. M. Forster's he'd liked to quote as a young man, the one that had represented to him then the consummate spirit of independence and personal loyalty, his own contempt for archaic nationalism? Something like, "If I have to choose between betraying my friend and betraying my country, I pray for the strength to betray my country."

Anne and Peter rushed across the lobby into each other's arms, quite oblivious to the curious glances of tourists and businessmen, the stares of disapproving and fascinated Chinese.

"You crazy darling," Peter whispered as he held her tight. "It's been awful without you."

Though they went to the Blue Door out of some vague nostalgia and Peter's enthusiasm for the carp, they were hardly aware of either their surroundings or the food. Peter served absentmindedly as Anne spun out her tale, or at least part of it. The Zhengzhou railway station, the peasants' meeting, the battle in Kaifeng, the night at the police station. But not the document.

She was incredible. If only all that energy and intelligence could be channeled into something more constructive. "God! It was just as dangerous as I feared. You're lucky you're here to tell the tale."

"There's bound to be some luck involved when you get out of a situation like that unscathed. But maybe it was what you told me in our first conversation. The Chinese are civilized. Wasn't that the word? A slap on the wrist and out you go." Her sarcastic tone was unmistakable.

"You've changed the context a bit. I wasn't referring to violent mobs and provincial police chiefs." Why did she always have to have the last word? And just when he was feeling so glad to see her. Oh, the hell with it, he *was* glad to see her, and he'd been dying to share the Washington trip with her, though of course he couldn't tell her everything.

"I met Zolti in Washington."

"You're kidding! He doesn't even hold press conferences. No one meets Zolti. Where?"

"At La Pyramide. His wife, too. Looks just the way you'd expect. The ice princess."

"Oh, that's wonderful. What a scoop! The most mysterious woman in Washington. The American ambassador to China—accompanied of course by his invaluable aide—conducts high-policy talks with the NSC adviser in the very newest, most fashionable French restaurant in the Western Hemisphere. Really, that's almost as good a story as a Henan riot."

"It wasn't much of a high-policy talk." Had he said too much? Surely she'd realize that it was hardly possible for Carpenter and Zolti to meet without saying at least something significant, especially at a time like this. So he described the decor of the restaurant, the way Haggard, Zolti, and Mrs. Zolti looked, and the specifics of the dinner, through all five courses. He was the charming and amusing Peter Matthewson who had captured her from the beginning. It was she who was stroking his hand.

"Wouldn't you like to put your adventure to some use?" he then asked quietly.

"Presumably I am, if I can just manage to get someone to print it."

"No, I mean something more concrete than that. After you called me today, I told Carpenter you were here. He knew you were in Henan. He wants to talk to you, tonight if it's all right."

They looked at one another steadily, not unaffectionately but with a kind of resigned appraisal. It was what it was. They were who they were.

Anne sighed. Why was it that there seemed to be no other way for reporters to get out hot political stories except by being utilized

251

in the interests of one faction or another in some bureaucratic struggle. Even Watergate, that glorious monument to journalistic honor. Deep Throat had not, after all, been a deus ex machina. Of course, there were differences in factions. Even a few moral differences. There had been then; no doubt there were this time. But how did she know what kind of role Carpenter was playing?

"Damn it, Peter, why should I do that? How do I know what your darling ambassador is going to do with the information I give him? We're talking about the man who killed my Tianbei strike story, the very one who had you suggest that I lay off that kind of thing. Now he wants what officials always want from reporters, intelligence their own networks couldn't get, and you, my dear lover, are this man's messenger. What in the world am I to do?"

Peter's voice was grave and—what else?—yes, sincere. Whatever else you might fault Peter Matthewson for, you couldn't say he wasn't a first-rate diplomat.

"I'll give you two very important reasons why you should talk to him. The first is he's fighting the Washington hawks in a very critical struggle. That, you just have to take my word for, like I've taken your word a few times. The second reason has to do with a matter that you, not I, brought up the night of our first dinner here."

Anne looked at him questioningly.

"Do you remember giving a little speech about the fact that there were forces here that American policymakers either didn't know about or weren't analyzing correctly? Remember, when you told me about Zhang Zhaolin?"

"I remember." So that's what this was all about. Might not even be a bad idea, but damn it, let the ambassador do his own investigating. Why should she be doing favors for him? She'd already gotten herself far deeper into the world of high political intrigue than she wanted.

She shook her head. "I don't care to, Peter."

"How can you refuse to talk to Carpenter when he's doing just what you said we should be doing, looking at the other policy options? And you're the one with the information. The *only* one, Anne. It's really you or nobody." If she hadn't known Peter as well as she did, Anne realized, she would have been a little overwhelmed by him. The future ambassador, an embryonic persona.

"Don't try to appeal to my sense of heroism, Peter. Everybody's been doing that. I'm pretty well immunized by now."

252

Peter was holding both her hands in his and looking at her gravely. "I'm not really very interested in your sense of heroism. There's something else I'd like to appeal to, though."

"What's that?

"Whatever it is that we have together. All that garbage I threw at you the day before you left—I've thought a lot about it while you were gone. I was just wrong, and you were right, when you said we'd meant what we said to each other in bed. Anyway, I meant it. I love you, Anne. It's as simple as that. Can't you trust me?"

Trust him. What was he saying? Yet she knew, at that moment at least, that he was being completely honest. He did love her. It was impossible to look into his eyes and not believe that. And after all, no one was going to force her to say more to the ambassador than she wanted to say.

She sighed, but not without a hint of irony. "You're very persuasive. I hope it's not just your professional touch." She squeezed his hands affectionately. A relieved smile transformed Peter's serious face.

When the aproned host looked discreetly into the room, he saw the dinner guests entwined in a lingering embrace. Strange people, these Americans. They seemed to have no sense of propriety. Love-making had its place, of course. But seated at a dinner table covered with half-eaten culinary masterpieces . . . It really was offensive, but he would bring the soup in anyway. One could only teach the barbarians how to behave by setting a proper example.

It was only eight o'clock when they arrived at the embassy. Peter rapped on the door of Carpenter's outer office and a deep voice responded immediately, "Come in." They entered to find the ambassador on his way to greet them. Dressed informally—burgundy sweater, gray-flannel slacks—he was still entirely ambassadorial in appearance, larger than she'd expected—certainly six-three—broad-shouldered, his square-jawed face set off with a thick head of graying hair; an impressive, powerful presence. He took Anne's hand in a firm grip.

"I'm delighted to meet you. I appreciate your coming on such short notice." He waved them to a group of armchairs. "I understand from Peter that the three of us could form a Stanford alumni group in Peking if we were so inclined."

"So it seems." Oh dear, were they going to suffer through an hour of old-school preliminaries?

But the ambassador wasted no time. "I understand you've been on the spot recently at some very important events."

"Yes, that's right."

"You arrived right in the middle of the Zhengzhou railway strike."

Yes." She hesitated a moment, but there was no reason not to tell him at least the outlines of what happened to her. "I also saw one of the peasant demonstrations that are occurring in the area. And ended up in jail—well, something pretty close to jail—for my trouble."

"Well, that's very interesting. I didn't know anything about that. Did you?" he asked Peter.

"Not until about an hour ago."

"Obviously the American embassy has an interest in knowing if its citizens are arrested in the host country. Interesting that we hadn't been informed. Well," he said, smiling at Anne. "I'd say the *Washington Inquirer* is most fortunate to have such an enterprising and courageous correspondent here."

"Apparently they don't think so. They don't want my Henan stories. In effect, they've put me on ice. It looks as if I'm going to be either fired or transferred."

"I see." Carpenter stroked his chin thoughtfully. "Well, that's not really surprising, you know. I imagine something could be done about it, however."

So the negotiations were opening already. Unless she was very much mistaken, he was making an offer. "No, not surprising, but still disappointing." She really had to make her position clear to Carpenter. "I had the impression when my first story here was killed —the one on the Tianbei strike—that some of the pressure for killing it came from here at the embassy, to put the matter as politely as possible."

Carpenter smiled. "You're quite right. The Tianbei strike—at least at that time—was a different matter, from our point of view. There are very significant American business interests involved at Tianbei. We didn't feel we could afford to start a financial panic over something that might be an isolated, one-shot affair if we could

254

help it. But nationwide strikes, having nothing directly to do with foreign investments . . . That's another question. Now, perhaps we should have looked at Tianbei differently, as part of this general phenomenon, but we didn't have the information available to us that you now possess."

Not bad, Anne thought. An impressively cool performance so far.

"What I'd like to do," Carpenter continued, "is to review the situation—the domestic instability you've been encountering here and the opposition leaders you've either met or heard about."

He's a fast mover, Anne thought.

"I'll be quite frank with you, though I'm sure you must already have figured out my interests in this matter. It's absolutely critical that we—we, meaning this embassy, the State Department, the President—have as accurate an assessment as possible of what's happening in China. You're aware of our mutual commitments. I've seen some of your economic articles and they're very knowledgeable."

Flattering, too.

"You also know that we have mutual military commitments and that they're increasing all the time. You don't know the specifics and neither do most people, but it doesn't matter. Understanding the general direction is sufficient."

Not about to give me anything I don't already know, either, was what crossed her mind as she watched the ambassador closely.

"You know as well as I do that if the *Inquirer* is killing your stories, there are forces in Washington determining that. You can't get at those forces, and I'm not sure whether I can. But without information, we're nowhere. You have the information. Maybe together we can do something with it."

Anne proceeded systematically but carefully. She began with her encounter with Xiao Hong at the Tiananmen demonstration. Then the meeting with her at the restaurant and the reading of the rebel manifesto.

"What's their position on the Soviet Union?"

"They want to work out their problems. They used a phrase something like 'put the relationship on a proper footing.' "

"I see. And the United States?"

"They feel they're being used by us for strategic military reasons. They say they can't afford modernization and militarization."

"What about the border problem?"

255

"They're anxious to settle it."

Then there was the meeting with the Tianbei strike leaders and Wang Weilai.

"And how were your contacts made during this time?" Carpenter asked. He wasn't taking notes, but he had the concentrated look that Peter knew well. What he decided to remember, he would remember. Peter knew Carpenter had a certain contempt for the incessant scribbling of notes.

Anne smiled. "You know reporters don't like to disclose their sources."

Carpenter nodded. "It's not important. Just my own curiosity about how such connections are made. I read those LeCarré books too, you know."

Anne continued. "Charlie Rudd made arrangements to go to Henan to view the newly opened Shang sites, and I was able to go with him. Actually, I was also interested in seeing the archaeological discoveries." Anne rushed over this part of the story, uneasily. It was her only real deception, the only one that mattered. But Carpenter didn't stop her. Charlie Rudd's interest in archeological sites was of no interest to the ambassador.

"I'd like you to describe the scene in the Zhengzhou Railway Station as specifically as you can," he said instead.

"I really wasn't able to see much." But it seemed safe enough to tell everything she remembered.

"My, my." Carpenter got up and walked, head down, to the other side of the room and back. "It's certainly fortunate we have reporters who manage to go where they're forbidden. Please continue. This is all extremely interesting."

There was the wait of several days in the empty hotel on the outskirts of Kaifeng.

"That was when the border fighting broke out, wasn't it? Did you hear anything about it?"

"The hotel staff just informed us in a very cursory way. We listened to the radio, the BBC and the Voice of America, and got the routine reports. But when I finally made connections with the rebels and went to a meeting of the peasants who were planning the demonstration, I heard something very interesting. I have no way of judging it, but . . ."

Carpenter's expression was intent. "Let's not worry about evaluating things at this point. You're a trained observer. Just tell me what you saw and heard. We'll try to put it together later."

"The rebel leader Wang Weilai said that the border conflict was provoked by a faction in the Chinese government working with, as he put it, American henchmen. He said the border war was started in order to put down domestic struggles. Sounds rather neatly conspiratorial. But the peasants at the meeting seemed to accept it."

Carpenter had a strange smile on his face, a smile that to Peter at least communicated a great deal. So his hunch had been confirmed, and he hadn't been wrong about the importance of getting to the Vice-President.

"Interesting, don't you think?" Carpenter observed, directing his remark to Peter.

"Very. Looks as if you were right."

"Well, it's not what a court of law would regard as evidence, but it's probably as close as we're going to get at this point. Conspiratorial. It certainly sounds conspiratorial, but that *is* the way the real world works, you know. When you sense a political conspiracy, I think you usually have a pretty good chance of finding one."

Were they talking about the same thing? It certainly didn't seem that way. She'd been the one to use the word "conspiratorial," but clearly the ambassador was talking to Peter about a different conspiracy.

"Was there anything said about the now deposed chariman of the Chinese border-talks team?"

"Zhang Zhaolin. Only that Wang referred to him as 'our friend' and said that the talks had been going well under him and—oh, yes —that 'we,' whoever that means, had sent a message to the Soviets telling them there was widespread sentiment in China for resolving the border problem."

"Oh my." Carpenter's tone was grim. "*That* we were not on top of, and I'm afraid it may put us in a whole different ball game. I think we'd better talk for a minute about this rebel leader Wang whatever his name is."

"Wang Weilai," Anne said. "I don't really know anything about his background. He's obviously an intellectual, quite young, perhaps in his early thirties, very self-assured, handsome, charismatic. At the two meetings where I saw him, both the Tianbei strikers and the peasant leaders seemed to accept his authority without any

257

question. The woman rebel leader who was my original contact told me everybody in the country knows about him."

Things were going very well. Peter was enormously pleased. Amazingly, he'd gotten Anne on the team. He finally felt relaxed enough to interject a contribution of his own.

"He seems to be sort of a legendary figure. One of those romantic Robin Hood bandit heroes who appears from time to time in Chinese history. Quite a few editorials are being written against him these days. He's not mentioned by name, of course, but obviously everybody knows who's being talked about."

"As I recall from my brief study of Chinese history, it's not uncommon for the bandit hero of today to become the celestial emperor of tomorrow. Am I correct about that?" Carpenter asked.

"Correct."

His next remark surprised them both. "I think I'd better meet this young man," he said to Anne. "Do you think you could arrange it?"

There was a period of stunned silence. Anne's mind began to race. So this is what it's all about. Not just information, but actually making the connection. What a nightmare! An intermediary. Not an unprecedented role for a journalist, not in U.S.-China relations anyway. That she knew. One could even end up like Edgar Snow, honored by both sides. But it was a very particular role, not at all the same as reporting the news.

Maybe, though, it didn't have to seal you in for life. Why not just do it, and then be done with it? After all, she had no commitment either to Carpenter or Wang, and at least Carpenter seemed prepared to get her stories published in exchange.

The ambassador had astutely kept quiet.

"I'll do it if I can. I can't guarantee anything, you understand that."

"Of course. That's all I expect. Now—"

"You said earlier you thought something could be done about my problems with the *Inquirer*," Anne interrupted. "Since you had sufficient influence to get my strike story killed, perhaps you could use the same influence to get my pieces published." She spoke firmly. She felt very sure of her ground now.

The ambassador was not the slightest bit surprised. "That's not as easy as you make it sound," he said. "It's far easier to kill news than it is to get it printed." He smiled. "I'm sure I'm not telling you anything you don't know. Let me think it over for a few minutes, but let's just go on as if I'd said yes."

Was he bluffing her into committing herself? Impossible. He must know that unless she had some equal commitment from him before she walked out the door tonight, the Wang Weilai contact would never be made. There seemed no reason then not to dump the big problem in the ambassador's lap. For him, it would no doubt be a choice bit of intelligence. For her, it was a burden she would just as soon place in official hands.

"There's something else, then, that you should probably know about." She looked uneasily at Peter. "Peter, I'm sorry. There's something I didn't tell you about. I just didn't feel I could."

The muscles of Peter's face tightened and his mouth became hard. Suddenly she wished she could discuss this with the ambassador alone.

Anne blurted out the information abruptly. "Wang Weilai handed me a document, a secret American document detailing military plans with China. It was titled *Consolidated Guidance—China 10.* It was classified 'Royal Security' and was apparently a copy from the desk of the Navy Chief of Staff."

"Oh my God," Carpenter murmured.

Peter was livid. "What were you doing, keeping something like that to yourself? You should have told me. You had a responsibility to tell me." He was speaking to Anne alone, his voice harsh and reproachful. It was as if he'd forgotten Carpenter was in the room.

"I have no responsibility—" Anne began, but the ambassador cut her off.

"Get yourself together, Peter," he said with obvious irritation. "This is no time for that sort of thing."

Carpenter had never had the privilege of having a Royal Security document addressed to him, but he was well aware of what they were. These were undoubtedly the secret military plans that Haggard had been sent to implement under the direct orders of the President.

He'd known there were two Washington tracks. You couldn't operate for long without understanding that elementary truth. Of course, the big question, the question that nobody really seemed to know the answer to was: Which track was the President on, State's or Zolti's? Probably neither. He prided himself on his pragmatism.

Clearly, he had absolute faith in Zolti, but there was also the Vice-President. The President didn't seem to like him, but he did listen to him. These were the same intangibles that Carpenter had been working with all along, but now, at least, some real information had fallen into his hands.

"That may be the most important part of your whole adventure," Carpenter said to Anne. "Naturally, I'd like to have the document as soon as possible."

"I don't have it. It was stolen from my suitcase in the hotel in Kaifeng while I was being held at the police station."

"I see," Carpenter said softly. Too softly. "So this isn't any imagined conspiracy. You're obviously being watched closely." He got up and paced the room, his anger and tension apparent in his long, deliberate steps.

"Did you read it carefully?"

"No," Anne replied, chagrined. How could she have let some absurd fear keep her from reading it? "Not the details, but I remember the table of contents quite accurately."

"Let's hear it."

Anne closed her eyes—it was very convenient to have a photographic memory—and rattled it off. She ended her recitation by saying, "Maybe I'm more naive than I should be, but I was quite stunned. Warhead transfer from South Korea to Haerbin. I assume that means nuclear warheads."

"Couldn't mean anything else. The details would have been interesting, but more to a military man than to me. This is all I really need to know." For now Carpenter knew a great deal. But what about the border incident? One couldn't be certain, but were Americans involved in that too? If they were, Haggard must be a key figure. There were still a lot of unanswered questions. Probably some of them could be answered better in Washington than here. Only one thing was utterly clear. Whatever forces were moving things, they were moving very fast.

Worse yet, Carpenter had heard nothing from Geoffrey Butler since he'd returned to Peking. Their discussion had certainly been reported to the President, so the lack of response was hardly reassuring. He'd give Butler an immediate scrambler-line call and see if he could find out where matters stood. However, the situation was already passing the point where one should be dealing with intermediaries, even good ones. He'd have to reach the President directly, but first he had to have some idea of where the President stood. In all the discussion about the arming of China, the one thing he thought had been declared off limits was nuclear weapons. And now nuclear warheads from South Korea might be on their way here at this very minute. No doubt he'd be the last to know. But was the President better informed than he? With that horrifying thought, he turned his attention back to Anne Campbell.

"I can't go into all the details with you at this point, but I want you to know that you've performed a great service in getting this information to me. If we have any luck and a little time on our side, we might be able to avert an enormous catastrophe. Meanwhile, I can't help but think that you personally are in quite a dangerous situation. Are you aware of that?"

"I've tried not to think too much about it," Anne replied soberly, "because I didn't see what I could do about it. But yes, I'm afraid I do understand the implications of having a secret military document removed from my suitcase."

"I'll put some of our intelligence people on that matter right away, but to tell you the truth, I'm not too optimistic. With the kind of business you got caught up in, there's going to be so much disinformation circulating that it might be hard to tell who's working for whom for a while. I think we should get you out of China. Don't worry about the *Inquirer*. As far as I'm concerned, young lady, we have a deal. I'll get the problem of your pieces straightened out one way or another to your satisfaction. But, in return, I do want you to do that one last thing for me before you leave."

"You really want me to try to put you in contact with Wang Weilai?"

"I do. It's a shot in the dark, but I think we have to try it. He's obviously a key figure in this whole mess. I've been saying for years that we should think about dealing with power shifts before they happen, not after. It seems history has given me the opportunity to practice what I preach."

"I'll try, of course. I don't know where Wang Weilai is, and I have no idea how much access my contacts now have."

"I understand that. However, you seem to be the only person who has even the remotest chance of reaching him. . . . And I want you to do something else, something you were obviously planning to do anyway."

"What's that?"

261

"Get your stories written up—all of them—Tianbei, the Zheng-zhou railway strike, the peasant demonstration, something about Wang Weilai. This is Wednesday night. Let's give it about thirty-six hours or so. By Friday morning, if you haven't heard that the *Inquirer* will take them, call Peter first for my instructions and then send them off to the *Times*. I have a friend there who I think will want to print them. But give it that long. I have a little business with Washington in the meantime."

The ambassador stood up. The meeting was over. "I'm very grateful to you for coming. I hope we can meet sometime in more leisurely circumstances and I can hear all the details we haven't gotten around to. But for now I've taken up enough of your time, and given you quite a load of work to do."

Anne smiled. He was a pleasant enough man. "You have indeed, and it's been made more complicated at this point because I've just been assigned a new secretary-interpreter who is unquestionably a spy."

Carpenter frowned. "So they've put a direct watch on you. That's not good. Yes, we'd better get you out of here in a hurry."

CHAPTER

18

Anne and Peter left the embassy in strangely high spirits. It wasn't as if either of them had many illusions about the limits of individual initiative in geopolitics. But there were those brief historical moments when cracks opened up, when the rare journalist or diplomat could rush right through, actually influence policy, put a small individual mark on the making of history. Maybe this was such a time.

They went down the steps hand in hand, exchanging conspiratorial smiles, and once inside the back seat of the embassy car, fell into each other's arms.

"Have you forgiven me for yelling at you in there? I was an ass. I was stunned that you'd kept anything like that from me."

"Of course you were mad. What an embarrassing spot I put you in! I'm really sorry. Let's never mention it again."

"We're going home to the Peking Hotel?" Peter murmured in her ear. It wasn't a question so much as a confirmation.

"Of course," she replied affectionately. It all seemed like some sort of floating dream now. Anything could happen. Her stories would be published and everyone would know the truth. Ambassador Carpenter and Wang Weilai would meet, work out a principled agreement, and together open the door for a triangular détente among the superpowers. Charlie Rudd would forgive her, knowing she'd done the right thing. She might marry Peter, or at least live happily with him for a long time. Nothing seemed beyond possibil-

263

ity. "Now that Mrs. Tan is gone, we won't even have to go through that nonsense of signing you in." She said it with a brightness, almost a delight, she hadn't realized she still possessed. She was fine, and it would all work out.

Peter drew his face away from hers and let his hands fall to her shoulders. "And what are we going to do about your going away?" he asked, his voice suddenly filled with emotion. "How can you leave Peking when it's perfectly obvious I can't live without you?"

She felt a great glow of affection for him. "You know I have to leave."

"I know you have to leave. When Tom Carpenter says you're in a dangerous situation, that you should leave as soon as possible, I don't want you to stay. But how am I going to find you again? I want to be with you—not just going to bed with you for a few hours in a hotel room, but going to bed with you every night and getting up with you in the morning. I think we might like living together, Anne. I'd even like . . ." His hands slid from around her shoulders to the back of her neck.

"What?" she smiled.

"I'd even like to be married to you, though this is an absurd moment to suggest it. In my modest opinion, this has all turned out to be something pretty wonderful. I'd like to hold on to it." The gentle but insistent pressure of his hands on the back of Anne's neck brought them together in a deliciously drawn-out kiss.

"Yes, let's hold on to it," she murmured, her eyes half closed. "After all, there are probably a lot of possibilities."

"Like? . . . "

"Like the *Inquirer* sees the errors of its ways. Of course, they're too embarrassed to give me back my Peking job, but they move me upstairs to a wonderful, newly created position, number-one roving Asia correspondent. I can wander around wherever I want, fly in to see you every few days, and establish a villa in some exotic spot where we can hide away for weeks at a time."

"Hm, sounds all right, but that's a lot of flying. Why don't you just stay in your villa? I'll come for very long weekends that start on Wednesday. I hope it's overlooking the water somewhere."

"Yes, definitely overlooking the water. Well, yes, I could stay in the villa and write my book."

"Your book?"

"Yes, of course. Everybody who goes to China writes a book.

264

About my China adventure. Don't you think I could get a monster advance?"

"Absolutely. Your adventure is incomparably more interesting than anyone else's."

"And I'll be the only foreigner the new leader of China trusts enough to give interviews to."

"Definitely. That in itself will get you a million." Peter laughed as he put his arm around her shoulders. "Okay, now it's my turn. I've got an even better scenario. I don't want to have you off in that villa, no matter how nice it is. Too far away. Besides, you're forgetting about all the heavy politics. See how you like this one. Carpenter gets the policy back on line. A major U.S. disaster is averted for once, thanks partly to your articles which get sent off to the *Times* on Friday. The *Times* offers you their post here. You can thumb your nose at those obsequious slobs at the *Inquirer* and return on a white horse—famous, virtuous, and out of danger. And then we'll find an old Peking house with a courtyard, hire the cook from the Blue Door, and spend our evenings at home behind our wall making love."

"That's wonderful! Your script wins." Anne leaned her head contentedly on his shoulder. "Where did this crazy, lovely Peter Matthewson come from? I thought you were one of those careful, proper, foreign-service types moving slowly but surely up the ladder to your own ambassadorship."

"I am. That's one side of me. The other side is my wildly romantic personality—firmly repressed but still extant. All it needed was the right stimulus to burst into furious bloom."

"Maybe it's good I'm leaving for a while. You might wake up in the morning and find you didn't approve of being taken over by this wildly romantic personality."

"Every morning you were away on that crazy trip I woke up depressed, knowing I was going to have to make it through another day without you. No, the testing's been done. Why do you think I'm making all these desperate proposals?"

"I love your desperate proposals, especially the one about the old Peking house with the courtyard." Suddenly her voice became serious. "I'll try, my darling, to work things out so I'm not too far away. Maybe we'll have to settle for one of those overpriced Hongkong crackerbox apartments for a while—and a lot of commuting."

Neither spoke for the rest of the way. Everything had been said

265

that could be said. They understood each other and knew they'd made a kind of contract, though they didn't know how it was to be worked out. But it was enough. Fingers intertwined, thigh against thigh, lips on lips—it was enough. Everything was understood. Everything would work out for the best.

Anne's room in the Peking Hotel, her practical, prosaic bed was their own special private world. They made love as if one of them was about to depart on a long, long journey.

It was two o'clock when Peter left, uncoiling carefully so as to disturb Anne as little as possible. He ran his hand gently down the length of her smooth body and kissed her tangled hair.

"I love you. I'll see you Friday," he whispered in her ear.

She mumbled a sleepy response, but the sound of the door closing woke her up. She lay in the dark, enjoying the melting sensation in her limbs, savoring the half-conscious state between waking and sleep. For a few precious hours, time had been suspended, and the realities of stolen documents, bureaucratic struggles, military plots, riots, strikes, and demonstrations had been displaced by a fragile moment of pleasure.

Anne pulled herself awake. She had to finish writing the stories right now, before that fool of a new secretary arrived. She jumped out of bed, put on her robe, poured hot water into a cup of instant coffee, and put paper in her typewriter.

The work went rapidly. She'd already made a good start the previous afternoon, and the events of her Henan adventure were sharply etched in her mind. Anne knew she'd have to take a careful look at what she'd written later when she wasn't in such an over-stimulated state, but she felt quite sure that the words reflected the power of the reality.

It was close to eight in the morning when she ended the final story, the one on the riot in Kaifeng. Suddenly, she felt exhausted, overwhelmed by an intense sense of loss. Everyone was gone. The young rebel woman; Tan Yulan; Charlie Rudd—yes, particularly Charlie Rudd; and even . . . for some strange reason Peter came to mind, but that was impossible. She pushed the thought away. It must be because the very tenor of the life she'd established here had been torn to shreds. She was tired. That was it. She realized that if she so much as closed her eyes, she would fall into unconsciousness instantly, sitting here at her desk before her open typewriter. There were just a few more matters that must be taken care of, then she could sleep.

In the back of her mind, disturbing her, was her agreement to contact Wang Weilai for the ambassador. Had she overstepped herself in her desire to get her stories out? How would she even get in touch with him? It wasn't as if she had any choice in the matter. There was only one possibility. She rang the buzzer by the door, hoping the right room attendant would respond.

He was there within seconds, almost as if he'd been expecting her summons.

"You knew I was in Henan," Anne began tentatively.

"Yes." He was noncommittal.

"I saw a lot. My train arrived in Zhengzhou right in the middle of the railway workers' strike." His face now expressed an undisguised interest in what she was saying. "Your comrades made contact with me in Kaifeng and took me to a meeting of peasants who were planning a demonstration, which I went to. It turned into a riot with soldiers fighting peasants."

His voice was still quiet, but very emotional. "Is it true what we've heard, that some of the soldiers refused to fire on the people?"

"Yes, I think so. At least some of them anyway."

"You've helped us a great—" he began in that earnest "foreign friend" tone she was now accustomed to.

She waved impatiently. "Not yet. Don't thank me too soon. My newspaper won't print the stories and they may also fire me."

The young man was plainly shocked. Anne went on hastily before he could speak. She didn't want any more gratuitous homilies about her assistance or heroism. She knew now that Chinese young people like him simply couldn't understand the realities of her world and job.

"I have to ask you to do something that might turn out to be important, though—more important than my stories, which I promise you I'll get printed one way or another." He nodded.

"I was invited to see the American ambassador here last night. I told him what I'd seen in Henan. He's an intelligent man. He understands that something important is happening in China. He wants to meet Wang Weilai."

There was no change of expression in the young man's unsmiling

267

face, but he was scrutinizing Anne intently, as if he could read in her eyes the real significance of this remarkable message. She knew what he must be thinking: Is this a trap? What's the real reason behind it? Have we been wrong? Is this woman an American spy? For just a moment she wondered herself. There was little she could say to reassure him, but she tried.

"I know you want to continue the relationship with the United States if it can be worked out on a basis that's acceptable to your movement. Xiao Hong said that, and so did Wang Weilai. How can you do that if you don't talk to a representative of the United States? It's really a rare opportunity, an American ambassador who actually takes the initiative in asking to meet with a rebel leader. History may not give you another chance like this."

The young attendant put the empty cups on a tray, replaced the thermos with a fresh one. He didn't speak until he was almost at the door.

"We'll see if it can be arranged," he said quietly. It could mean anything.

Then, as he opened the door, Anne remembered something. "Oh, and thank you for watering my plants while I was away."

"You're welcome. I'm glad to be of service," he said cheerfully. That seemed to be his true response.

He closed the door and Anne picked up the phone. She gave the operator the number of the Chinese Foreign Ministry, the old number she'd used for Tan Yulan. "This is Anne Campbell at the Peking Hotel," she said to the female voice at the other end of the line. "I'd like to leave a message for a man named Lin Yaoping who's just been assigned to me as a secretary-interpreter." There was no response, so she continued. "He met me at the airport yesterday, so he knows I've just returned from a very tiring trip. I'm not feeling well. I'm going to spend the day sleeping. Please tell him I won't need his help today."

"I will inform him," the voice responded.

Anne hung up with a feeling of great relief. Everything was done that needed to be done. She stumbled the few feet from her desk to the bed and, still wearing her robe, fell onto it. Pulling the blankets up around her ears, she instantly fell deeply asleep.

◆

268

After her day of sleep, Anne proceeded carefully to repair her wounded nervous system. A very long, very hot bath with lots of bubbles that cascaded onto the bathroom floor; for her very quiet supper, that best of tonics, a large bowl of noodle soup, in her very quiet room. For her psyche, she had something else in mind—an evening at the International Club.

The crowd crushed together elbow to elbow. There was the clinking of glasses; the familiar roar of English, French, and Japanese; and that familiar feeling, at least for this moment, of being the old Anne Campbell, a first-rate journalist among her peers. She easily shrugged off a few curious questions about where she'd gone. There was too much excitement about the border war, the rumors of strikes and riots, for anyone to concentrate long on her. Soon she found herself pleasantly alone with Michael Crimmins. His florid face maintained its customary expression of amused cynicism.

"Well, love," he said. "My guess is you've really gotten around since I saw you last." He held up his hands, palms out, in mock defense. "No, don't tell me. I won't intrude on your professional secrets, but we do still have a bit of business to take care of, don't we? I hate to be so ungentlemanly, but I'm afraid you owe me fifty bucks. There's no hurry, of course. I just didn't want you to forget."

She *had* forgotten. "God, I'm glad you reminded me, Michael. You were right, of course. You always are, and more important, I never really had a chance to thank you for taking that story to Tokyo for me. It seemed very important at the time. I still think it was, in fact, but the *Inquirer*, as you've noticed, disagreed, and continues to do so about everything I propose. Most vehemently, I'm afraid. Why don't I give you a check right now."

Michael, who was seldom embarrassed by anything, looked embarrassed. "I was only kidding you. In typical fashion, I just wanted to remind you about the prescience of my prediction. But I can see you've gone right ahead and done more of the same. Are you leaving soon?"

Anne, her arm squeezed close to her body by the press of the crowd, was scribbling out a check on top of her bag. She looked up startled. "What brought that question to mind?"

"There aren't that many possibilities, are there? If you're filing hot stories and your paper won't print them, it would seem to be only a matter of time before they recall you, or the Chinese expel you, or both."

269

"Not bad, Michael. You're a pretty good investigator yourself," Anne responded, handing him the check. "What do you think one should do under such circumstances, all hypothetical, of course?"

"Write everything up. Keep the facts filed away in your head in case the stories are confiscated, and sell them to somebody else, because now they really matter."

"Indeed! And what's made you come to that conclusion all of a sudden?" It was relaxing to fall into Michael's style of friendly sarcasm.

"I've spent the better part of my life out here, you know. I've been around for a lot of revolutions, big and small, coups, power shifts, changes of the guard—in Vietnam, Laos, Cambodia, Indonesia, the Philippines, Pakistan, India, you name it. By now, I have a sixth sense about when the turn is coming. It's not really a matter of strikes and demonstrations. Those are just the facts of life. It's how they begin to come together—the cumulative effect of a lot of separate and dispersed actions."

"And that's what's happening here?" Anne was no longer sarcastic.

"I think so. I really do think so." It was unusual for Michael to sound anything but bored. That in itself was significant. For many years Michael Crimmins had predicted shifts in Asian politics well in advance of anyone else, and usually with remarkable accuracy.

"You're right, Michael—about the *Inquirer*, I mean. I don't think they're going to print any of my stuff."

Michael smiled sardonically. "Of course not. Too close to Washington power. I told you that before. Maybe you should come and work for us for a while. We English really have only one serious stake in this whole China thing—oh, some business interests naturally, like everyone else—but strategically, only Hongkong. Everyone's been pretty relaxed about that for the last few years. The Chinese have made it quite clear that they like having us there with our capitalist methods and our police force." He shrugged. "Naturally, a little xenophobic nationalism could alter all that, but it hasn't happened yet. There are plenty of British papers that would snap up your stories in no time."

"I'm not to that point yet." Anne's voice was thoughtful. "But I might be sooner than I'd like." She couldn't help wondering: Could the ambassador really be trusted? After all, maybe she couldn't get through to Wang Weilai, or maybe he would simply refuse to see the ambassador. Then what? Perhaps Carpenter would decide that if she couldn't come through with her part of the deal, he had no obligation to fulfill his. But she wouldn't think about it. Not anymore. Not here. Not tonight.

The crowd swirled past Michael and her, this way and that, to the bar for drinks, to distant groups of friends, to other more interesting conversations. Everyone who passed had a few words to say to Anne. Where had she been? What was happening? How big was it? Were the reports accurate? She gave Michael a look of mock desperation and he picked it up immediately.

"Why don't we find a quieter corner for our next drink," he said. "We'll evaluate the progress of the new revolution and figure out who to sell your stories to. And now that I've just made a quick fifty, we might as well make an evening of it. I'll show you the latest Peking night spots."

271

CHAPTER

19

It was close to one in the morning when Anne got back to the hotel. It had been a lovely, capricious evening of bar and restaurant hopping. As Anne walked down the long corridor to her room, she was humming happily and just a little drunkenly. It was so empty and quiet, now that the rooms in this area were all being repainted. Lucky she'd convinced the management to hold off on hers until she left Peking.

She turned the key in the lock, opened the door, and reached automatically for the wall switch to turn on the overhead light. She clicked it back and forth a few times, but nothing happened—must be broken. A trace of annoyance disturbed her mood. Some ridiculous thing was always breaking down. The room was very dark. Anne left the door ajar so the hall light would shine in while she walked to the standing lamp by the side of the sofa.

How cold the room was! Someone must have left the windows open, for the drawn curtains were blowing into the room. Suddenly, the door to the hall closed and she was standing in darkness. Anne froze. Every nerve in her body was taut. The hazy euphoria of an evening of drinking vanished in a surge of adrenaline.

A dim light snapped on, the small lamp by the side of her bed, and now she could see them, the two men on either side of the open window—short, wiry, ugly in their dark Western suits and black shirts. They were holding pieces of braided rope in their hands. Anne whirled quickly. A third man, huskier than the others, his face and neck fat, was standing just inside the door holding a blackjack in his thick hand.

A triangle of killers . . . With an intuitive flash, Anne understood it immediately. They were going to throw her out the window. Their steps very slow and calculated, they began to slide toward her, proceeding with the terrifying deliberateness of slow-motion film. Their movements seemed routine, unhurried, almost choreographed.

In the seconds in which she was assessing the situation, Anne's heart pounded furiously, but her mind was lucidly clear. The bell rope in the alcove. She must reach it. She must manage to hold them off until help came. All of her athletic instincts surfaced. She took a sudden two-step feint toward the bathroom, and as all three men lunged toward her, bounded in the opposite direction throwing herself through the alcove curtains. The rope . . . The rope . . . It was there against the wall. She grabbed the end of it with both hands and pushed the button with all the force she had.

Instantly, the three men crashed through the curtains and were on top of her. Powerful hands twisted her arms fiercely and pulled her off the rope. Her legs were grabbed from behind and she was on the floor, being dragged back into the room, her face rammed into the carpet. She understood only one thing. She must grab something, make it hard for them to move her. With all her strength, she twisted violently from side to side. The hand gripping her right arm loosened slightly and she reached desperately for the bottom of the alcove curtain.

Her legs were being pulled out of their sockets, but she wasn't moving, she wasn't moving. There was a sudden sharp blow on her wrist. She felt her fingers loosening. Then suddenly, the curtain crumpled to the floor and they were all submerged in the folds. Anne flipped over on her side, her arms free. Miraculously, she was on top of one of the men, his fat loathsome face under hers. With wild but deliberate fury, Anne pushed her thumb into his eye socket. There was a howl of pain.

But the other two had her again, her arms forced behind her back, her ankles locked in an iron grip. She pushed her shoulders against the floor. They could only move her slowly, but she knew she was moving. She concentrated on loosening her muscles and letting herself go as limp as possible. Out of one eye, she watched the bottom of the familiar furniture sliding by. Her bed was approach-

273

ing. With a flailing motion, using every ounce of strength she had, she wrenched an arm free and grabbed the metal leg of the bed. She crooked her elbow around the bed leg and thrashed her whole body furiously. In the midst of all the grabbing, hitting, pulling, she somehow realized that although her opponents were strong and muscular, she was taller than any of them and certainly outweighed the two thin ones. Why didn't they just kill her? No, they were determined to drag her to the window.

She couldn't hold out much longer. Her arm was viciously wrenched loose and a screaming, sickening pain shot through it. It was limp, motionless, and she was firmly in their grip. Her arms—the one making her dizzy with pain—were pinioned behind her back. Two men were pushing her to her feet. She was screaming. She could hear her own voice. A hard hand was clapped over her mouth. They pushed and pulled. Anne felt the blow of a knee in her back. She fought to keep her feet on the floor, but she could feel herself being lifted up. Reserves of strength she didn't know she had surfaced and surfaced again. By the sheer resistance of her body, Anne made them struggle for every inch of ground.

The four interlocked bodies staggered like a drunken quartet. Anne was now conscious of the cool air from the window blowing in her face and knew she was fighting for her life. With one last, desperate surge of strength, she pulled them to the side. They swayed with her, but she couldn't hold them there. She felt the grip of hands around her ankles again and knew she was being lifted up, every limb now firmly locked in a viselike hold, and a heavy hand covering her whole face. She couldn't open her mouth, couldn't see, couldn't breathe, but she could sense the nearness of the window.

The three assassins had been surprised. They'd expected this to be a simple job—an unarmed woman caught off guard in a sixth-floor room in the middle of the night. Just pick her up and drop her out the window. They'd done it dozens of times, with much tougher customers than this one. No shooting, no injuries were the instructions. It had to look natural enough to pass an autopsy. No problem there, either. They were professionals. But this one! Who would have expected her to fight like a tiger? Crazy, she didn't have a chance. And so big! No one had prepared them for that. An American giant, some kind of an athlete. It hadn't gone well at all. Too much noise. There were probably injuries. The room was torn to pieces. It wasn't supposed to look like that. But they had her now. Just another couple of inches.

A sudden screech split the air. It was terrifying, primeval, a bloodcurdling cry of attack. Anne hit the ground with a shock, and scrambled to a sitting position, dazed, paralyzed with fear, but she hadn't been dropped to the sidewalk below. The three killers were facing the door. Three white-jacketed hotel attendants confronted them. There were two men, one her familiar messenger, and a woman pointing a gun. One of the men held an iron club menacingly in both hands and was moving slowly toward them. The other twirled a strange device above his head, two sticks connected by a chain. Nunchaku sticks. Anne had never seen the weapon, but a Hongkong friend had once described one to her. A mad, medieval instrument, he'd said, weird, but absolutely deadly. Anne scrambled to the darkness of the corner of the room, ducking down behind the end of the sofa.

For a split second all the actors were poised, suspended in time and space, ready to spring. The hand of one of the gangsters slid almost imperceptibly down his side, but it was already too late for guns. In a great explosive leap, the young man whirling the nunchaku sticks above his head was across the room, the killer just as quickly diving for his attacker's knees. But the gyrating sticks, expertly spinning lower, struck the head in mid-descent. There was the chilling thud of smashing skull, and as Anne watched in horror, the chain was adeptly wrapped around the neck, the two sticks jerked swiftly outward, and it was over, the body on the floor with the head slightly askew, the neck broken.

The room was a wild, spinning scene, the mad pirouetting of a Peking opera's frenzied climax. In the moment that his companion went down in a broken heap, the stocky killer holding the blackjack lunged at the woman. He was fast, an acrobat, flying through the air; but she was faster, backing up nimbly, giving space for her partner with the iron bar to wield his weapon. The bar came down unhesitatingly, irrevocably. The blackjack fell to the floor, released by the now uncontrolled hand. The limbs folded. The black-suited body sprawled in the middle of the room.

The third gangster rushed toward the bathroom, ducking beneath the sweep of weapons. As he dashed past her shelter behind the sofa, Anne from her sitting position swung her legs in front of the running figure. Off balance and arms flailing, the assassin crashed into the wall, and the two men with their fearful weapons were upon him. Anne turned away from the massacre. A thud of iron on bone, a ghastly howl, and the whole thing was over, the room was still. Three crumpled bodies lay on the floor soaking the carpet with blood.

Anne and the three attendants looked at each other, stunned. The young woman laid her gun carefully on the coffee table, went into the bathroom, and returned with a glass of water for Anne.

"Are you hurt?"

"Not very much, considering what they had in mind. I think my arm is broken."

The young man who had wielded the iron bar with such deadly efficiency knelt on the floor and gently pressed Anne's arm at the wrist, the elbow, the shoulder. "Yes, broken," was all he said.

"We must move quickly now," the woman said.

Anne was still frozen in the grip of the nightmare just past. Of course they must move quickly. But where? To do what? She leaned against the sofa. "If you hadn't gotten here when you did, I would have been splattered on that street out there by now," she murmured.

The man who had looked at her arm was still squatting near her. "That was our responsibility, to see that nothing happened to you, and we almost failed. Someone slipped up very seriously. These gangsters"—he gestured contemptuously toward the heap of bodies —"these filthy gangsters should never have been permitted to get in here. We'll have to find out later who was responsible for that." He stood up. "We have to get rid of the bodies and get you out of here. You must go to your embassy and arrange to leave China immediately."

"Leave immediately? But now it's all over." Anne felt stupefied. It couldn't possibly be real.

"It won't be long before whoever was trying to kill you will find out the attempt failed. Then there will be another attempt, and the next one will be much more carefully planned." He waved his hand again at the bodies. "These are professional killers. From their dress and methods, it's obvious they're from Hongkong, and there are more of them where these came from. I don't know who was trying to kill you, but this is not the way people carry out such things here, no matter how fierce the struggle."

276

Hongkong killers! Who wanted to kill her by using Hongkong assassins?

The three attendants were already at work, each one dragging a body toward the door.

Anne staggered to her feet. "Here, let me help you. Let me do something," she said. Her arm was throbbing with pain. When she stood up, she felt faint and nauseous.

"You can't do much with your arm like that," her messenger said. "But you could stand watch in the hall while we get rid of the bodies. Even though there's usually no one around at this hour, you never can tell."

The four of them stood next to the three lifeless bodies heaped on the floor. Anne stared in horror at the smashed remains of faces, now raw and ragged hunks of butchered meat.

"Don't look," the woman said sharply. She was briskly removing the pillowcases from the pillows on Anne's bed. She swiftly placed one over each of the mangled heads. Anne was suddenly sick to her stomach. She rushed into the bathroom and threw up in the toilet. She wanted nothing so much as to lie down on the cold bathroom floor and stay there forever. But the attendants were by the door, waiting patiently for her to pull herself together. She rinsed out her mouth, splashed her face with cold water. What was she doing! . . . When every second counted, she was allowing herself the luxury of falling apart. Embarrassed, she returned to the room.

"I'm sorry. I'm all right now. What do you want me to do?"

Her room attendant looked at her kindly. "Don't be sorry. Of course you're upset. They came very close to killing you. Do you think you'll be able to stand watch in the hall for us?"

"Of course. Of course. I'm over it now," Anne replied brusquely. "What are you going to do with the bodies?" You didn't just kill people and go on doing whatever you'd been doing before. "And you . . . What's going to happen to you?"

The three looked at each other, knowing, almost ironic looks.

"We're going to throw the bodies down the service elevator shaft. There's no reason for anyone ever to look there," the woman said.

The young man that Anne hadn't seen before tonight continued, "They won't be discovered for a week, until the bodies begin to smell."

"And where will you be by then?"

"Far away from the Peking Hotel," the woman said. "Our assignment here was to watch out for you, among other things. A week from now, we'll have other tasks to carry out."

To watch out for her! So Tan Yulan and her successor had been assigned to watch her for one reason and these three for another! How many different Chinese factions might be watching one's every move, and who knew what their political purposes might be. Her three rescuers and the ambassador were right: The sooner she got out of China the better.

The old-fashioned side lamps were burning dimly in the long hall. The woman snapped off the switch nearest them. The center area was suddenly dark, but the lights remained lit at either end of the corridor. The service elevator was in a back hallway off the end of the main corridor. It had been decided that if Anne saw anyone arriving by the passenger elevator at the opposite end of the hall, she should warn the three by switching on the lights outside her room. Then she was to delay whoever emerged from the elevator. It would take them five minutes at the most to dispose of the bodies, but they had to have that five minutes.

The silence in the hallway was almost palpable. The dim lights at either end cast a muted glow on the dark patterned carpet. In between, the darkness revealed only the cumbersome shape of a slow procession. Each of the three had hoisted one of the limp bodies over a shoulder. They were quiet in their cloth shoes, but the weight of a human body gave a plodding thud to their steps. For Anne, nothing existed but a consciousness of sound and the sight of the strange group all black on white—the white jackets of the attendants, the white pillowcases over the bloody heads, black suits, black pants, black hair blending into the darkness.

The group seemed to move with excruciating slowness. Anne felt as if she were pushing them forward with the strength of her own will. They were almost to the lighted area at the far end of the hall when suddenly that too was plunged into darkness. They'd reached the light switch and turned it off. She could barely make out the silhouettes of the lumpy moving shapes. They were so close to being safely out of sight.

Then with a sound magnified out of all proportion by the silence and her nervous concentration, Anne heard the passenger elevator bumping its way through the shaft. There was time, there was time . . . They were almost at the end of the hall, she was sure, but they still had to have a few more minutes. She clicked on the light outside

278

her room and ran to the passenger elevator at the opposite end of the hall, her mind spinning dizzily.

She stood in front of the closed elevator door listening to the sound coming closer. What could she say, what could she do that would delay someone for a few minutes? Anne drew a deep breath and straightened her shoulders. She glanced nervously toward the dark end of the hall. She could see nothing, no glimpses of white in the blackness. Had they disappeared into the side corridor or was she just unable to see them in the darkness?

The thumping came closer. The elevator had reached her floor. But as Anne stared at the closed doors, waiting for them to open, the sound continued, going downward, diminishing little by little, thumping steadily. Anne leaned against the wall beside the elevator door. Her hands were shaking. They'd made it.

She ran breathlessly down the long dark hallway. As she reached the doorway leading into the service corridor, Anne almost plunged into the arms of the woman and her messenger. "All right?" she whispered. They nodded and motioned in the direction of her room. The three of them hurried back together. Once the door was closed behind them, Anne looked around at the chaos. The alcove curtain was crumpled in a heap on the floor, her bed torn to pieces, the spread and blankets on the floor, pillows tossed across the room, straight chairs knocked over. On the pale green rug with the floral center—under the window, near the bathroom door, in the middle of the room—there were dark stains. The two attendants surveyed the room coolly, as if assessing the damage and determining what would be needed to get things back in shape.

The woman turned to Anne. "Our other comrade is getting a car to drive you to your embassy. Gather up what you need as quickly as possible. Can you get what you need in that shoulder bag? It would be better not to take a suitcase."

Anne moved automatically. She put together the stories she'd written, a few odds and ends from the bathroom. Thank God she had a few codeine pills left over from some long-forgotten dental work. She swallowed one, hoping it wasn't too old to blot out the overwhelming pain of her arm. She threw together some under-wear, her jewelry, a toothbrush—it was always necessary to have a toothbrush, for some absurd reason. That was all she could think of.

The two attendants were already at work, the woman on her hands and knees with an enamel basin full of soapy water and a stiff scrub brush, rubbing fiercely at the bloodstains on the rug, the man putting the furniture back in place, hanging the curtains, gathering up the bedclothes. Anne was wearing her tweed pants and a sweater, her uniform here. Quite suitable for making a quick getaway from Peking, she thought ironically, as she slipped off the red brocade jacket she'd been wearing all evening and put on her own familiar down jacket. The red jacket had been an accessory to her strange adventure here—appropriate that it be left behind. She could offer it to the young woman. But no, she'd probably be insulted at being given a foreigner's Chinese dress-up clothes. Better just to leave it.

"Ready?" the man asked.

"Ready."

The woman barely looked up from her scrubbing. But surely one must say something.

"Good-bye, and thank you for everything," Anne said awkwardly. The woman who had been so terse got up and, smiling warmly, shook Anne's hand formally but strongly. "Don't thank us. We thank you. You've risked a great deal to help us." To the very end, assumptions she couldn't respond to. Anne just smiled weakly and pressed the woman's hand.

It was the same with the man. Strange, she thought, as she followed him down the dark hallway to the side corridor and into the cavernous service elevator. This man had come in and out of her room several times a day for the entire time she'd been in Peking. He'd brought her messages and carried them back. He'd been responsible for knowing her every move, for protecting her safety, and, finally, for saving her life. Yet she didn't even know his name or his reasons for doing what he did. Where had he come from and where would he go now? It was too late for all those questions.

They rode down to the basement in silence, staring at each descending floor through the triangular pattern of the sliding iron doors. At the bottom of this shaft were three bloodied bodies, now smashed beyond all recognition. She wondered what the silent, sweet-faced young man beside her was thinking. It was impossible to tell.

Before she got into the waiting car, he too shook her hand formally. There was something very touching about his simple "Thank you." Then, at the last second, he added, "Tell your ambassador we're doing our best to reach Wang Weilai. He's not far from Peking, and a meeting may be possible. Tell him we understand

280

how important it is, and we hope for success." He and Anne stood for a few seconds, looking into one another's eyes, as if each would read the other's thoughts.

"Thank you," Anne said quietly. "And good luck." He nodded gravely. As the car drove off, she could just see his white-jacketed figure in the darkness, his arm raised in a gesture of farewell.

CHAPTER

20

It was three in the morning when Anne was ushered into the ambassador's office. He and Peter were seated on opposite sides of the huge desk, every inch of which was covered with papers and folders, coffee cups, and overflowing ashtrays. Both men were in their shirt-sleeves, Peter gray with fatigue, the ambassador rumpled and grim-looking. When they saw her, they both jumped up, their startled expressions telling her that she really looked as much of a wreck as she felt.

"What happened?"

"It seems someone's trying to get me killed." A brave attempt at her old style, but Anne's voice was shaking. Peter gently helped her to a chair.

"Are you hurt?"

"I'm pretty sure my arm's broken."

Carpenter was already on the phone. "A doctor will be here in a minute," he said hanging up. "Let's hear what happened." As she talked, his frown deepened.

When she mentioned that everything about the assassins indicated they had been brought in from Hongkong, she caught the look that passed between Carpenter and Peter.

"It's not the normal way they go about things here, even when murder's involved, is it?"

Peter shook his head. "I've never heard of anything like it."

"Neither had the three people who saved me." She still couldn't bring herself to identify them as hotel attendants. Some residual reporter's instinct for preserving sources, she imagined. "What do you think it means?"

"I hate to think," Carpenter said, tight-lipped. "All I know is we should get you out of here fast. Now finish your story."

"There's not much more, really. They threw the bodies down the elevator shaft and put me in the car that brought me here. They also emphasized I should get out of the country immediately."

"As soon as the doctor takes a look at that arm, I want you to be on the first possible plane. I should never have asked you to make that contact for me."

"Well, that might be the bright spot in all this. The last word is that Wang Weilai is somewhere near Peking, and they're trying to get through to him. Of course, they couldn't give me any idea of what the chances are."

"Of course," Carpenter said and shook his head. He gestured wearily at the masses of papers on the desk. "The whole thing is unraveling. Peasant rebellions all over the country, the army fighting pitched battles with striking miners at Anshan and several railroad centers." He pressed his fingers against his forehead as if holding off pain. "And we still have no idea what the Soviets are doing. It's relatively quiet up there, but the troop movements are ominous. Now there's an unnerving new component in the west, some sort of Moslem uprising among the Xinjiang minorities in the border areas. No matter what his influence, I doubt whether Wang Weilai and I could come up with a comprehensive enough scenario to handle all those variables. Even assuming anyone would be interested in it." His tone was bitter.

"A Moslem uprising. Oh God," Anne groaned. "As if Baluchistan weren't enough."

"It's all Central Asia. Those people have no loyalty to either the Russians or the Chinese." Peter sounded very tired.

"Unfortunately, it's the Russians who have the troops there," the ambassador added.

"And Washington?"

"The status quo prevails. We're to stay on course. Steady as she goes." The ambassador's tone had become increasingly derisive. Then, abruptly, it turned businesslike. "Enough of that. Let's deal with the immediate problems and then get you out of here. What happened to your stories?"

283

Anne tapped her shoulder bag, on the floor beside her.

For the first time, there was a glimmer of a smile on Carpenter's face. "It's nice working with a professional. I'm going to get you on the first plane to Tokyo. It's obvious you'd be safer there than in Hongkong. You haven't heard anything from the *Inquirer*, I take it?"

Anne shook her head.

"Okay, I'll see what I can do about that problem. Meanwhile," he said, handing her a slip of paper on which he'd just been scribbling, "send the stories off to this guy at the *Times* as soon as you get to Tokyo. And while you're at it, write out another piece on the plane about CG 10 and the attempt to kill you. That should send a little fur flying in Washington. Let's just thank God those fools broke your left arm."

Peter's and Anne's eyes met. This wasn't exactly the way they'd planned things only twenty-four hours ago. There was a pained silence. Carpenter was not insensitive to it.

"Let's wind this up so you two have a few minutes to yourselves before the plane."

Money, passport, visa, a phone call bumping a businessman off the plane, and the doctor, roused from his bed. A very bad break. He asked no questions. Must be X-rayed as soon as she got to Tokyo. No cast until then. A temporary splint and sling. Pain? Yes, the codeine hadn't done much good. Some pills to put in her bag.

The ambassador excused Peter. There wasn't much more that could be done until the Chinese government offices began to open up in the morning. Peter could spend the remaining time with Anne before the car arrived to take her to the airport. Carpenter was sending along a military escort, nothing elaborate, just a Marine in the front seat. Then Peter should get a few hours sleep. They'd begin work again at 8:30 in the morning.

Peter and Anne sat close together on a sofa in one of the reception rooms, her good hand tightly gripping his. Peter's arm held her shoulder gently, just touching the sling.

"This situation scares me," Anne said at last. "It feels awful. I'd like to smuggle you onto that plane with me."

"I'd like it too, but not because of the situation. We're always stepping to the brink. A few days of hot television news and we'll undoubtedly be right back in the old routine. I'd just like to be going with you. How are we ever going to put our lives together?"

Anne noticed again how exhausted he looked. She shook her head, but made an effort to smile. "We're either going to have to get ourselves assigned to the same part of the world or open up a Chinese restaurant together."

It didn't have quite the same tone of just a day ago, but it was the easiest way for both of them to leave it. They were used to international plane flights, long distance phone calls, hotel life; and anyway, what else was the twentieth century good for if not for removing the old barriers of distance?

As they held each other in a last, fierce embrace, Peter murmured, "Here's looking at you, my reckless love."

How unfortunate, a crazy voice in Anne's head said, that she hadn't brought along her Dietrich slouch hat. A woman traveling alone in exotic places should never be without a hat to make her exit *comme il faut.*

Tom Carpenter knew he could make it through this day, but how many more? Three hours sleep the night Anne Campbell left and the same last night. It wasn't enough. He already felt irritable, and here, first thing in the morning, one of the few household rules he'd ever made had been broken! Awaiting him on his neatly set breakfast table, a letter. He thought he'd made it perfectly clear the very first week at the embassy, breakfast was sacrosanct. Newspapers yes, but nothing else. Business began the minute he stepped into his office, not one second before.

Yet here it was, a large white envelope addressed to "Ambassador Thomas Carpenter, U.S.A.," right next to his glass of orange juice where he couldn't possibly miss it. He tore it open impatiently.

"Mr. Wang agrees to your request for an appointment. You will be expected tomorrow evening at 7:00 P.M. in the Bamboo Room of the Peking Duck Restaurant."

It hit him immediately, but he still couldn't quite believe it. That wild shot in the dark. He put the letter in his pocket. Wang Weilai. The most notorious rebel leader in the country couldn't have figured out a better way to impress him. Right by his orange juice! He'd have to check embassy security immediately.

Carpenter put cream in his coffee and stirred absentmindedly. Were they really going to meet in the Peking Duck Restaurant?

285

Unlikely. Probably an intermediate connecting point. Well, it had been his idea. Now there was nothing to do but ride the tiger. If this were Central America, he wouldn't go, at least not without a squad of security men armed to the teeth. But here? He'd have to trust his instincts.

There was probably no point in taking any security men at all. If these people were interested in kidnapping him, they would certainly have sufficient forces. He couldn't go alone, though. He needed someone who spoke Chinese, who understood what he was doing, and that person was Peter. He could depend on him to have a cool head and know when to keep his mouth shut. Of course, there had been that inappropriate outburst with Anne Campbell, but that was understandable. As long as she wasn't around, Peter would be fine. He'd performed admirably on the Washington trip.

No armed escort, he was sure about that now, but he couldn't imagine going into an unknown and potentially dangerous situation like a lamb to the slaughter. All foreign service officers were given antiterrorist training, including marksmanship. He had never had much to do with guns, but just as he excelled at most things, he'd excelled at shooting. When the course was finished, he'd put the guns away. Tonight, however, he would take one out, perhaps the smaller and less conspicuous Walther, the PPK, would be the best. Peter would have to carry one too.

That day and the one that followed were as exhausting and frustrating as Carpenter had anticipated. Every phone call, every dispatch brought news of a new crisis, and all of his urgent communications with Washington resulted in either maddeningly bland official responses or silence. In China, the peasant rebellions and strikes were spreading, even though the Army had managed to put them down in a number of places. The Moslem uprising in Xinjiang was impossible to analyze. Reports filtered in of armed horsemen sweeping across the desert and back to their mountain refuges. No one even seemed to know what their demands were. The Sino-Soviet border was the murkiest of all. The Russians were continuing to move in massive numbers of troops, but there was an unnerving lull in the fighting.

When Carpenter appeared at 6:30, Peter was in the outer office, waiting impatiently.

"Ready?"

"Ready." Peter patted the pocket of his Burberry and grinned.

286

Carpenter had decided to go in the ambassador's limousine, all flags flying, with the Chinese driver whom he'd always assumed must be a police agent. Certainly, Mr. Wang did not expect him to sneak disguised into the largest and most popular restaurant in Peking. The arrangements, whatever they were, must include the known presence of the American ambassador at the Peking Duck Restaurant.

"Tell the driver I want him to stay here," he instructed Peter when they arrived. The driver spoke some English, but Carpenter preferred to address him indirectly. It was always good to maintain some distance. "We'll be at least two hours, maybe longer, but the car is to stay here, and he is to be with it. Also tell him we're having a very important dinner meeting and are not to be disturbed under any circumstances. Underline that."

The Bamboo Room was at the end of the corridor on the third floor. The waiter seemed to be expecting them. He waved them into the small private dining room, said to Peter, "The arrangements for your dinner have already been made," shut the door, and disappeared.

Their contact was already seated in one of the armchairs in the corner of the room. Compact, young, and obviously tough, he rose, stepped to a lacquered screen, and motioned to them. The screen concealed a door. They followed him down a dim stairway, out into the night, and into the back seat of a car parked nearby.

"My God," Carpenter whispered. "This is fantastically well organized. These people, whoever they are, are everywhere. It's starting to remind me of stories I've been told about the last days in Saigon."

Their driver took them rapidly from the crowded center of the city onto commercial side streets, everything now closed but an occasional restaurant, and soon into an industrial section that neither of them had ever seen.

Suddenly, their car turned into a huge factory surrounded by the customary high brick wall. Sprawling buildings, many lighted, surrounded them. The yard through which they were driving was alive with factory workers, and somewhere they heard the distant roar of machinery.

Carpenter was looking intently out the window. "See if you can catch any signs identifying this place."

Peter squinted. "The building over there has big characters on it. Maybe when we get a little closer I'll be able to read them."

The driver had slowed down for people walking in the roadway. The characters on the wall were well lighted.

"The North China Locomotive Works."

Carpenter whistled softly through his teeth. So this was the rebels' stronghold. "I think we weren't mistaken to take this man seriously."

They stopped in front of a large administration building and followed their silent driver up the few steps and into the front door. It was spartan inside, gray and rather shabby, with naked light bulbs strung along the ceiling of the corridor.

Their guide knocked briefly on one of the doors, indistinguishable from the rest, and swung it open for them. It was the standard factory reception room. Peter had seen others like it before. There was a row of stiff chairs, a long wooden table covered with dark green felt, and on it tall, lidded tea mugs, a teapot, large ceramic ashtrays with bright packs of cigarettes—a room replicated a million times throughout this ceremonial country, its ambiance altered only by the changing power constellation represented by the presiding officials. As one regime displaced another, the rotating cadres who rose to the top officiated here with equal graciousness and authority over the shifting statistics that foreign guests scribbled assiduously in their notebooks.

The official who rose courteously this time was Wang Weilai. He had his cohort—several men on either side, one woman next to him —but he was the overwhelming presence. Startlingly handsome, a filmmaker's revolutionary, he had something more than mere good looks, Carpenter decided. Charisma, that was the word, that strange, magical gift of the gods.

The American guests were seated opposite Wang Weilai and his phalanx, the ambassador face to face with the leader. Looking across the table, Peter noticed there was something peculiar. In all such reception rooms, revolutionary ancestors gazed sternly and benevolently down from the walls. Marx, Engels, and Lenin were almost always there; Stalin and Mao had had their ups and downs; and other Chinese leaders had had brief spells of glory—but invariably some version of this classic pantheon was there. On this dingy wall, however, there were five blank, conspicuously white spaces. What could that mean?

The tea was poured, the cigarettes passed. The ambassador began.

288

"Thank you for arranging our meeting. I understand you had to make a special trip."

Wang Weilai smiled slightly. "My work requires constant traveling. It was no problem. If the representative of the United States feels we have reason to talk, that is sufficient cause for me to make a trip to Peking. Besides"—he waved his hand in the direction of the factory yard—"there were other things I wanted to see."

Carpenter was not unaware of the thrust of Wang's response. Courteous, open to cooperation, yet indicating the magnitude of his own power base. "Your people seem to be taking control of things all over the country, if the reports we're getting are accurate. As foreigners, though, we have no sense of whether all these strikes and peasant uprisings are really part of a coordinated movement. You seem to be saying they are."

Wang Weilai's tone was quite neutral. "Your government will have to draw its own conclusions, Ambassador Carpenter. You have excellent intelligence sources, I'm sure. I will assure you, however, that we expect to be victorious—if not this month, next month, next year, a decade from now. The time is of no importance. We are certain we will win because we represent the interests of the people, who are joining forces against their common enemy. At some point your government will be forced to come to terms with us. It's to your credit that you have grasped this earlier than most."

"And what proof can I offer my government that your expectations are accurate? That you are a leader it should deal with?"

"None. You must know that there are never any preliminary guarantees in history. You have no choice but to assess what you see. Perhaps you are familiar with the old Chinese saying, 'He who loses power is a bandit; he who wins power is a king.' At the moment I am a bandit, but it is always wiser to make your arrangements with such bandits before they become kings, not after. Otherwise, your dealings with my enemies may jeopardize our future relationship."

Carpenter was fascinated and repulsed. The arrogance of this dazzling young man was beyond belief. Yet it was clearly true. He could indeed become king. "And what would such arrangements entail?"

"As you are aware, many of the weapons being used to put down the just struggles of the Chinese workers and peasants were furnished by the United States. Those weapons are already here. We

289

will have to take them away from the Army as we've done before and use them ourselves, but there must be no more. We have every interest in maintaining the relationship with the United States, but your military aid to the Chinese government now in power must cease immediately."

The man's audacity was astonishing. "I'm sure, Mr. Wang, that you know as well as I the reason for that military aid. It is what your country asked for—begged for, in fact—to protect itself against the Soviet Union. Some of that American military equipment is being used at this very moment against Soviet troops on the Chinese border."

Wang Weilai was entirely composed, the chain of cigarettes that he smoked the only hint of possible strain. "These matters are far more complicated than they appear on the surface. For example, Zhang Zhaolin, the border-talks chairman who supports our policies, was recently involved in serious negotiations with the Russians about the border problem. As you may know, he's now in jail. It is your allies, not mine, who put him there. Perhaps if it were not for the American military influence in China, there would be no border crisis at this moment."

"You seem to be saying that you're not overly concerned about the escalation in the border fighting."

"No. It's very serious, very dangerous. It may already have gone past the point where it can be turned around. But one thing is absolutely clear: It will never be turned around with the present policies and increased American weapons."

"I take it you're in favor then of returning to your old relationship with the Soviet Union." Carpenter was aware that his voice was rising.

Wang Weilai smiled condescendingly. "It seems very difficult for both the United States and the Soviet Union to understand that our relationship with one of you does not negate the possibility of a relationship with the other. Let us make sure we understand each other in this matter. The overriding interest of the United States in opening relations with China was to use China as a counter to the Soviet Union. Playing the China card, you call it. It is for this reason that your country is now engaged in a dangerous military escalation, the planned arming of China with your nuclear weapons."

Carpenter was ready for this. "The reporter you gave that document to has told me about it. I hope you realize it's no more than

290

a contingency plan, one among many that various branches of my government have prepared." He had to speak carefully now. "You must understand that few in my government would be in favor of actually implementing such a proposal."

"In this case, Mr. Ambassador, I'm afraid I may be better informed than you. Although it was useful to receive such a document, we have far more concrete and frightening information than that about your nuclear upgrading program in China. You would perhaps be surprised at the work your military units have already done to improve, if that is the word, our nuclear facilities in Xinjiang."

Carpenter had an urge to shout, "Not *my* military units," but he stopped himself. So Haggard had done far more damage than even he had imagined.

"It could hardly be said that this was truly in China's interests. However, what's past is past. We will take our own steps to rectify the situation here . . ."

Now what does that mean? Carpenter wondered.

". . . but what's important is the future. We're also aware that there are those in China who hope to play the American card, encouraging the barbarians to fight the barbarians. I am not interested in either of those games. Our policy is to seek equitable relations with both the superpowers."

Carpenter thought it best to change the subject somewhat. "I fear you're oversimplifying Sino-American relations when you describe them in purely military terms. Economic relations are at least as important. Certainly that has always been one of my major interests in the relationship."

"I'm aware of your background, Mr. Carpenter. You represent the multinational wing of American capitalism that favors trade over war. We understand that it is the more progressive wing of moribund capitalism. No doubt that's why you're here today."

Moribund capitalism! Carpenter thought. My God, what language. "It's a very attractive idea, getting along with both the superpowers, but if it were so easy, don't you think somebody would have tried it before? The Soviets hate China. You must know that. What makes you think they'd be interested in your kind of terms?"

Wang Weilai spoke in that patient Chinese tone that was so infuriating. "The world is changing, Mr. Ambassador. The old men, with their strategies of winnable wars, are dying. There are no

291

winnable nuclear wars. And in the nuclear age, there are also no winnable conventional wars among the superpowers. Only small countries can now afford that luxury. Perhaps what we're proposing couldn't have been done before now, but there's a new generation coming to power here, in the Soviet Union, in Europe, and even, I suppose, in the United States. In any case, the fact is we're going to have to get along whether we like each other or not."

Ambassador Carpenter did not enjoy being lectured to. He glanced discreetly at his watch. It was time to get to the nitty-gritty. "Your proposal?"

"That your government immediately cease its military assistance, nuclear or otherwise, to the present Chinese government."

"And in return?"

"In return, our movement will guarantee the protection of American property and citizens and leave the way open to future peaceful and constructive relations between you and ourselves."

It was incredibly audacious. Between the government of the most powerful nation on earth, and some disparate rebel forces. And yet . . . it must have looked the same in Iran.

"We would like your government's answer as soon as possible."

"This is hardly a matter that can be decided quickly. Surely you understand that. I believe you said you had decades."

"That's one possibility. The other is that the situation will move very rapidly. There is an internal struggle going on, but at the same time, there are Soviet forces on two of our borders. We must know where the United States stands at this moment."

The men on either side of the table stood up. Thomas Carpenter, the ambassador from the United States of America, and Wang Weilai, the Chinese bandit king, shook hands.

"I'll take this up with my government and let you know as soon as possible."

"Good. Beginning the day after tomorrow, my representative will visit your embassy every other day until a reply is received. Here's the code word that will identify him." Wang reached into his pocket, pulled out a small envelope, and handed it to Peter.

So, from the very start, they were prepared for everything, Carpenter thought, as Wang escorted them alone to the door, shook hands again, and bid them a final farewell.

Their driver wove his way through the still busy factory yard and then sped out of the dark industrial district.

"They'll think I've lost my mind, but I've got to let Washington know about the whole thing—Haggard, the document, and all." Carpenter sank back against the seat and thrust his hands into his pockets. His right hand struck the cold steel of his small pistol. He'd completely forgotten it. What an absurdity that would have been.

There hadn't been such an air of crisis to a WASAC meeting since the rebellion in Baluchistan had broken out, and from that had come the playing of the China card. This morning that game was strewn over the table in complete disarray. Zolti's haughty air appeared to be undented by the disaster. If anything, he was more overbearing than ever; but to those familiar with his moods, there was a defensive quality to his hauteur.

"You've all read the briefing papers, I assume." Zolti spit out the words. He was extremely displeased that the President had insisted on including sections of Ambassador Carpenter's mad report. It was the sort of stuff that the President had, in the past, shared only with him. This time, however, the President had gotten on his high horse and insisted. Since WASAC had been created as a crisis-management task force, it had to know more about the situation, including the decision on nuclear arms. That indicated only one thing to Zolti: a lack of trust in himself. And now these jackals around the table had their tongues hanging out, waiting to tear him to shreds. Let them try. The President wanted them to come up with a plan. If Carpenter was any example, what a joke that would be.

It was the general from the Joint Chiefs who first sprang to the attack. "I just don't understand it," he said in his sternest commanding-officer style. "Our decision for a massive military upgrading was made on the assumption that the Chinese government was stable. We were given assurances that that was the case. That was the foundation for our entire plan. What's wrong with our intelligence sources? This same thing happens over and over again."

Frederick Soames often chose to ignore the blanket criticism thrown at his bailiwick, but this was beyond ignoring. He wasn't going to have another Iran pinned on the CIA. His voice was icy. "You seem to have forgotten the report I gave this meeting the very day the China-card option was decided upon. If your memory needs refreshing, I'd be glad to go over my notes from that meeting. Do

293

you recall my saying something about underground organizations of unemployed youth and peasant uprisings?"

"Well, perhaps you didn't emphasize them enough," the general muttered gruffly. "Your reports always include demonstrations and uprisings. It wasn't clear that something of this magnitude was going to happen."

"As I recall, I was told that our analysis was outdated." Soames took a perverse pleasure in the disaster. After the way Zolti had put him down at that meeting, at least he had the satisfaction of knowing he'd been right.

"Forget about that, forget about it," Schneider from the Pentagon snapped. "We made our military commitment to the Chinese; nothing wrong with that. I'm not convinced these strikes and rebellions can't be handled. It's been done plenty of times before. Now's the time to keep the hardware moving in, when the government needs it. What I'm concerned about is the Russians. What are we saying to them? Why don't we know what the hell they think they're doing there?"

"The Russians are fighting the Chinese over that old border problem. They know we're not involved." Zolti spoke unhesitatingly.

"How do they know we're not involved?" It was Mason Graves from State.

"I informed them of it."

"And they believed you?"

"I don't know why they shouldn't." Zolti was livid. It was enough that the President didn't have confidence in him without having to put up with the nastiness of a fool like Graves. Implying *he* was lying!

With obvious satisfaction, Graves threw his ace on the table. "According to Ambassador Carpenter's report, the Chinese rebel forces know more about our secret military plans than this committee does. Would you care to explain that to us? When we agreed only you and the President would have access to the top-security aspects of the military plans, we didn't realize you intended to distribute them publicly."

Zolti was white. "Every person in the Pentagon is going to undergo lie detector tests."

"Again?" Graves asked mildly.

"The Pentagon!" It was Schneider.

294

"Yes. There's every indication of Soviet espionage." Zolti was going on the attack now. "And they're in the State Department, too, Graves!" he shouted. "We know that. We'll get them. There's going to be a cleanup of the whole place."

"But it was a leak from *your* staff, Zolti. It had to be."

"No, not my staff. It was the military."

Now the general was shouting. "How dare you implicate the military! There was nothing in Ambassador Carpenter's report that implicated the military!"

"Ambassador Carpenter knows very little about the military situation."

"That's right. That's the point," Graves cut in. "Carpenter says that General Haggard, who *is* directly in charge of the military program, is involved in all sorts of strange activities. What the hell is Haggard up to? You know, and nobody else here does."

The volume of Zolti's voice matched that of Graves's.

"I don't like your insinuations. Lowell Haggard is doing a brilliant job in China. He's the best thing this government has going for it."

"And what's this brilliant man doing now? Getting us all ready for an insane nuclear war with the Russians, or just stirring up more trouble in China of the sort that's being reported not just by Ambassador Carpenter, but on the front page of the *Times* this morning? We don't even know where Haggard is, for God's sake. All hell is breaking loose, and we don't even know where he is."

Zolti's eyes were blazing. "I know where he is, Mr. Graves," he hissed. "He's right where he's supposed to be. There are a few matters which are still in the hands of only the President and myself, and the whereabouts of Lowell Haggard is one of them."

Around the table, the men hunched aggressively forward.

"And what about the main point in the Carpenter report, Professor Zolti?" Soames's voice was heavy with sarcasm. "Are we going to consider it or are we going to shelve it as usual until it's too late?"

Mason Graves had himself under control again. This was his department. Carpenter was his man. Thank God there were still ambassadors who took some initiative, even if they usually ended up getting sacked or being forced to resign—Sullivan in Iran, White in El Salvador—he ticked them off in his head.

"I don't see what we have to lose by agreeing to this man Wang's conditions, at least temporarily. We halt the shipment of weapons.

The Chinese have got plenty already. We do some more investigating of this opposition movement. Meanwhile, things will continue to develop in China, and we'll have a better idea of whether they really have any strength or not."

"You don't see what we have to lose!" Zolti leapt to the feet. He couldn't believe that anyone, even Graves, would seriously consider Carpenter's idiotic proposal. "Everything, that's what, everything! China, that's what we have to lose."

"We lost China once before," the general agreed solemnly. "We can't afford to do that again."

"You can't lose China," Soames retorted. "You can only make the wrong decision about which horse to back."

"Yes? Well, Carpenter's horse isn't even in the running. Who ever heard of the guy anyway?"

"Who ever heard of Khomeini? Who ever heard of Castro, or Mao? We never hear about these people until it's too late."

"There's no way we could agree to a condition like that even if we did know who we were dealing with. We have a military commitment to the Chinese government. What are we going to do, tell them we've changed our minds on the basis of one crackpot report?"

"I assume you're referring to Ambassador Carpenter's analysis. And what about the report by that reporter in the *Times* this morning, if corroboration is needed. As far as I can see, she's accurate enough on the military upgrading program, so why should we assume she's any less so on the strength of the rebels?"

"Much as I dislike learning about my government's policies in the press, there's some sense in what Graves says." It was Soames. "Our own reports tally with what she has to say. And Carpenter's report indicates that this woman knows what she's talking about. She certainly passed accurate information on to him and—"

It seemed as if Zolti would simply explode. "This is insane!" he burst in. "We have information that this woman is a Russian agent."

Graves was livid. "Are you claiming Ambassador Carpenter's involved with—"

"Yes! They cooked it up together to undermine our relations with the present government of China."

"Have you gone completely mad? Do you think she hired three goons to kill herself to make her story look good, or didn't you read the rest of Carpenter's report?"

"She could easily have faked it!"

296

"Oh, for God's sake . . ."

"Gentlemen this is getting out of hand and off the point," Schneider from the Pentagon cut in. But it was too late. Everyone was shouting across the table now. The general was shaking his head. Everything was wrong. None of the solutions were good. You couldn't run a military program like this. Good God, what was the matter with these foreigners. Fists pounded the table, arms flailed in the air.

The meeting never really adjourned. The WASAC members straggled out of the room, arguing as they went. It was the shortest WASAC meeting on record, and nothing had been resolved. Zolti would recommend to the President that United States China policy remain on course.

CHAPTER

21

Tokyo itself had been a shock. Anne hadn't been in China for long, and yet the Chinese world had become her overwhelming reality. She was exhausted, more mentally than physically, and more disoriented than she could ever remember being, but she had trained herself to be efficient under stress, and almost mechanically did what had to be done. First, her arm. Then the difficult matter of wiring her resignation to the *Inquirer*. She could have, probably should have phoned them, but she didn't want to have Larry or some editor she'd never heard of treat her patronizingly, angrily, kindly, condescendingly, or whatever else they considered appropriate at the moment. The more she thought about it, the angrier she felt about the way they'd handled the whole thing and *her*. Handled was the word. The hell with them. She sent the stories, including the lead one she'd written on the plane, to Carpenter's friend on the *Times*, and then collapsed in her hotel room.

But she couldn't sleep. Even a sleeping pill didn't help. Her mind just refused to be turned off. Why? She was safe here in this comfortable Tokyo hotel room, far away from the watchful surveillance of both protectors and assailants. She'd done what she'd had to do with the *Inquirer*. As for the *Times*, what would be would be. It was entirely out of her hands now, so what was this knot that wouldn't come untangled?

As she lay there in the dark, waiting, Paul Engleberg's name crossed her mind. His shadow had hung over her from the beginning. But she definitely wasn't the next Paul Engleberg. She'd crossed a line that was qualitatively different. Not only had she almost gotten herself killed, but she'd been used or misused by just about everyone. Carpenter, the *Inquirer*, Wang Weilai—yes, even her dear Peter. Not to speak of the people who had tried to have her assassinated, whoever they were. And Charlie Rudd, the only person who hadn't used her, she had used, wrecking his life in her own single-minded way.

Paul had said he'd had no regrets. He'd felt it was worth it, and for him it clearly had been. Good stories, his honor unquestioned, his reputation intact. But something different had happened to her. She was not naive. She'd gone to China sure she knew what she was doing, and maybe she had. But power, the workings of power had fouled her up. That was the crux of this knot. In Paul's case, the demands of power had dictated silence. For him, as it would have been for her, the response to that dictate was clear: to speak as long as you could. But her situation had turned out to be so impossibly different. There was that old cliché, information was power. She'd been the one with the information—and the access—that those in power needed. It was her own independent news instincts that had led her there. That and a few twists of fate, and everything had followed as she crossed some shadowy line into the world of the power holders. It probably wasn't even her fault. Perhaps it was simply immutable, this uneasy liaison between the gatherers of the news and the users of information. But was it worth it? Would it make any difference at all even if her pieces were printed?

And Peter? Wang Weilai had used her for her access, Carpenter for both access and information, but would she ever have become so involved if it hadn't been for Peter? How conscious had he been of using her? Not in any sort of crass, deliberate way—she knew him better than that—but just because he believed in his world and couldn't help wanting to draw her into it.

Ah, Peter—charming, loving Peter. What had she been doing, having such a self-indulgent romance? He'd never pretended to be anything but himself, and she'd never pretended to be anything but herself, and they'd convinced themselves that that was enough. Yet they knew: At least she knew, if not before, certainly now. They would be forever pulling each other into uncongenial orbits. They would make each other feel guilty, used, betrayed. Leave it alone. Leave it the way they'd left it when they'd said good-bye. It was what it was, a Peking romance, a small jewel in her life, pristine in its way. Peter would always be Peter. When they ran across each other someday, she'd only remember the good things.

To her amazement, when she woke out of her drugged sleep it was morning and there was already a cable from the *Times* awaiting her. Phone calls quickly followed, then intensive checking of her and her information, and finally, rarity of rarities, they began to run her stories, the pieces of a *Times* outsider in front-page serial form, beginning with her account of the plan to nuclear-arm China and ending with the story of her own near-death. Everything fit, day by day. There were peasant uprisings. She had a story. There were strikes. She had a story. Troop movements on the border intensified. They used an updated version of her original speculative piece on Zhang Zhaolin. It was incredible. She had tears in her eyes as she read the first piece.

They paid her well, but they had their own China correspondent in place, and she knew they wouldn't have a China job to offer her. Still, she remained in the limbo of her Tokyo hotel room, half paralyzed, waiting with unaccustomed passivity for she hardly knew what to happen.

About a week into her stay, the phone call came. From the same man on the *Times*. And what an offer! She couldn't believe it.

"You'd be based in Mexico, but with the whole Central America beat, Guatemala in particular right now. I know you're an Asia person, but this post has just opened up and we want you. It's not just your stories, but your resourcefulness that's impressed us."

Anne, holding the receiver, sat down on the bed.

"Do you want some time to think it over?"

"No. No, I don't need any time. I'll take it. I'd love to take it."

Central America. The conflagration in the American backyard. Vietnam had seemed so far away. China was China, forever the Middle Kingdom. It could live with the United States or without it. What was it that Charlie Rudd had said? "The relationship with America was a minuscule event in aeons of Chinese time." Something like that, anyway. But on our own linked continents, there was no escaping reality. Did one even have to ask whether it was worth going after the facts? She felt the knot beginning to untangle.

Spanish. She must brush up on her Spanish. A million things. She must start reading. Pack. Make plane reservations.

Peter. Immediately, this minute, before she became too cowardly

300

to do it, she must phone Peter. She was going to Mexico City. That was all she'd need to tell him. She was going to Mexico City. He'd know.

It was one of those incomparable Peking spring days, the essence of April, clouds of blossoms quivering in the limpid air. One had to make an effort to resist the magical transformations of such a northern Chinese spring, but Peter did. Events had been compacted fantastically. The answer from Washington had come back more rapidly than Carpenter had expected. It had taken the President and whoever was advising him, still Zolti no doubt, no time at all to reject any possibility of making further contact with the rebel forces for the time being. For the time being! As if there were any time to waste. Peter knew Carpenter was considering the advisability of resigning. But for Peter, there could be no such thought. He was a career foreign service officer, not an appointed ambassador.

To make your little mark on history, he thought wryly. That's what he and Anne had each hoped to do. Obviously, if the ambassador couldn't do it, with his position, his background, his connections . . . Peter sighed. Maybe Anne was right and the best possibility was a well-aimed shot from the fourth estate, but what a crazy life that was. The work of the press had never attracted him. In fact, he'd always had a certain disdain for it, and his association with Anne had hardly demonstrated to him that there was more dignity to the profession than he'd suspected. But Anne. Damn it, he missed her. It wasn't just their afternoons of lovemaking, though that was no small loss. Without her, he was unspeakably bored. Yes, bored, a strange malady when you were living in the center of a maelstrom, every hour a dispatch about a new uprising. Was the army going to be effective? Would there be splits in the officer corps? What did the rumors of defections mean? He was worn down with it all, and there was no one to talk to, no one who said wonderful, funny things and could get him out of his own head for a while. So, she was off to Mexico City. It was inevitable. It was the Anne he loved. He couldn't imagine that it was anything but temporary, and anyway, there were planes from Peking to Mexico City.

Meanwhile, he had to go on living. Last night he'd even tried going out to dinner with one of the women at the embassy, the assistant to the cultural attaché. He'd always noticed that she was pretty in an earnest sort of way, and nice. And nice she was. He'd never been so bored in his life. The evening seemed interminable as she talked about the relative influences of Buddhism and Taoism, Chinese bureaucracy, and the difficulties of working out cultural exchanges. Oh, Anne, it wasn't going to be so easy to replace you. Better to spend his evenings alone and brooding.

"Peter, can you see it from your window?" It was Carpenter's secretary, peering in his door.

"See what?"

"What's the matter with you? Can't you hear the noise?"

And then he could, whatever it was, in the distance, and gathering volume very quickly. Inside the embassy there was the sound of running, of voices calling back and forth.

"Doesn't anyone know what it's about?"

"Are you sure they're coming here?"

"Well, look. Jesus, they're coming right here."

He turned to the window. The people—good God! A dark blue sea of people, sweeping everything before them, carrying banners by the hundreds, red flags, sky blue flags (blue flags, what did that mean?), placards on sticks, gigantic cartoons, and—was it possible? —red-tasseled spears. They were shouting slogans, vast rhythmic chants, shaking their fists in the air, and marching steadily in the direction of the embassy's front gate. A group broke ranks and ran to the gate with bullhorns, loudspeaker equipment, some sort of a makeshift platform. By the time the thousands came close, there was already a passionate young man thrust up above the heads of the roaring crowd, waving his arms. The slogans were impossible to hear, but Peter picked out "Americans" and "foreign imperialists."

Suddenly, the iron gates burst open and the swirling, storming crowd poured into the embassy's front yard. Within seconds the area was packed, demonstrators everywhere, on the walls, in the trees, on the roof of the building.

Peter whirled around. Carpenter was standing behind him. "What happened to the PLA guards?"

"I don't know. Swallowed up." The ambassador's expression was grim. "Maybe they joined the demonstrators."

"And our Marines?"

"I'm not about to order half a dozen Marines to fire on a hundred thousand people. I've instructed them just to try to politely hold the

302

people where they are. I'm going to go down and offer to talk to the leaders. I want you to do one little thing in the meantime."

"What?"

"I want you to send a message to Washington. Don't make it complicated. Just tell them we're O.B.E. They'll understand what happened."

Then, on his way to the door, Carpenter paused. "Too bad neither of us thought to ask Wang Weilai for one of his calling cards."

He was a survivor. That was the term the foreign press used to describe him, and it was quite accurate. Tang Chen had joined the revolution when he was in his twenties and had survived, even surmounted, the bloody factional struggles of more than four decades; but the struggle going on now was trickier than most. Too many people out in the streets. Of course, you had to get your forces into the streets. That's what twentieth-century politics was all about. But they were much harder to manage when the ferment began down below rather than at the top. It could be done. During the Cultural Revolution, the Party, under attack, had done a brilliant job of turning the masses against each other. But the price had been terrible.

The one cardinal rule of managing these mass political struggles was: Make sure you have the Army with you. That had been Mao's ace in the Cultural Revolution, the crafty old fox. He'd kept the Army firmly in his hands by naming that sycophant Lin Biao as his successor. Then when he'd put down the rebellion he'd initiated, he'd gotten rid of Lin. Absolutely brilliant, and almost impossible to duplicate. In the past few years, the Army had become a mess. Too many changes of policy, too much loss of prestige. And that Taiwan business. The People's Liberation Army, from the humblest private to the most powerful general, had been nurtured on the battle cry, "Liberate Taiwan." The Americans, foolish children of a four-year presidency, had undermined them all on that one.

No, he didn't like the way things were developing. The Army was starting to disintegrate in one part of the country after another. His own secret reports told him a great deal more about that than anyone else in the leadership even suspected. Little wonder he was extremely apprehensive about the border fighting. When he and

303

Lowell Haggard made their plans, he hadn't doubted he'd be able to turn things around the moment he wanted to. But something had happened. The anarchic disease of local control—warlordism it used to be called—was affecting the northern military operation. The commanding officer had turned out to be a crazy hothead. He *wanted* to fight the Russians! He thought this was some kind of patriotic crusade to save the motherland. Madness. Tang Chen had started the machinery to have him removed from his command, but it might already be too late. It seemed the Russians were taking it all too seriously.

Well, he'd had his contingency plans ready for a long time. A point finally came when you decided you wanted to spend your few remaining years in peace and contemplation. He wasn't defeated. He felt quite sure he could come out on top one more time, using the skills sharpened in a thousand battles. Men like Wang Weilai needed men like him, but the truth was he was tired of it. His daughter had been admitted to MIT. His younger son had been concentrating on buying San Francisco real estate. Everything was ready for him, and it was pleasant to realize that in addition to his family, he would have a few American friends as well. He looked forward to some long pleasant evenings with Lowell Haggard.

Tang Chen glanced out the window. The helicopter was arriving. Right on time.

Another hotel room. Another continent. Anne stood at the edge of America, looking west. Before her lay the benign enclosure of San Francisco Bay, the late afternoon light turning the Golden Gate Bridge to structured fire against the distant waters.

She was reluctant to leave her place by the window. The view was familiar from long ago and somehow, for all its grandeur, personal. But she was conscious in spite of herself of the sterility and loneliness of the room. Was this really her life? No one to talk to. No one now to hold her hand. No Hank or Peter or even a good old Charlie Rudd.

She looked at her watch impatiently. Enough brooding. She was meeting friends for dinner, but not until 7:30. Automatically, she clicked on the TV, and stood frozen before it. The picture! An enormous blue and black Chinese crowd, photographed from above,

304

surging forward then back, banners flying, a muted roar of sound. Glimpses of the familiar green-leafed poplar trees that lined the city streets, an occasional impersonal modern building.

"The American embassy in Peking has been surrounded for hours now. We have no communication with anyone inside."

The camera zoomed close to the crowd, the distorted shouting faces, the fists, the mouths forming angry slogans.

Anne sank into a chair. Oh, Peter. My God.

"It's not clear who the leaders here are or what they're demand-ing, or whether this mob in Peking has any connection with the riots reported throughout the country. We're safe here for the mo-ment, but we can see cameras being smashed, and TV and newspa-per people being escorted out of the riot zone. We don't know how long we'll be able to transmit. We'll stay here as long as we can. For the moment though, we're going to switch back to you in New York, Bob."

No, no! Stay! Don't leave them!

But they were in the studios, the calm confident face of the anchorman on the screen. "We'll be keeping you posted as the news reaches us. All we can report at the moment is that the American embassy in Peking is under siege, by what group is not known. Reports of riots continue to come in from all over China. Fighting with government troops is reported in several areas. Now to Wash-ington."

Washington. What a laugh. Now the experts in Washington would explain it all, the ones who'd been carefully holding their hands over their eyes so they wouldn't see anything to disturb their precious strategies. Anne got up and walked nervously back and forth, her eyes still riveted to the screen.

It was Stefan Zolti leaving the White House, surrounded by reporters and cameramen. He was frowning. Shouted questions were lost in the hubbub, but his answers were clear and angry. "Yes, of course it's a very serious situation. . . . No, we don't know who we're negotiating with. . . . The President is being fully informed. . . . The Chinese government? Chinese government headquarters are also surrounded. Nothing more, nothing more. I have no further statements." He disappeared into a long black car.

Then the somber face of the Pentagon correspondent. "We have a special dispatch, as yet unconfirmed by Washington sources. In Xinjiang Province in western China, a major Chinese nuclear installation is reported to be in the hands of Moslem insurgents. They have announced over Xinjiang radio stations the capture of American military personnel including an American general, Lowell Haggard. Pentagon sources have not confirmed this report, nor have they confirmed that General Haggard, one of the country's leading satellites experts, is even in Xinjiang. This is all we have at present. We'll keep you informed as the Xinjiang situation continues to develop. Back to you, Bob."

The news blared on—the shallow pontificating, the idiotic commercials, shots of the raging crowd once again—but Anne turned her back on it. Did I abandon you, Peter, my dear conservative Peter, there on the front line? What an irony. I said I wanted to smuggle you onto the plane, but how could that have been? It wouldn't have been you, or me either. You'll be all right. You will. Don't you remember? The civilized Chinese. You'll be all right. You have to be.

She turned again to the window. Beyond the bridge, the glimmering, fading light spread over the rolling expanse of blue. California, the newest of the new world, and China, the oldest of the old, facing one another across the ocean called pacific.

AN HISTORICAL NOTE

Since it is well understood by the readers of contemporary political novels that any resemblance to actual people and events is entirely coincidental, it seems only fair to point out that a few matters in this book are based closely enough on verifiable realities to warrant particular note.

Among the Chinese names mentioned in the book, there is one less well known to foreigners than those of famous figures such as Mao Zedong, Zhou Enlai, and Deng Xiaoping, but a real one nonetheless. That is Wei Jingsheng, the famous young leader of the early "democracy movement" which based its legitimacy on Article 45 of the 1978 Chinese constitution, guaranteeing the rights to freedom of speech, the press, association, demonstration, and strike. Wei was arrested in March 1979 and formally charged with having provided foreign reporters with military intelligence regarding the Chinese invasion of Vietnam. In October 1979 he was sentenced to fifteen years in jail.

The banned transcript of Wei's dramatic defense, which he conducted himself in a heavily guarded show trial, appeared unexpectedly in poster form, covering fifty-eight feet of Democracy Wall. When removed by the authorities, it was circulated underground in China. Taking the offensive throughout, the twenty-nine-year-old editor went down in a storm of rhetoric, stating that "opponents of democracy," not he, were the real counterrevolutionaries in China. He admitted talking to friendly journalists, saying that these conver-

307

sations only "enhanced friendship and deepened understanding between our countries," and that the "intelligence" he was accused of transmitting, specifically the names of People's Liberation Army officers, was not secret, but simply general knowledge.

The Chinese government's extreme sensitivity to its people's contact with foreign journalists surfaces periodically. Article 12 of the provisional regulations issued in 1979 by the State Council states, "The journalistic activities of resident correspondents shall not go beyond the limit of normal news coverage." There has been no clarification of what the limits of normal news coverage might be. In February 1982, however, a Chinese newspaper editor, Li Guangyi, former chief editor of the *China Finance and Trade Journal*, was sentenced to five years in jail for allegedly disclosing to a foreign journalist, thought to be Japanese, information about a meeting of the Party Central Committee the preceding June.

As Tan Yulan told Anne, Democracy Wall was closed down in 1979; but she neglected to mention what other reports indicate, namely that it was turned into a wall for posting advertisements.

The manifesto that Xiao Hong read to Anne is fictional, but it is similar in style and content to any number of such manifestos issued by young democracy activists and editors. One of the most famous of them was posted in Canton in 1974. Its author, thirty-five-year-old Wang Xizhe, was finally arrested in 1981. The definition of "democracy" varies considerably in these publications, ranging from liberalization led by the Communist Party to the formation of a democratic republic with a two-party system.

Democratic demands have also appeared in other sectors of society. Labor unrest over the past several years has included the call for unions independent of Communist Party control, particularly during the 1981 period of intense union activity in Poland. The Chinese press reported, critically, on the demand for Polish-style unions in such major cities as Shanghai, Wuhun, and Xian. In April 1981, Chen Yu, a deputy chairman of the All-China Federation of Trade Unions, admitted to the existence of such problems, notably in a steel mill in the northern industrial city of Taiyuan. Although the right to strike, like freedom of speech, was theoretically guaranteed by the 1978 constitution, the Chinese press warned firmly against strikes, slowdowns, and independent union activity. One practical response of the Chinese authorities has been the promotion of popularly elected workers' congresses within individual enterprises, thus preventing the formation of nationwide comprehensive unions along the lines of Poland's Solidarity.

The example of Poland seems not to have been lost on either workers, democracy dissidents, or Party officials. In a 1981 issue of an underground journal, *Flag of Theory*, an editorial described bureaucratic privilege in Poland before discussing its counterpart in China in these terms: "In a China facing economic collapse since the downfall of the Gang of Four, bureaucratic cliques still vie to build private villas. At a time when the suffering masses go without adequate food and shelter, how can such people in good conscience build luxurious housing for Party secretaries, generals, and even for their own children?" During the same period, internal Party circulars analyzed the Polish situation, compared it with the Chinese one, and came up with remarkably similar conclusions as well as serious warnings on the need for Party self-discipline, reform, and attention to the problem of bureaucratic privilege.

In the description of the general conditions of the peasantry in this book, there is nothing beyond information that is common knowledge—that is, the breaking up of the communes, the increase in private farming, the prosperity of some peasants accompanied by the impoverishment of others, and a growing inequality in the countryside. Peasant uprisings are in the realm of speculation, though there have been reports of such occurrences as demonstrations of hungry peasants converging on Peking. An increase in the traditional evidence of rural poverty—begging, theft, and prostitution—is reported with regularity. There have even been reports of a return of concubinage and the selling of daughters.

The condition and mood of the peasantry—80 percent of the Chinese population—has always been the great unknown factor in analyzing and predicting events in China. Ever since the first European traders were confined to special enclaves in southern Chinese cities, foreigners, if fortunate, have generally come to know only a relatively small number of Chinese in the major urban centers: Peking, Shanghai, Canton, Nanking, Tianjin. For most Chinese in these same cities, the world of the peasants is similarly distant and alien. It was for this reason that Edgar Snow's 1938 classic, *Red Star Over China*, was such a remarkable journalistic breakthrough; for in it, he gave the world, and many in China as well, their first view of Mao Zedong's peasant army that would soon sweep to victory. Should a Western journalist ever have Anne Campbell's fictional

309

opportunity to attend a secret meeting of peasant rebels and observe a peasant uprising, it would be another significant reportorial coup.

Whether the disparate protests of unemployed youth, democracy activists, workers, and peasants ever merge into the kind of rebellion described in the book is, of course, something only history will reveal. Official fears that such a phenomenon could conceivably come about, however, may be inferred from the fact that China enjoys the distinction of being the only staunchly anti-Soviet country in the world that rushed to express its approval of the Polish military regime.

There are free-trade zones in China: several in the southern part of the country near the Hongkong border, and another planned for the Fujian coast opposite Taiwan. Their conditions for foreign investment are the same as those described in the book for Tianbei. However, there are as yet no northern trade zones in China. The name Tianbei was created from the "Tian" of the industrial city of Tianjin and "bei" meaning "north."

Similarly, the early Shang city that Anne and Charlie went to Henan to see still exists only in the imagination. As Charlie reminds Anne, the city of Ao was discovered in the first decade after Liberation, and bronzes preceding the great works of the late Shang period were found there. This laid to rest most doubts about the indigenous development of bronze technology. However, it is also true that evidence from a still earlier period has not yet been found. The area around Kaifeng, one of the earliest centers of Chinese civilization, would be one logical place for such a discovery, if it is ever made, though historical tradition has the Shang king moving to Ao from a location farther east.

Regrettably, some of the more ominous military matters referred to in the book are not purely fictional. In the chapter describing the first WASAC meeting, there is a reference to Brezhnev's reaction to Sino-American military relations as stated to Chaban-Delmas in Moscow. What he actually said was that he "would not tolerate the nuclear arming of China" and "after the destruction of Chinese nuclear sites by our missiles, there won't be much time for Americans to choose between the defense of their Chinese allies and peaceful coexistence with us." This story, which made headlines in Europe, appeared on page 15 of the *New York Times*, January 30, 1980.

The acquaintance of the fictional Lowell Haggard and Tang

Chen is said to have begun in the course of the presentation to the Chinese of a gift from the Nixon delegation—satellite photos of Soviet troop dispositions on the Chinese border. It is not clear, at least to this writer, whether or not this exchange actually did take place. Rumors that Nixon and Kissinger brought such photos with them to China were prevalent in Washington at that time, but there were also denials.

We must hold Tang Chen and Lowell Haggard responsible for their own wild plans. However, they were not operating entirely in the realm of fantasy. The analysis of the Lin Biao affair, which gave Haggard his idea for a border provocation, is one presented as his own view by Roger Glenn Brown, then a senior CIA analyst, in his article "Chinese Politics and American Policy" in the Summer 1978 issue of *Foreign Policy*.

The descriptions of concrete ways in which the United States might upgrade Chinese conventional and nuclear forces against the Russians are similar to those outlined in a February 1979 *Armed Forces Journal* article, "U.S.'s Toughest Message to the U.S.S.R.," by "Justin Galen" (the pen name of a former senior Department of Defense civilian officer).

Most important, of course, is the matter of the *Consolidated Guidance* document. With the exception of Point 4, the transfer of nuclear warheads from South Korea to Haerbin, the provisions in the table of contents are modeled on a Department of Defense policy planning guidance document, *Consolidated Guidance 8*. *CG 8*, as it seems to be known in the trade, was leaked from the Pentagon and reported in the *New York Times* on October 4, 1979, in an article by Richard Burt, "Study Urges U.S. Aid to Chinese Military," and also by William Safire in a column titled "Louder Than Words." The provisions of *CG 8* were also referred to in the August 26, 1980, hearings before the House Subcommittee of Asian and Pacific Affairs as part of the prepared statement of Banning Garrett, Research Associate, Institute of International Studies, U.C. Berkeley.

The idea of transferring warheads from South Korea was entirely General Haggard's stroke of genius, and he must receive full credit for it.

ABOUT THE AUTHOR

Nancy Dall Milton, who taught at the Peking First Foreign Languages Institute from 1964 to 1969, is the co-author of *The Wind Will Not Subside: Years in Revolutionary China*, among other books. She now lives and teaches in San Francisco.